At the Edge
of the Abyss
A Declassified Documentary History of the Cuban Missile Crisis

Red and Black Publishers, St Petersburg, Florida

Library of Congress Cataloging-in-Publication Data

At the edge of the abyss : a declassified documentary history of the Cuban Missile
Crisis.
    p. cm.
    ISBN 978-1-934941-89-8
1. Cuban Missile Crisis, 1962--Sources.
    E841.A8 2010
    972.9106'4--dc22

                                                                    2010015085

Red and Black Publishers, PO Box 7542, St Petersburg, Florida, 33734
Contact us at: info@RedandBlackPublishers.com
        Printed and manufactured in the United States of America

Introduction

In the last two weeks of October 1962, the world came closer to nuclear warfare than it ever has. For 14 tense days, United States President John F Kennedy and Soviet Premiere Nikita Kruschev stood eyeball to eyeball, each with his hand on the nuclear trigger. In the end, both sides blinked.

The object of contention was the island of Cuba. Ruled by the dictator Fulgencio Batista, Cuba had been the vacation hotspot of the Caribbean, with wealthy American tourists and jetsetters lounging at the opulent casinos and hotels in Havana. In 1959, however, a Cuban lawyer named Fidel Castro, at the head of a band of bearded guerrillas, succeeded in overthrowing Batista. At first, the US looked on in benign neglect, considering it as just another Latin dictator being overthrown by his own people. By 1960, however, Castro declared himself a socialist, nationalized and confiscated American-owned property in Cuba, and openly allied with the Soviet Union.

In the midst of the Cold War, the United States could not allow the Russians to have a base so close to the US, and the CIA began a whole series of efforts to overthrow Castro and install a pro-US strongman again. Some of the CIA's efforts were, quite frankly, nutty — including a plot to dust Castro with a powder that would make his beard fall out, and another plot to spike his drink with LSD so he would give an incoherent speech and discredit himself. Far more deadly in intention, however, were the various plans carried out jointly with the American Mafia (which had owned all the confiscated Cuban casinos) to assassinate Castro. When President Kennedy took office in 1961, the CIA already had a covert plan to use an army of Cuban exiles to invade Cuba at the Bay of Pigs and provoke a popular uprising to oust Castro. The plan failed disastrously, and the entire brigade was killed or captured.

In the wake of the Bay of Pigs failure, the US military carried out a constant surveillance of Cuba, launching periodic overflights using the U-2 spy plane. The US announced an economic embargo against Cuba in February 1962, and in September 1961, Congress passed a resolution authorizing the use of American military force in Cuba if American interests were threatened. The Pentagon planned a large-scale military exercise in the Caribbean to take place in October 1962.

To the Soviet Union and Cuba, all signs seemed to point to an imminent American invasion. Determined not to lose his only base in the Western Hemisphere, Kruschev decided to send large amounts of military supplies to Cuba, including MiG jet fighters, IL-28 bombers, anti-aircraft surface-to-air (SAM) missiles, and other arms. And, in a calculated move, he also decided to introduce medium and long-range nuclear missiles.

The arrival in Cuba of growing amounts of Soviet military hardware was detected by the US in early October, 1962, and increased U-2 overflights and satellite reconnaissance were ordered. On October 14, a U-2 flight photographed what was clearly a Soviet SS-4 nuclear missile site. Subsequent spy planes detected SS-5 sites. There were also long-range Ilyushin bombers, capable of carrying nuclear weapons to the United States. The Cuban Missile Crisis had begun — though at this time everything was kept secret and the American public had no idea it was now under a nuclear gun.

The Joint Chiefs of Staff unanimously recommended the bombing and immediate invasion of Cuba, but the political leadership countered that this would provoke the Soviets to invade West Berlin, and lead to world war. Instead, it was decided by Kennedy to impose a naval "quarantine" on Cuba, in which ships from the American Navy and from various Latin American countries would stop all inbound vessels and search them for missiles. Kennedy was gambling that the Soviet Union would not use force to prevent their ships from being stopped. At the time, the President did not know that the Russian ships were being escorted by Soviet attack submarines. He also did not know that (as recently declassified Soviet documents later revealed), in addition to the missiles, the USSR had already placed a number of active tactical nuclear weapons, including aerial bombs and short-range rockets, in Cuba and had authorized their use, under restricted circumstances, in the event of an American invasion. The nuclear abyss was far closer than either side realized at the time.

Although Kennedy had attacked the Eisenhower-Nixon administration during the campaign for supposedly allowing a dangerous "missile gap" to develop, giving the Russians a chance for nuclear superiority, when he became President, Kennedy learned the actual reality – it was the United States who had a huge advantage. The US possessed some 5,000 nuclear weapons capable of reaching Russia, while the Soviets had fewer than 350, including the 40 launchers in Cuba, that could reach America. Nevertheless, even 350 nuclear weapons would be enough to remove the United States as a functional society. If the Cuban Missile Crisis led to full-scale nuclear war, the results would be catastrophic.

On October 22, over a week after the missile sites had been found, Kennedy broke the secrecy and, in a televised address, told the nation about the missiles and about the naval quarantine. It would take about three more days for the approaching Soviet freighters to reach Cuba. Messages from the Soviet Union declared that the "blockade" was illegal and that Soviet ships had been instructed to ignore it.

On October 25, the American military was placed at DEFCON 2 ("Defense Condition 2", the step immediately preceding full-scale war).

That same day, at the United Nations Security Council, the Soviet ambassador to the UN denied that the USSR had placed any missiles in Cuba (like the Soviet Ambassador to the United States, he had not been told of their existence by Moscow). This prompted US Ambassador Adlai Stevenson to produce the U-2 aerial photographs of the missile bases.

The next day, a crucial incident occurred that was not revealed until the Soviet archives later became available to researchers. The destroyer USS *Beale* had tracked a Soviet submarine, the *B-39*, in the quarantine zone and, when it refused to surface, dropped a number of depth charges. Unknown to the Americans, the *B-39*, a "Foxtrot" class attack sub, was armed with a nuclear torpedo, and was under orders to use it if attacked. With its batteries almost dead and American depth charges exploding all around, the submarine faced a stark choice—either surface and be vulnerable to American fire, or attack immediately. According to Soviet accounts, the sub's captain, Valentin Savitsky, and the commander of the local sub fleet, Vasili Arkhipov, argued furiously, with the Captain going so far as to activate and load the nuclear torpedo before finally deciding to surface. It was a decision that single-handedly prevented World War Three.

On October 27, a surface-to-air missile shot down an American U-2 over Cuba, killing the pilot. War seemed imminent. The US began moving troops and aircraft for the planned bombing and invasion of Cuba, and also placed its forces worldwide on notice to prepare for nuclear war if the Russians responded with military force.

During this time, a flurry of diplomatic action was happening behind the scenes. On October 25, newsman John Scali of ABC was contacted by Soviet diplomat Alexander Formin (who was in reality the KGB Station Chief in Washington) to ask Scali to use his government contacts to sound out a proposal – the USSR would withdraw its missiles from Cuba if the US in turn agreed not to invade Cuba. Later that same day, a message arrived from Kruschev (now known as "the first message") offering the same solution.

The next day, however, while the Americans were considering this offer, a "second message" arrived from Kruschev, now declaring that the USSR would remove its missiles from Cuba only if the United States removed its own intermediate-range Jupiter missiles from Turkey and Italy. Although the US had itself already begun making inquiries to its allies about making a similar proposal, this new message indicated a hardening of the Soviet attitude, and Kennedy pessimistically concluded that war was now all but certain. But in a last-ditch desperate attempt, Kennedy decided to simply ignore the "second message" entirely and instead respond to Kruschev's first offer, agreeing that the US would make a no-invasion pledge in exchange for the UN-supervised removal of the missiles. To everyone's relief, Kruschev agreed to talk.

With this breakthrough, the crisis broke. On October 28, Kruschev announced that the missiles would be withdrawn. In exchange, the United States announced that it would not invade Cuba or interfere in Cuba's internal affairs. And, in a separate diplomatic agreement that was never announced publicly, the US also agreed to withdraw its Jupiter missiles from Turkey and Italy.

By November, the crisis was over. The only one not happy with the terms of its resolution was Fidel Castro, who had not been consulted by anyone during the entire negotiation.

The documents that follow are the declassified versions from both American and Soviet archives. They trace the history of the crisis from the discovery of the Soviet weapons in Cuba to the Kennedy-Kruschev agreement.

Timeline of the Cuban Missile Crisis

1962

July 26; Castro announces that the USSR is helping him defend Cuba, and declares that an American attack would produce "world war".

August 10; The CIA, after monitoring the movement of Soviet cargo ships in the Black Sea, tells Kennedy that the Soviets may be attempting to ship nuclear missiles overseas, probably to Cuba.

August 29; U-2 photos reveal SAM anti-aircraft sites at the locations where the missiles will later be found. Construction of the missile launch site has not yet begun.

August 31; Senator Keating tells the White House that there is information that missile bases are being constructed in Cuba. Keating's information apparently came from the CIA, who in turn got it from Cuban exiles.

September 4; Kennedy talks with Soviet Ambassador Dobrynin about the military buildup in Cuba. Dobrynin assures Kennedy that the weapons are defensive and that no Soviet missiles will be deployed in Cuba.

September 7; The Pentagon begins formulating contingency plans for military action in Cuba.

September 27; Contingency plans for US military intervention in Cuba are finalized.

September 28; Aerial photos of Russian ships bound for Cuba show large crates on their decks, containing nuclear-capable IL-28 bombers.

October 1; Analysts inform McNamara that there are indications of missile bases being constructed in western Cuba. McNamara orders the joint chiefs to draw up contingency plans for airstrikes against Cuba and a naval blockade.

October 9; Kennedy orders U-2 flight over Cuba to look for evidence of missiles. Weather delays the flight until October 14.

October 14; The U-2 flight takes aerial photos of western Cuba.

October 15; Morning; Photo-analysts identify Soviet SS-4 medium-range missiles and launchers in the photos. They are capable of reaching the southeastern United States, but do not yet appear to be operational.

Afternoon; The CIA is informed of the photos, but Director John McCone is on a plane and out of contact. The photo-analysts are asked to consult with missile experts to confirm their conclusions.

Late evening; The photos are shown to Defense Secretary Robert McNamara and National Security Advisor McGeorge Bundy. They decide to wait until morning, when they have better information to present, before telling the President.

October 16; 0845; Bundy tells the President of the missiles. Claiming a cold, Kennedy returns to the White House.

1145; Kennedy calls a meeting of top-level advisors (the "Executive Committee" or "ExComm") to discuss the matter. Military options are discussed. More U-2 flights are ordered.

1830; The ExComm meets again. More discussion on military options.

October 17; Morning; Photo-analysts identify Soviet SS-5 intermediate-range missile launchers. They can reach virtually the entire continental US. These launchers too do not yet appear to be operational, and no actual missiles can be seen.

Afternoon; The idea of a "surgical strike" to take out the missile sites is rejected as impractical. Opinion divides between a fullscale invasion and a naval blockade.

October 18; 1100; ExComm debates airstrikes, followed by invasion.

1430; Debate over blockade. Airstrike and invasion is seen by some as immoral. President Kennedy also leans toward blockade.

1700; Kennedy has a pre-scheduled meeting with Soviet Foreign Minister Gromyko, concerning a possible visit to the US by Kruschev in 1963. Gromyko is unaware that missiles have been placed in Cuba, and Kennedy does not tell him he knows about the missiles.

2100; ExComm meeting. By now, most administration officials favor the blockade (called a "quarantine").

October 19; 1100; ExComm forms two working groups, one each to explore the airstrike/invasion and blockade options.

Early afternoon; The two teams meet and discuss. The blockade option wins out.

Evening; Discussion centers on probable Soviet reaction to various options.

October 20; 0900; Work begins on TV speech to be made by Kennedy about the crisis.

1430; Kennedy rejects the military plans and adopts the blockade plan. TV speech is scheduled for October 22. Adlai Stevenson brings up the idea of withdrawing Jupiter missiles in Turkey as part of a settlement deal. Kennedy decides it is too soon to be making such concessions.

Evening; The Bureau Chief of the *New York Times* asks several administration officials what all the secret meeting is about. He is given a partial briefing, and is asked for national security reasons not to run a story.

The CIA estimates that about 16 of the SS-4 missiles in Cuba are now operational.

October 21; 1000; Kennedy formally approves the blockade plan. Press Secretary Pierre Salinger is told for the first time about the crisis.

1130; Tactical Air Command General Sweeney briefs the President, telling him that he cannot guarantee that an air strike would take out all the missiles. Kennedy directs Sweeney to be prepared for air action if the blockade fails.

1430; Admiral George Anderson briefs the National Security Council about the blockade plan. It is determined that any ship attempting to run the blockade will have its rudder shot off to disable it.

Several newspaper reporters now have pieced together most of the story — they are asked by the White House to withhold publication until after the president's TV address.

October 22; 1055; American Ambassadors around the world are instructed to brief friendly governments in the UK, West Germany, France and elsewhere, about the missiles and the planned "quarantine".

1200; The Strategic Air Command begins placing its B-47 and B-52 nuclear bombers on alert.

1700; Congressional leaders from both parties are briefed at the White House on the missile crisis.

1800; Secretary of State Rusk gives Soviet Ambassador Dobrynin an advance copy of the President's speech.

1900; President Kennedy tells the nation about the missile crisis.

October 23; 1906; President Kennedy formally signs the order for the naval quarantine. Low-level reconnaissance flights begin over Cuba. Moscow raises the military preparedness of its forces.

1930; Robert Kennedy is told by Ambassador Dobrynin that there are no missiles in Cuba, and that Soviet ships have orders to defy the US blockade.

2215; The blockade line is drawn in closer to Cuba, from 800 miles to 500 miles, to give the Soviets more time to consider their position.

October 24; Early morning; All but one of the Soviet ships en route to Cuba are reported to have reversed course. Later, it is determined that at least three Russian ships are approaching the quarantine zone. Soviet submarines are also reported in the area.

1000; The quarantine officially goes into effect.

1025; Two Russian ships at the quarantine zone are intercepted by the USS *Essex*. They stop. Kennedy orders no further interceptions to be made for one hour, until the situation is clear. No Russian ships attempt to run the blockade.

1925; Kruschev sends a message to Kennedy declaring that the blockade is illegal and he has instructed his ships not to respect it.

October 25; 0715; The Soviet ship *Bucharest*, which is not believed to be carrying military equipment, is allowed to pass through the blockade without being stopped.

Afternoon; American UN Ambassador Adlai Stevenson presents aerial photographs of the Cuban missile sites to the UN Security Council.

1700; Intelligence briefing indicates that work is accelerating on the missile sites and more SS-4 missiles might now be operational. US forces are placed at DEFCON 2, and permission is given to load live nuclear weapons aboard US aircraft.

October 26; The Russian submarine *B-36* is depth-charged by American destroyers and surfaces.

1300; American reporter John Scali is contacted by a Russian diplomat and is asked to determine from his government contacts whether the US would be interested in a diplomatic effort to trade removal of the Cuba missiles in exchange for an American pledge not to invade Cuba.

1800; "The first message" arrives from Kruschev, offering a missile withdrawal in exchange for a no-invasion promise.

October 27; 0900; "The second message" arrives from Kruschev, declaring that the missiles would be withdrawn from Cuba only if corresponding American missiles were taken out of Turkey and Italy.

1200; An American U-2 plane is shot down by a SAM anti-aircraft missile over Cuba. A second reconnaissance plane is damaged by antiaircraft fire.

1600; During a briefing, Kennedy receives word that the U-2 had been shot down. He decides not to retaliate, but orders that if any more planes are attacked, the SAM sites would be bombed.

1615; ABC reporter Scali meets again with Soviet KGB Section Chief Formin, asking why the offer from Kruschev suddenly changed. Formin blames it on "miscommunication".

1945; Robert Kennedy meets with Ambassador Dobrynin and offers to remove American missiles from Turkey and Italy in exchange for removal of the missiles in Cuba.

2005; President Kennedy sends a letter to Kruschev confirming the missile deal.

October 28; 0600; CIA reports that all 24 SS-4 missiles in Cuba are now operational. Although work is proceeding on the SS-5 sites, no actual SS-5 missiles seem to have entered Cuba yet.

0900; Kruschev send message accepting the missile-trade solution. The US publicly pledges not to invade Cuba, and secretly pledges to withdraw the Jupiter missiles in Turkey and Italy. The crisis ends.

1700; Soviet technicians begin to dismantle the Cuban missiles.

The Documents

Central Intelligence Agency Memorandum

Washington, January 19, 1961.

SPECIAL GROUP MEETINGS—CUBA
19 January 1961
1. Mr. Willauer presented the highlights of a paper which he had prepared following meetings of the special contingency planning group. He concluded that several major aspects of the overall plan require clarification or further decision, citing the following: (a) the use of U.S. air bases for strikes before and after D-Day, (b) staging of the invasion force, possibly from the U.S., (c) specific action, including timing, to get support of other Latin American countries, (d) how and when to recognize a provisional government, (e) the possibility of having to provide considerably more overt support than originally planned.
2. Mr. Dulles noted that the next ten-day period poses a number of problems from the standpoint of policy approval. In

answer to a question, Mr. Barnes said we are not planning specific overflights in the immediate future but urged that we be in a position to service requests as quickly as possible. The Group agreed that dispatches by sea can be continued without further approval at this time. It was also agreed that a high level meeting, to include the new Secretaries of State and of Defense should be arranged as soon as possible to reaffirm basic concepts.

3. Mr. Merchant said that the Department of Justice is not now prepared to take any action against Masferrer. The Group agreed this seemed reasonable under the circumstances.

4. Mr. Merchant reported the opinion of Assistant Secretary Mann that President Ydigoras may be overthrown in the next few days, perhaps by leftists in the Army or Air Force. Mann had urged that it be agreed that no Cuban trainees be placed at the disposal of Ydigoras and that plans for evacuation on very short notice be firmed up. It was noted that Mr. Mann and Col. King are in close touch on this matter.

Memorandum
Washington, January 22, 1961, 10 a.m.

SUBJECT
Meeting on Cuba

PARTICIPANTS
The Secretary of State
The Secretary of Defense
The Attorney General
The Under Secretary of State-designate
The Under Secretary of State for Political Affairs
Chairman of the Joint Chiefs of Staff
Mr. Allen W. Dulles

Mr. Paul Nitze
General Bonesteel
Ambassador Hugh S. Cumming
Mr. Thomas Mann
Ambassador Whiting Willauer
Mr. Richard Bissell
Mr. Tracy Barnes
General David Gray
Colonel Cecil Shuler
Mr. Joseph W. Scott

The Secretary called on Mr. Mann to give a resume of activities regarding Cuba in the diplomatic field over the last several months. Mr. Mann said that several months ago he had talked with members of the Latin American diplomatic corps and had indicated to them that the United States wanted to know whether the OAS system could prevent Castro's exportation of communism elsewhere in the hemisphere. The reaction of most members of the corps was that they wanted to know first where the Kennedy administration and the Quadros administration would stand. A short time ago, the Colombian Ambassador suggested to Mr. Mann that he go to Colombia and talk with President Lleras, who had once been Secretary General of OAS and who could be expected to be eager to see the OAS used in an effort to stop Castro. Mr. Mann then presented at some length a procedure for lining up support in the OAS for sanctions against Castro. He mentioned that a complicating factor was the problem posed by the Trujillo regime in the Dominican Republic. He then listed the possible lineup in the OAS which might favor effective action against Castro if properly approached. In summary Mr. Mann felt that the basic choice was whether we go it alone or multilaterally. (After the meeting, Mr. Mann made clear to some of the participants that the multilateral approach he had in mind should proceed simultaneously with the development of action plans in other fields and should in any case provide us with a realistic estimate of multilateral possibilities within about a month from the time soundings were begun.)

At this point, Mr. Merchant noted that two distinctions should be made regarding possible Latin American support for action against Castro. First a distinction should be drawn between the attitudes of governments and the attitudes of peoples within Latin American countries. A second distinction should be made with regard to the difference between what governments would be willing to support publicly and what they would be willing to support only privately.

Ambassador Willauer said that one of the matters that had captured his attention from his position in the field was how the fear engendered by Castro had dried up private capital activities in all of Latin America. Not only American firms, but also local sources of capital were seeking to escape.

With reference to the distinction between governmental and public attitudes, the Secretary asked Mr. Mann whether we might be in some rather tight situations in a number of countries of the hemisphere if Moscow pushed the button, i.e., with respect to pro-Castro movements in a number of countries. Mr. Mann said this would definitely be the case and mentioned Venezuela and Colombia as examples. As a further example of this [censored] mentioned that he had a private meeting with [censored] had been brutally frank. [censored] mentioned he would send the Secretary a memorandum on his talk [censored].

The Secretary asked whether a systematic review had been made of possible actions under the Monroe Doctrine. He thought we ought to know what would be the legal situation under the Doctrine with regard to differing levels of action. Mr. Mann replied that a lot of thought had been given to this but as far as he was aware no systematic study had been made of it. He mentioned that Mr. Arthur Dean had recommended a young lawyer to study this problem. Mr. Mann felt that we should have outside legal advice on it.

The Secretary next asked at what point did we begin to consider that Castro had gone beyond the watershed in Cuba, adding that it seemed clear there was little hope now. Mr. Mann indicated it was difficult to name a specific point. There were a number of things that Castro had done that led to the conclusion that he had crossed the watershed. One early action on his part was his initiative in seeking ties with the Sino-Soviet bloc, which he had undertaken before we had acted on sugar quotas. Mr. Mann then listed other actions on Castro's part such as expropriation of land, setting up the militia, etc. He summarized by saying that history may indicate that Cuba had been one of the most rapidly communized states—faster even than those in Eastern Europe. He pointed out that Castro has complete control, something totally different from the situation in the traditional dictatorships in Latin America.

Mr. Bowles asked whether we had an estimate on the economic needs of Cuba and how far the Sino-Soviet bloc would likely go to meet them. Mr. Mann indicated there was such an estimate which needed, however, to be updated.

The Secretary then called on General Lemnitzer to review the military situation in Cuba. After having emphasized the extreme sensitivity of some of the information he was about to give, General Lemnitzer estimated that the Revolutionary Army had 32,000, the Revolutionary National Police 9,000, the Militia over 200,000. He said that Cuba was an armed camp. They had received more than 30,000 tons of arms and equipment over the past five or six months. This buildup had made a decided change in the U.S. contingency plans to deal with it. He said there was no evidence of jet aircraft, missiles, or nuclear weapons; on the other hand, about 100 Cuban pilots were being trained in jet aircraft in Czechoslovakia. Their return to Cuba would add a new dimension to the problem.

With respect to Guantanamo, the General identified the critical problem for us as being the water supply. In response to a question from the Secretary he said there was no evidence of a buildup of Cuban forces around Guantanamo. He also indicated that very precise rules of engagement had been worked out for our aircraft in the area of Cuba. These included hot pursuit into Cuban airspace. The Secretary wanted to know whether the Cubans knew about this. The General said that they did not.

The Secretary then asked whether the Cubans had any air-strike capability against Miami. The General replied they didn't have much now but when the pilots now training in Czechoslovakia return and if jet aircraft became available for them this would change the picture.

The Secretary then called on Mr. Dulles to outline the program for which he has been responsible with regard to Cuba. Mr. Dulles said that last March 17th the President had approved a covert action program to eliminate Castro. There had been three major lines of development under this program. The first was the political front, the second the psychological front, and the third was training Cubans for paramilitary activities. With regard to the political front he indicated that a vehicle had been created, the FRD, to enable the Agency to pull together as many of the disparate anti-Castro groups as possible. At one time there had been 184 anti-Castro refugee groups. He thought that on the whole the FRD was a reasonable representation of the anti-Castro political spectrum now inside Cuba. It covered the range from a little to the right to a little to the left of center. There were no Batista-ites or Communists in the FRD. The essentials of its program were the restoration of the Cuban constitution of 1940 and the original reforms announced by Castro, which had been subsequently laid aside. He then mentioned that under the mechanism of the FRD they had proceeded with psychological and paramilitary activities. Under the former he mentioned Swan Island, WRUL and certain radio stations in the Miami area, publications such as *Avance, El Mundo, Diario de la Marina* and *Bohemia*.

Mr. Dulles next described the paramilitary training activities going on at Retalhuleu in Guatemala. Under cover of the FRD, he said, we now have about five to six hundred highly trained Cuban foot soldiers. These have been trained by three Special Forces teams from Fort Bragg. The head trainer considered them the best-trained men in Latin America. In addition, we had sixteen B-26's, four or five C-46's and seven C-54's. At the present time, we had six active communications teams in Cuba and were planning to put in small paramilitary teams of six to eight men whose mission would be to try to line up resistance in Cuba.

The Secretary asked what was the estimated strength of resistance in Cuba at the present time and Mr. Dulles said he thought we could count on about 1,000, who were somewhat scattered. The Secretary then asked whether we have a capability to establish a going resistance movement without use of U.S. forces. Mr. Dulles said this would necessarily depend on how many came over to the dissident side. He said that our present Cuban force in training would reach 700 to 800. He then went on to mention the difficult problem of keeping them in Guatemala. At the best, we had six weeks to two months left before something would have to be done about them.

Mr. Dulles then said that in the normal course of events the Agency would continue drops—the next ones were scheduled for January 25-26—but that policy guidance was now needed from the new administration. He mentioned that the 5412 Group had met weekly and it had heretofore been possible for him to get his guidance from that Group. He said that at the moment what he needed was policy guidance on the following matters: (1) continuance of training, (2) introduction of small teams into Cuba with sabotage and communications capability, and (3) drops of food and supplies to dissidents now in Cuba. Mr. Barnes added that guidance was also needed on infiltrating political leaders into Cuba. He mentioned Artime and Manuel Ray.

Secretary McNamara asked what size Cuban force was considered necessary to buildup enough strength to overthrow Castro. Mr. Dulles said he thought that our presently planned Cuban force could probably hold a beachhead long enough for us to recognize a provisional government and aid that government openly. Secretary McNamara then asked whether the estimate was that time was strengthening or weakening us. Mr. Dulles replied that it now was weakening us. This could change if people in Cuba got hungry, but this might be a long time off. Food was still being sent to Cuba from the United States. General Lemnitzer interjected to say that Castro's popularity might be going down but his grip was getting tighter daily.

Mr. Bowles asked whether we knew of any cliques in the Castro hierarchy. Mr. Dulles said we didn't think there were any; that it now seemed to be down to the hard core. Mr. Bowles recalled the division between Trotsky and Stalin. Mr. Dulles replied that they didn't see any such division in the Cuban picture. He said he believed that the Castro regime had plans to export Castro's communism; that they already have power among the people in the Caribbean countries and elsewhere, particularly in Venezuela and Colombia.

The Attorney General said that about five days ago he had been approached by a former attorney of Castro's who was till close to Raul Castro, who had indicated that Raul might be going over into counter-Revolutionary efforts, principally against Che Guevara. The attorney had asked him what were the prospects for cutting off petroleum shipments to Cuba in the event of Raul's defection. He expected the attorney, who is now in Cuba, to return shortly with more on this.

Turning to the possibility of recognizing a provisional government, the Secretary indicated that seizing the Isle of Pines would have a number of advantages. Mr. Dulles said it had indeed a number of advantages but one major problem was how could dissidents in Cuba join up with a force landed there. General Lemnitzer said the Isle of Pines was heavily defended. Ambassador Willauer said that his first reaction had been very much in favor of trying to seize Pine Island. The head of the Special Forces team training the unit in Guatemala, however, had informed him that they would expect to lose roughly 50% of an invading force. He also brought up the possibility of a counter-attack by Castro forces from Cuba itself. The Secretary then said he was thinking about a two-step operation; first the establishment of a beachhead on the Isle of Pines and then moving on to Cuba itself. In this connection he asked whether we had a Puerto Rican ranger battalion and General Lemnitzer said we did not.

The Secretary next asked whether we anticipated any problem about restaffing Cuban personnel at the Guantanamo base. General Lemnitzer said there was no problem about this at the moment. About 1,000 Cubans lived on the base. The rest lived outside. The Secretary asked what about the possibility of putting the force now in Guatemala on the base at Guantanamo. General Lemnitzer replied that there might be some problem of concealment and an action of that sort might justify an attack against the base. The Secretary then asked in terms of contingency planning how many U.S. divisions were being thought of. General Lemnitzer in reply said two plus or maybe three.

The Secretary then commented on the enormous implications of putting U.S. forces ashore in Cuba and said we should consider everything short of this, including rough stuff, before doing so. He said he felt we might be confronted by serious uprisings all over Latin America if U.S. forces were to go in, not to mention the temptation that the commitment of such forces in Cuba would provide elsewhere in the world. In this connection he again mentioned the possibility of a physical base on the Isle of Pines for a provisional government which we could recognize. This he thought would be a powerful step forward. What we needed was a "fig leaf." A Cuban provisional government on the Isle of Pines, for example, could sink Soviet ships carrying supplies to Castro with less danger than would be the case with direct involvement of U.S. forces.

The Secretary then asked Mr. Dulles if he could say offhand how much money the Cuban operation had cost to date. Mr. Dulles said that it had cost about $6 million last year and $28 million was earmarked for the first six months of 1961. The Secretary asked him whether he could use a quarter of a billion dollars. Was there a possibility, for example, of suborning a unit on the Isle of Pines. This in the long run would be much cheaper than using U.S. forces directly. The Secretary also mentioned that we should inquire into the possible usefulness of a pacific blockade with a carefully and publicly defined mission. In elaboration he mentioned the possibility of "making some international law." Should we, for example, announce that the introduction of jet aircraft into this hemisphere by the Bloc would be regarded as a violation of the Monroe Doctrine. It would then be the Bloc's responsibility if they chose to "escalate" in the face of such an announcement.

General Lemnitzer then asked permission for General Bonesteel to show a chart of several possible courses of action in ascending scale which had been drawn up for contingency planning purposes. General Bonesteel summarized the chart and said that in his view we needed an overall national plan. The Secretary agreed and said it was clear a task force was needed to devote itself to the development of such a plan. He thought that the task force should be composed of representatives of State, Defense, and CIA. Mr. Dulles said that perhaps also representatives of Treasury and Justice should be included as needed.

Mr. Merchant commented that the inadequacies of the original March 17th plan only began to become apparent in November and mentioned that the intelligence community had brought out an estimate in the first part of December concluding that time was running against us in Cuba. He then mentioned that we were now working against some important deadlines. Among these were the shakiness of the Ydigoras regime, and the so-called "shelf-life" of the Cuban unit in Guatemala. The possibility of bringing the Cuban forces to the United States raised the question of how overtly the United States was prepared to show its hand. These problems were of an immediate nature, and another reason why policy guidance was needed as soon as possible.

Mr. Dulles said he hoped that the 5412 Group would be continued and could resume its meetings as soon as possible. The Secretary concluded by saying he would try to work out some arrangement about this tomorrow or the next day.

(At the end of the meeting, Ambassador Willauer gave the Secretary a memorandum he had written for Mr. Merchant on January 18 which outlined a number of major issues on which policy guidance is needed. The memorandum was a reflection of views developed at the first meetings of a tripartite (State, DOD, and CIA) task force on the Cuban problem which had been chaired by Ambassador Willauer. A copy is attached to the original of this memorandum.)

Memorandum

Washington, January 28, 1961.

MEMORANDUM OF DISCUSSION ON CUBA

PRESENT

The President, The Vice President, the Secretary of State, the Secretary of Defense, the Director of Central Intelligence, the Chairman of the Joint Chiefs of Staff, Assistant Secretary Mann, Assistant Secretary Nitze, Mr. Tracy Barnes, Mr. McGeorge Bundy

The meeting began with a description of the present situation in Cuba by the Director of Central Intelligence. The judgment expressed without dissent was that Cuba is now for practical purposes a Communist-controlled state. The two basic elements in the present situation are a rapid and continuing build-up of Castro's military power, and a great increase also in popular opposition to his regime.

The United States has undertaken a number of covert measures against Castro, including propaganda, sabotage, political action, and direct assistance to anti-Castro Cubans in military training. A particularly urgent question is the use to be made of a group of such Cubans now in training in Guatemala, who cannot remain indefinitely where they are.

The present estimate of the Department of Defense is that no course of action currently authorized by the United States Government will be effective in reaching the agreed national goal of overthrowing the Castro regime. Meanwhile, the

Department of State sees grave political dangers to our position throughout the Western hemisphere in any overt military action not authorized and supported by the Organization of American States.

After considerable discussion, the following proceedings were authorized by the President:

1. A continuation and accentuation of current activities of the Central Intelligence Agency, including increased propaganda, increased political action and increased sabotage. Continued overflights for these purposes were specifically authorized.

2. The Defense Department, with CIA, will review proposals for the active deployment of anti-Castro Cuban forces on Cuban territory, and the results of this analysis will be promptly reported to the President.

3. The Department of State will prepare a concrete proposal for action with other Latin American countries to isolate the Castro regime and to bring against it the judgment of the Organization of American States. It is expected that this proposal may involve a commitment of the President's personal authority behind a special mission or missions to such Latin American leaders as Lleras, Betancourt and Quadros.

Finally, it was agreed that the United States must make entirely clear that its position with respect to the Cuban Government is currently governed by its firm opposition to Communist penetration of the American Republics, and not by any hostility to democratic social revolution and economic reform. The President intends to deal with this matter himself in the State of the Union Address

The President particularly desires that no hint of these discussions reach any personnel beyond those most immediately concerned within the Executive Branch.

McGeorge Bundy

Memorandum
Washington, April 18, 1961.

I think you will find at noon that the situation in Cuba is not a bit good.

The Cuban armed forces are stronger, the popular response is weaker, and our tactical position is feebler that we had hoped. Tanks have done in one beachhead, and the position is precarious at the others.

The CIA will press hard for further air help—this time by Navy cover to B-26s attacking the tanks. But I think we can expect other pleas in rapid crescendo, because we are up against a formidable enemy, who is reacting with military know-how and vigor.

The immediate request I would grant (because it cannot easily be proven against us and because men are in need), but the real question is whether to reopen the possibility of further intervention and support or to accept the high probability that our people, at best, will go into the mountains in defeat.

In my own judgment the right course now is to eliminate the Castro air force, by neutrally-painted U.S. planes if necessary, and then let the battle go its way.

McG. B.

Program Review, Operation Mongoose

18 January 1962

THE CUBA PROJECT

I. Objective
The U.S. objective is to help the Cubans overthrow the Communist regime from within Cuba and institute a new government with which the United States can live in peace.

II. Concept of Operation

Basically, the operation is to bring about the revolt of the Cuban people. The revolt will overthrow the Communist regime and institute a new government with which the United States can live in peace.

The revolt requires a strongly motivated political action movement established within Cuba, to generate the revolt, to give it direction towards the object, and to capitalize on the climactic moment. The political actions will be assisted by economic warfare to induce failure of the Communist regime to supply Cuba's economic needs, psychological operations to turn the peoples' resentment increasingly against the regime, and military-type groups to give the popular movement an action arm for sabotage and armed resistance in support of political objectives.

The failure of the U.S.-sponsored operation in April 1961 so shook the faith of Cuban patriots in U.S. competence and intentions in supporting a revolt against Castro that a new effort to generate a revolt against the regime in Cuba must have active support from key Latin American countries. Further, the foreignness (Soviet Union and Bloc) of the tyranny imposed on the Cuban people must be made clear to the people of the Western Hemisphere to the point of their deep anger and open actions to defend the Western Hemisphere against such foreign invasion. Such an anger will be generated, in part, by appeals from the popular movement within Cuba to other Latin Americans especially.

The preparation phase must result in a political action organization in being in key localities inside Cuba, with its own means for internal communications, its own voice for psychological operations, and its own action arm (small guerrilla bands, sabotage squads, etc.). It must have the sympathetic support of the majority of the Cuban people, and make this fact known to the outside world. (It is reported that the majority of Cubans are not for the present regime, but are growing apathetic towards what appears to be a hopeless future or the futility of their status.)

The climactic moment of revolt will come from an angry reaction of the people to a government action (sparked by an incident), or from a fracturing of the leadership cadre within the regime, or both. (A major goal of the Project must be to bring this about.) The popular movement will capitalize on this climactic moment by initiating an open revolt. Areas will be taken and held. If necessary, the popular movement will appeal for help to the free nations of the Western Hemisphere. The United States, if possible in concert with other Western Hemisphere nations, will then give open support to the Cuban peoples' revolt. Such support will include military force, as necessary.

III. Estimate of the Situation

Our planning requires sound intelligence estimates of the situation re Cuba. The latest National Estimate (SNIE 85-61) of 28 November 1961 contains operational conclusions not based on hard fact, in addition to its intelligence conclusions; this is a repetition of an error in the planning for the unsuccessful operation of last April.

The planning indicated herein will be revised, as necessary, based on the hard intelligence estimate of the situation by the U.S. Intelligence community. A new National Intelligence Estimate (NIE 85-62 on Cuba), due on 23 January, apparently has been postponed until 7 February.

It is recognized that one result of the Project, so far, has been to start the collection of Intelligence on Cuba in depth, to provide facts on which to base firm estimates and operations.

IV. Initial Phase (30 Nov 61-81 Jan 62)

A. Establish a U.S. mechanism for the project

Status: The President's directive of 30 November 1961 was implemented by creating a U.S. operations team, with Brig. Gen. Lansdale as Chief of Operations, and with tasks promptly assigned. His immediate staff are Mr. Hand and Major Patchell. Representatives of Secretaries and Agency Directors are:

State — Woodward (Goodwin, Hurwitch)

CIA — Helms

Defense — Brig. Gen. Craig

USIA — Wilson

B. Intelligence Support

Status: CIA made a special survey of U.S. capabilities to interrogate Cuban refugees in the USA (1,700-2,000 arriving per month) and on 16 January approved a program increasing the staff at the Opa Locka Interrogation Center in Florida from the present 2 people to 34. CIA will build up agent assets (positive intelligence assets inside Cuba are very limited and it has no counter-intelligence assets inside). Special intelligence assets will be exploited more fully. The Cuba Project needs far more hard intelligence in depth than is presently available. CIA will require further assistance from Defense and other U.S. organizations in this intelligence effort, and is submitting specific qualifications for personnel on 19 January.
C. Political platform for peoples' movement inside Cuba.

Status: State has sketched in a broad outline. CIA is to produce the firm platform statement of aims for which the Cubans who will operate inside Cuba are willing to risk their lives, and upon which popular support can be generated.

D. Nucleus for popular movement

Status: To date, CIA has been unable to produce the necessary political action agents for this purpose. Upon re-evaluation of its capabilities, CIA now hopes to complete spotting and assessing eight to ten Cuban political action agents by 15 February, from among Cubans available in the United States. The minimum need for the Project to be effective is 30 such political action Cubans and CIA is tasked to make a priority search for them among Cubans in the U.S. and Caribbean area.

E. Deployment of nucleus

Status: CIA is tasked to select 20 localities within Cuba where political action groups can be established. Initial selection and plans for establishing these action groups are now due 1 February. Havana, and localities in the provinces of Camaguey and Las Villas will receive priority consideration, according to present intelligence. Planning on this must be adjusted as firmer intelligence is acquired.

F. Diplomatic actions

Status: State is concentrating on the OAS Meeting of Foreign Ministers, which opens 22 January, hoping to get wide Western Hemisphere support for OAS resolutions condemning Cuba and isolating it from the rest of the Hemisphere. A companion resolution, to offer OAS relief directly to the suffering Cuban people (similar to U.S. relief to Russia, 1919-20) is being considered, as a means to reach the Cuban people sympathetically without going through their Communist government. The OAS meeting is to be supported by public demonstrations in Latin America, generated by CIA, and a psychological campaign assisted by USIA.

The major task for our diplomatic capability is to encourage Latin American leaders to develop independent operations similar to this Project, seeking an internal revolt of the Cuban people against the Communist regime. This is yet to be initiated by State and must be vigorously pressed.

G. Economic warfare

Status: This critical key to our political action Project is still in the planning stage under State leadership. State is basing future economic actions, including plans for an embargo on Cuban trade, on the outcome of the forthcoming OAS meeting. Meanwhile, State has chaired an Economic action group, which agreed on developing 13 actions. 15 February is set for a report on implementing plans, so that actions can be initiated. CIA was unable to undertake action to sabotage the sugar harvest, which commences about 15 January, and upon which Cuba's one-crop sugar economy depends. (Sabotage of transport, mills, sugar sacking and cane fields was explored.)

H. TV intrusion

Status: Equipment to enable TV intrusion of Havana TV broadcasts has been reactivated on a small vessel under CIA control. CIA plans to attempt intrusion on 22 January during Castro's forthcoming speech and parade demonstrations.

I. Special sabotage support

Status: State has explored, with negative results, the feasibility of pre-emptive action with respect to tanker charters (most Bloc shipments to Cuba are carried in Western bottoms). CIA has initiated action to contaminate POL supplies for Cuba, although visible results (stoppage of some Cuban transport) are not expected until mid-1962. [censored]

J. Military actions

Status: Defense has been tasked with preparing a contingency plan for U.S. military action, in case the Cuban people request U.S. help when their revolt starts making headway. This contingency plan will permit obtaining a policy decision on the major point of U.S. intentions, and is looked upon as a positive political-psychological factor in a peoples' revolt, even more than as a possible military action. Defense also has been tasked with fully assisting State and CIA, as commitments of Defense men, money, and materiel are required.

K. Major elements of the population

Status: Both State and CIA are continuing to explore their capabilities (with results largely negative to date) for mounting special group operations inside Cuba focused upon dynamic elements of the population, particularly [censored] through Labor contacts to reach the workers. Other elements include enlistment of the youth and professional groupings. Special consideration is to be given to doing this through Latin American operational contacts. This is vital to the success of our political action nucleus when CIA can put it into place.

L. Outlook

Status: As reported to the Special Group last week, there has been a period of a realistic second look at CIA capabilities to mount the required clandestine operations against Cuba, and a subsequent start in "tooling up." After this second look, CIA has concluded that its realistic role should be to create at least the illusion of a popular movement, to win external support for it, to improve CIA operational capability, and to help create a climate which will permit provocative actions in support of a shift to overt action. This outlook, although arrived at thoughtfully within CIA, is far short of the Cuba Project's goals. CIA must take yet another hard look at its potential capabilities, in the light of the following tasking, to determine if it cannot make the greater effort required.

V. Target Schedule

A. Intelligence

Task 1: NIE 85-62 on Cuba due 7 February (CIA).

Task 2: By 15 February, Opa Locka Interrogation Center to be made an effective operation for collection and processing of intelligence (CIA with support of Defense, State, I&NS, FBI).

Task 3: Intelligence collection from Cuban refugees elsewhere than Miami area. CIA to survey other refugee points (*[censored]* etc.) and on a priority basis to ensure maximum coverage of all such source points. 15 February target date.

Task 4: CIA to continue its re-examination of intelligence assets, with priority on agents inside Cuba, and report on capability by 15 February. Also included is coverage of intelligence through third country sources, particularly those having diplomatic relations with Cuba.

B. Political

Task 5: CIA to submit plan by 1 February for defection of top Cuban government officials, to fracture the regime from within. The effort must be imaginative and bold enough to consider a "name" defector to be worth at least a million U.S. dollars. This can be the key to our political action goal and must be mounted without delay as a major CIA project.

Task 6: CIA to complete plans by 1 February for Cover and Deception actions, to help fracture the Communist regime in Cuba. Defense, State and FBI are to collaborate on this.

Task 7: By 1 February, CIA to submit operations schedule for initiating popular movement within Cuba. This must include localities selected inside Cuba, assessment of selected Cubans, their infiltration, activity assignments, and political platform. One section must deal with the "underground," assess its true status and plans to use it.

Task 8: State to follow up the OAS meeting by having U.S. Embassies in Latin America exploit all opportunities to enlist local sympathy for the Cuban people and to increase hostility towards the Communist regime in Cuba. State to submit report on results of this assignment by 13 February, so further planning can be programmed.

Task 9: By 15 February, State to submit an inventory of operational assets in the Caribbean area, including capabilities of local governments or groups to mount operations on their own, to help achieve the Project's goals. Plans for early use of such capabilities are due by 19 February.

Task 10: CIA to submit operational schedule for using assets in the Caribbean area to achieve the Project's political action goals. The objective of working on dynamic elements of the Cuban population (such as workers, farmers) is underscored. Due 19 February.

C. Economic

Task 11: State to prepare recommendations to the President on U.S. trade with Cuba, as follow-up to OAS meeting. (If the minimum result of the meeting is an agreement to condemn Cuba as an accomplice of the Sino-Soviet Bloc and adoption of a general statement that Cuba presents a threat to the peace and security of the Hemisphere, State is prepared to recommend to the President that remaining trade between the U.S. and Cuba be barred.)

Task 12: State to plan, with Commerce and other U.S. agencies, on how to halt the diversion of vital items in the Cuban trade.

Due date 15 February. Cooperation of other OAS nations, particularly Canada and Mexico, is to be explored by State.

Task 13: State with Commerce and others involved, to plan on how to make "positive list" items to Latin America be subject to the same licensing procedures as applied to such shipments to other parts of the free world. Due 15 February.

Task 14: State to obtain from Commerce proposal to amend present export controls of technical data (petrochemical, communications equipment) so that Cuba is treated the same as the Sino-Soviet Bloc. Due 15 February.

Task 15: State by 15 February to submit recommendations on issuance of transportation order (T-3) under authority of the Defense Production Act of 1950 forbidding U.S.-owned vessels to engage in trade with Cuba.

Task 16: State plan due 15 February on feasible extension of U.S. port treatment now given to Bloc and Cuban vessels to charter vessels of Bloc and Cuba (Treasury to advise on this).

Task 17: State to report by 15 February on feasibility of harassing Bloc shipping by refusing entry into U.S. ports (statedly for security reasons), if vessels have called or will call at Cuban ports.

Task 18: [censored]

Task 19: State to report by 15 February on possibilities for obtaining the discreet cooperation of the National Foreign Trade Council to urge U.S. shippers to refuse to ship on vessels which call at Cuban ports. (Commerce to assist on this.)

Task 20: State to report by 15 February on possibilities to obtain the discreet cooperation of the U.S. Chamber of Commerce and the National Association of Manufacturers to influence U.S. firms having subsidiaries abroad to adhere to the spirit of U.S. economic sanctions. (Commerce to assist on this.)

Task 21: CIA to submit plan by 15 February for inducing failures in food crops in Cuba. *[censored]*

Task 22: State to report by 15 February on status of plans to gain cooperation of NATO allies (bilaterally and in the NATO forum, as appropriate). Objective is to persuade these nations to take steps to isolate Cuba from the West.

Task 23: State to report by 15 February on status of actions undertaken with Japan, which has comparatively significant trade with Cuba, along lines similar to those with NATO nations.

Task 24: CIA to submit plan by February on disruption of the supply of Cuban nickel to the Soviet Union. *[censored]*

D. Psychological

Task 25: USIA to submit plan by 15 February for the most effective psychological exploitation of actions undertaken in the Project, towards the end result of awakening world sympathy for the Cuban people (as a David) battling against the Communist regime (as a Goliath) and towards stimulating Cubans inside Cuba to join "the cause."

Task 26: CIA to submit by 15 February its operational schedule for a psychological campaign to provoke a relaxing of police state control within Cuba. This is to include effective means of publicly indicting "peoples' criminals" for justice after liberation of Cuba (not only individual top officials, but members of the Vigilancia, etc.).

Task 27: CIA and USIA will report on progress as of 15 February in developing identification of the popular movement inside Cuba, as with songs, symbols, propaganda themes.

Task 28: By 15 February CIA will report on plans and actions for propaganda support of the popular movement inside Cuba. Included will be exactly what is planned for use by the movement inside Cuba, and feasibility of using smuggled food packets (such as the "I Shall Return" cigarette packets to Philippine guerrillas in World War II) as morale boosters in generating the popular movement.

E. Military Action

Task 29: Defense to submit contingency plan for use of U.S. military force to support the Cuban popular movement, including a statement of conditions under which Defense believes such action would be required to win the Project's goal and believes such action would not necessarily lead to general war. Due 28 February.

Task 30: CIA to submit by 15 February its operational schedule for sabotage actions inside Cuba, including timing proposed for the actions and how they affect the generation and support of a popular movement, to achieve the Project goals.

Task 31: CIA to submit specific requests to Defense for required support by Defense as early as possible after its plans firm up. Requests for all major needs are expected by 23 February.

Task 32: Defense will submit plan for "special operations" use of Cubans enlisted in the U.S. armed forces. Due 28 February.

VI. Future Plans

By 20 February, it is expected that sufficient realistic plans for individual tasks will have been received, and initial actions started, to permit a firm time-table to be constructed. Since the President directed that the Chief of Operations conduct the Project through the appropriate organizations and Departments of the Government, and since these U.S. organizations are mainly in the initial inventory and development of capabilities phase concerning assigned tasks, a precise operations timetable as of today would be too speculative to be useful.

CIA has alerted Defense that it will require considerable military support (including two submarines, PT boats, Coast Guard type cutters, Special Forces trainers, C-54 aircraft, F-86 aircraft, amphibian aircraft, helio-couriers, Army leaflet battalion, and Guantanamo as a base for submarine operations). Also, CIA apparently believes that its role should be to create and expand a popular movement, illusory and actual, which will create a political climate which can provide a framework of plausible excuse for armed intervention. This is not in conformity with the Presidential directive now governing Project tasking. Actually, the role of creating the political climate and plausible excuse for armed intervention would be more properly that of State and Defense, if such an objective becomes desirable.

Soviet Memorandum

24 May 1962
Top Secret
Special Importance

One Copy
To the Chairman of the Defense Council
Comrade N.S. Khrushchev
In accordance with your instructions the Ministry of Defense proposes:

1. To deploy on the island of Cuba a Group of Soviet Forces comprising all branches of the Armed Forces, under a single integrated staff of the Group of Forces headed by a Commander in Chief of Soviet forces in Cuba.

2. To send to Cuba the 43rd Missile Division (commander of the division Major General Statsenko) comprising five missile regiments:

The 79th, 181st and 664th R-12 missile regiments with eight launchers each, in all 24 launchers.

The 665th and 668th R-14 missile regiments with eight launchers each, in all 16 launchers.

In all, 40 R-12 and R-14 launchers.

With the missile units to send 1.5 missiles and 1.5 warheads per each launcher (in all 60 missiles and 60 warheads), with one field missile technical base (PRTB) per regiment for equipping the warheads and rocket fuel in mobile tanks with 1.75 loadings per R-12 missile and 1.5 per R-14 missile at each launcher.

Deployment of the R-12 missiles is planned in the [*illegible*] variant with the use of SP-6. Prepared assembly-disassembly elements of the SP-6 for equipping the missile pads will be prepared at construction enterprises of the Ministry of Defense by 20 June and shipped together with the regiments. Upon arrival at the designated locations, personnel of the missile regiments will within ten days equip the launch positions by their own efforts, and will be ready to launch missiles.

For deployment of the missile, units armed with R-14 missiles, construction on site will last about four months. This work can be handled by the personnel of the units, but it will be necessary to augment them with a group of 25 engineer-construction personnel and 100 construction personnel of basic specialties and up to 100 construction fitters from State Committees of the Council of Ministers of the USSR for defense technology and radioelectronics.

For accomplishing the work it is necessary to send:

16 complete sets of earth equipment for the R-14 produced by [the machine] industry in the current year;

machinery and vehicles:

Mobile cranes (5 ton) — 10
Bulldozers — 20

Mobile graders — 10
Excavators — 10
Dump trucks — 120
Cement mixers (GVSU) — 6
Special technical equipment for [illegible] and testing apparatuses
Basic materials

Cement — 2,000 tons
Reinforced concrete — 15,000 sq.

meters (not counting access roads)
Metal — 2,000 tons
SP-6 sets — 30

GR-2 Barracks — 20
Prefabricated wooden houses — 10
Cable, equipment and other materials.

Further accumulation of missile fuel, missiles, and warheads for the units is possible depending on the creation of reserve space and storage in Cuba, inasmuch as it would be possible to include in each missile regiment a third battalion with four launchers.

The staff of the Group and of the missile division can expediently be sent from the Soviet Union in the first days of July 1962 in two echelons: the 1st echelon (R-12 regiments) and the 2nd (R-14 regiments).

3. For air defense of the island of Cuba and protection of the Group of Forces to send 2 antiaircraft divisions, including in their composition 6 antiaircraft missile regiments (24 battalions),

6 technical battalions, one fighter air regiment with MiG-21 F-13 (three squadrons — 40 aircraft), and two radar battalions.

With the divisions to ship 4 missiles per launcher, in all 576 missiles.

To send the antiaircraft divisions: one in July, and one in August, 1962.

4. For defense of coasts and bases in the sectors of probable enemy attack on the island of Cuba to send one regiment of Sopka comprising three battalions (6 launchers) with three missiles per launcher

on the coast in the vicinity of Havana, one regiment (4 launchers)

on the coast in the vicinity of Banes, one battalion (2 launchers)

On the southern coast in the vicinity of Cienfuegos to locate one battalion (2 launchers), planned for delivery to Cuba in 1962.

The Sopka complex is capable of destroying surface ships at a range of up to 80 km.

5. To send to Cuba as part of the Group of Forces:

a brigade of missile patrol boats of the class Project 183-R, comprising two units with 6 patrol boats in each (in all 12 patrol boats), each armed with two P-15 missiles with a range up to 40 km.;

a detachment of support ships comprising: 1 tanker, 2 dry cargo transports, and 4 repair afloat ships;

fuel for missiles: fuel for the R-13 and P-15 — 70 tons, oxidizer for the R-13 — 180 tons, oxidizer for the P-15 — 20 tons, kerosene for the S-2 and KSShCh — 60 tons;

two combat sets of the P-15 missile (24 missiles) and one for the R-13 (21 missiles).

Shipment of the missile patrol boats Project 183-R class, the battalions of Sopka, technical equipment for the missile patrol boats and technical batteries for the Sopka battalions, and also the missiles, missile fuel, and other equipment for communications to be carried on ships of the Ministry of the Maritime Fleet.

Shipment of the warheads, in readiness state 4, will be handled by ships of the Navy.

6. To send as part of the Group of Forces in Cuba in July-August:

Two regiments of FKR (16 launchers) with PRTB, with their missiles and 5 special warheads for each launcher. Range of the FKR is up to 180 km.;

A mine-torpedo aviation regiment with IL-28 aircraft, comprising three squadrons (33 aircraft) with RAT-52 jet torpedoes (150 torpedoes), and air dropped mines (150 mines) for destruction of surface ships;

An Mi-4 helicopter regiment, two squadrons, 33 helicopters;

A separate communications air squadron (two IL-14, five Li-2, four Yak-12, and two An-2 aircraft).

7. With the objective of combat security of our technical troops, to send to Cuba four separate motorized rifle regiments, with a tank battalion in each, at the expense of the 64th Guards Motorized Rifle Division in the Leningrad Military District, with an overall personnel strength of 7300. The regiments to be sent in June-July 1962.

8. Upon completion of the concentration of Soviet troops planned for Cuba, or in case of necessity, to send to Cuba on a friendly visit, tentatively in September:

A) A squadron of surface ships of the Navy under the command of Vice Admiral G.S. Abashvili (deputy commander of the Red Banner Baltic Fleet) comprising:

two cruisers, Mikhail Kutuzov (Black Sea Fleet) and Sverdlov (Red Banner Baltic Fleet);

two missile destroyers of the Project 57-bis class, the Boikii and Gnevny (Black Sea Fleet);

two destroyers of the Project 76 class, the Skromnyi and Svedushchii (Northern Fleet);

Along with the squadron to send one refueling tanker. On the ships to send one full combat set of standard ammunition (including one combat set of KSShch missiles –24 missiles) and standard equipment.

Sailing time of the ships 15 days.

B) A squadron of submarines, comprising:

18th Division of missile submarines of the Project 629 class [Trans: NATO Golf or G-class] (7 submarines each with 3 R-13 [SS-N-4] missiles with range of 540 km.);

a brigade of torpedo submarines of Project 641 class (4 submarines with torpedo armament);

two submarine tenders.

Sailing time for the submarines, 20-22 days.

If necessary, the squadrons can be sent separately. Time for preparation to depart, after 1 July, is 10 days.

Upon arrival of the squadrons in Cuba, they would be incorporated into the Group of Soviet Forces.

9. For rear area security of the Group of Forces in Cuba to send:

three hospitals (200 beds each);

one anti-epidemic sanitary detachment;

seven warehouses (2 for food, 1 for general storage, 4 for fuel, including two for automotive and aviation fuel and two for liquid fuel for the Navy);

one company for servicing a trans-shipping base;

one field bakery factory;

Create reserves:

in the Group—fuel and provisions for routine maintenance of the troops for three months;

in the troops—mobile (fuel, ammunition, provisions) by established norms;

for follow-up secure provisions for 25 days.

10. The overall number of the Group of Soviet Forces in Cuba will be about 44,000 military personnel and 1300 workers

and civilians. For transport of the troops and combat equipment in summertime a simultaneous lift of about 70-80 ships of the Ministry of the Maritime Fleet of the USSR will be required.

11. To establish a staff of the Group of Soviet Forces in Cuba to command the Soviet troops. To form the staff of the Group convert the staff of the 49th Missile Army from Vinnitsa, which has a well qualified integrated apparatus with support and service elements.

To incorporate into the staff of the Group a naval section, an air force section, and an air defense section. The Commander in Chief of the Group to have four deputies—one for general matters, one for the Navy (VMF), one for Air Defense (PVO), and one for the Air Force (VVS).

12. The form of dress envisioned for the troops sent to Cuba, except for the Navy, is one set of civilian clothes and one tropical uniform (as for troops in the Turkestan Military District).

13. Food for the personnel of the Group of Soviet Forces in Cuba will be arranged from the USSR.

14. Financial support will be paid on the same general basis as for other troops located abroad.

15. Measures for creation of the Group of Soviet Forces in Cuba will proceed under the codename Anadyr.

We request your review.

[signature]
R. Malinovsky

[signature]
24 May 1962 M. Zakharov
Prepared in one copy
on seven pages, no draft

Attested Colonel General S.P. Ivanov
[signature]

Handwritten Notes on back of May 24 Soviet Memorandum

24.5.62

The question of aid to Cuba was discussed by the Presidium of the CC of the CPSU. N.S. Khrushchev presented a report. Statements were made by Kozlov, Brezhnev, Kosygin, Mikoyan, Voronov, Polyansky and all other members of the Presidium and [illegible] approval of the decision.

The Decision

1. The measures in Anadyr are approved entirely and unanimously. The document was approved subject to receiving agreement by F. Castro.
2. A commission is to be sent to C— for negotiation. Comrade Biryuzov, Comrade Ivanov
[illegible]

25.5.62 11:00 AM

1. N.S. Khrushchev, Malinovsky, Gromyko, Andropov, Troyanovsky, Rashidov, Alekseyev [text missing]

[signed:] S.P. Ivanov

Attested: Colonel General S.P. Ivanov [signature]
24.5.62

10.6.62 11:00 AM

Presidium of the CC CPSU meeting, with participation also of Gromyko, Malinovsky, Zakharov, Yepishev, Biryuzov, and Chuikov.

Rashidov and Biryuzov reported.

Soviet General Staff Memorandum on Operation Anadyr

20 June 1962:
Top Secret
Special Importance

In One Copy
Diagram Of the Organization of the Group of Soviet Forces
for "Anadyr"
Commander of the Group of Soviet Forces
General of the Army I.A. Pliyev
Staff Deputies
(133 pers.)
Lt. Gen. V.V. Akhindinov First-Deputy — Lt. Gen.
Sections Of Av. P.B. Dankevich
Operational DirectorateFor Naval Affairs — Vice
(22 pers.) Adm. G.S. Abashvili
Col. N.A. Ivanov For Air Defense — Lt.
Intelligence Gen Av. S.N. Grechko
(11 pers.) For the Air Forces — Col.
Communications Gen. Av. V.I. Davidkov
(11 pers.) For Special Ballistics Armaments —
(6 pers.) For Combat Training —
Cartographic and Geodosy Maj. Gen. L.S. Garbuz
(9 pers.) For the Rear Services —
Meteorological Service Maj. Gen.N.R. Pilipenko
(8 pers.) Deputy — Maj. Gen.
Sixth Section Tech. Trps. A.A.
(4 pers.) Dement'ev
Personnel and Records
(7 pers.)
Eighth Section
(13 pers.)
Missile Forces (RV)
43rd Missile Division
665th Missile Regiment (R-14 with PRTB)
668th Missile Regiment (R-14 with PRTB)

79th Missile Regiment (R-12 with PRTB)
181st Missile Regiment (R-12 with PRTB)
664th Missile Regiment (R-12 with PRTB)
(Eight launchers per regiment)

Air Defense Forces (PVO)
11th Antiaircraft Division
16th Antiaircraft Regiment
276th Antiaircraft Regiment
500th Antiaircraft Regiment
4 battalions in each AA Regiment

Separate Radar Battalion
10th Antiaircraft Division
294th Antiaircraft Regiment
318th Antiaircraft Regiment
466th Antiaircraft Regiment
32nd Fighter Aviation Regiment
40 MiG-21s

Separate Radar Battalion

Air Forces (VVS)
561st FKR (Frontal Cruise Missile) Regiment
584th FKR Regiment
Each regiment with 8 launchers and PRTB

437th Separate Helicopter Regiment
33 Mi-4 helicopters
134 Separate Aviation Communications Squadron
11 aircraft

Ground Forces (SV)
302nd Separate Motorized Rifle Regiment
314th Separate Motorized Rifle Regiment
400th Separate Motorized Rifle Regiment
496th Separate Motorized Rifle Regiment

Naval Forces (VMF)
Submarine Squadron
18th Missile Submarine Division
7 submarines
211th Submarine Brigade
4 submarines
Two submarine tenders (floating support bases)
Surface Ship Squadron
2 cruisers, 2 missile destroyers, 2 destroyers
Missile Patrol Boat Brigade
12 missile patrol boats (cutters)

Sopka Missile Regiment
6 launchers

Aviation Mine-Torpedo Regiment
33 IL-28 aircraft

Detachment of Support Ships
2 tankers
2 dry cargo ships

1 floating repair ship
Rear Services
Field Bakery Factory

Hospitals (3 at 200 beds each)
Sanitary-antiepidemological detachment
Company to service entry to the bases
Food storage stocks (2)
Warehouse
Missile and aviation fuel stations (2)
Fuel oil for the Navy (2)
Chief of the Main Operations Directorate of the General Staff

Colonel General S.P. Ivanov
20 June 1962

Soviet Memorandum

6 September 1962

Top Secret (Sovershenno sekretno)

Special Importance (Osoboi vazhnosti)

Sole Copy (ekz. edinstven.)

To the Chairman of the Defense Council of the USSR, Comrade N.S. Khrushchev

I am reporting

I. On the Possibility of Reinforcing Cuba by Air.

1. About the transport by air of special warheads for the Luna and R-11M missiles. Tests have been conducted at the test range and practical instructions have been worked out for the transportation of special warheads for R-11M missiles, two on AN-8 aircraft, and four on AN-12 aircraft.

The alternatives for transport of warheads for the Luna missile are analogous to those for the R-11M.

The transport of special warheads by Tu-114 is not possible owing to the absence of a freight hatch and fasteners.

2. About the transport by air of R-11M and Luna missiles.

Practice loading, securing and transport of training R-11M and Luna missiles has been carried out on AN-8 and AN-12 aircraft, with 2 Luna or 1 R-11M missiles on AN-8 or AN-12 aircraft.

3. The size of the freight hold and carrying-capacity of AN-8 (5-8 tons) and AN-12 (7-16 tons) do not permit air transport of launchers, special earth moving machines, and field missile-technical bases (PRTB) for the R-11M and Luna missiles.

The Tu-114 aircraft, notwithstanding its large loading capacity (up to 30 tons) and long range (up to 8,000 km.), is not suitable for transport of missile equipment as it is not adapted in a transport mode.

II. Proposals of the Ministry of Defense for Reinforcing Forces of the Group in Cuba

In order to reinforce the Group of Forces in Cuba, send:

1) One squadron of IL-28 bombers, comprising 10-12 aircraft including delivery and countermeasures aircraft, with a mobile PRTB and six atomic bombs (407N), each of 8-12 kilotons;

[*handwritten note added*:] Send to Cuba six IL-28s with atomic warheads [*illegible*]   [signed] N.S. Khrushchev 7.IX.1962.

2) One R-11M missile brigade made up of three battalions (total: 1221 men, 18 R-11M missiles) with PRTB (324 men) and 18 special warheads, which the PRTB is capable of storing;
3) Two-three battalions of Luna for inclusion in separate motorized infantry regiments in Cuba.

[*handwritten note added*:] Three Luna battalions. N.S. Khrushchev 7.IX.62

Each Luna battalion will have two launchers and 102 men.
With the Luna battalions, send 8-12 missiles and8-12 special warheads.
For the preparation and custody of special warheads for the Luna missiles, send one PRTB (150 men).
The indicated squadron of IL-28s, one R-11M missile brigade with PRTB, and two-three Luna battalions with PRTB, and the missiles are to be sent to Cuba in the first half of October.
Atom bombs (6), special warheads for the R-11M missiles (18) and for the Luna missiles (8-12) are to be sent on the transport Indigirka on 15 September.
The Defense Ministry has just conducted successful firing tests of the S-75 anti-aircraft system against surface targets on level terrain. At distances of 24 kilometers, accuracy of plus or minus 100-120 meters was achieved.
The results of computer calculations indicate the possibility also of successful use against naval targets.
In order to fire against land or sea targets using S-75 complexes with the troops, small modifications in the missile guidance stations will be required by factory brigades together with some additional equipment prepared by industry.

Marshal of the Soviet Union R. Malinovsky [signature]

6 September 1962

Soviet Memorandum

8 September 1962
Top Secret
Special Importance

Copy #1
Personally
To the Commander of the Group of Soviet Forces in Cuba

The temporary deployment of Soviet Armed forces on the island of Cuba is necessary to insure joint defense against possible aggression toward the USSR and the Republic of Cuba.

A decision on employment of the Soviet Armed Forces in combat actions in order to repel aggression and reinstatement will be made by the Soviet Government.

1. The task of the Group of Soviet Forces in Cuba is not to permit an enemy landing on Cuban territory from the sea or from the air. The island of Cuba must be turned into an impenetrable fortress.

Forces and means: Soviet troops together with the Cuban Armed forces.

2. In carrying out this task, the Commander of the Group of Soviet Forces on the island of Cuba will be guided by the following considerations:

a) With Respect to Missile Forces

The missile forces, constituting the backbone for the defense of the Soviet Union and Cuba, must be prepared, upon signal from Moscow, to deal a nuclear missile strike on the most important targets in the United States of America (list of targets included in Attachment #1)

Upon arrival of the missile division in Cuba, two R-12 regiments (539 th and 546th) and one R-14 regiment (564th) will deploy in the western region, and one R-12 regiment (the 514th) and one R-14 regiment (the 657th) in the central region of Cuba.

The missile units will deploy to the positional areas and take up their launch positions; for R-12 missiles, not later than [illegible] days; for the R-14 missiles with fixed launch facilities [illegible] period.

With the establishment of launchers on combat duty, [illegible] regiments will maintain Readiness No. 4

b) With Respect to Air Defense (PVO) Forces

PVO forces of the Group will not permit incursion of foreign aircraft into the air space of the Republic of Cuba [illegible] and strikes by enemy air against the Group, the most important administrative political centers, naval bases, ports [illegible]. Combat use of PVO forces will be activated by the Commander of the Group of Forces.

The PVO divisions will be deployed:

12th Division — the Western region of Cuban territory [illegible]

27th Division — the Eastern region of Cuban territory [illegible]

213th Fighter Air Division will be deployed at Santa Clara airfield.

After unloading in Cuba of the surface-to-air missiles and fighter aviation will be deployed [illegible] and organization of combat readiness.

c) With Respect to the Ground Forces

Ground forces troops will protect the missile and other technical troops and the Group command center, and be prepared to provide assistance to the Cuban Armed Forces in liquidating [illegible] enemy landings and counterrevolutionary groups on the territory of the Republic of Cuba

The independent motorized rifle regiments (OMSP) will deploy:

The 74th OMSP, with a battalion of Lunas, in the Western part of Cuba in readiness to protect the Missile Forces and to operate in the sectors Havana and Pinar del Rio;

The 43rd OMSP, with a battalion of Lunas, in the vicinity of Santiago de las Vegas in readiness to protect the Command of the Group of Forces and to operate in the sectors Havana, Artemisa, Batabano, and Matanzas;

The 146th OMSP, with a battalion of Lunas, in the area Camajuani, Placetas, Sulu...[*illegible*], in readiness to protect the Missile Forces and to operate in the sectors: Caibarien, Colon, Cienfeugos, Fomento;

The 106th OMSP in the eastern part of Cuba in the vicinity of Holguin in readiness to operate in the sectors Banes, Victoria de las Tunas, Manzanillo, and Santiago de Cuba.

d) With Respect to the Navy

The Naval element of the Group must not permit combat ships and transports of the enemy to approach the island of Cuba and carry out naval landings on the coast. They must be prepared to blockade from the sea the U.S. naval base in Guantanamo, and provide cover for our transport ships along lines of communication in close proximity to the island.

Missile-equipped submarines should be prepared to launch, upon signal from Moscow, nuclear missile strikes on the most important coastal targets in the USA (List of targets in Attachment #1).

The main forces of the fleet should be based in the region around Havana and in ports to the west of Havana. One detachment of the brigade of missile patrol boats should be located in the vicinity of Banes.

The battalions of Sopka should be deployed on the coast:

One battalion east of Havana in the region of Santa Cruz del Norte;

One battalion southeast of Cienfuegos in the vicinity of Gavilan;

One battalion northeast of Banes in the vicinity of Cape Mulas;

One battalion on the island Piños in the vicinity of Cape Buenavista.

The torpedo-mine air regiment will deploy at the airfield San Julian Asiento, and plan and instruct in destroying combat ships and enemy landings from the sea.

e) With Respect to the Air Force

The squadron of IL-28 delivery aircraft will be based on Santa Clara airfield in readiness to operate in the directions of Havana, Guantanamo, and the Isle of Pines.

The independent aviation engineering regiments (FKR) will deploy:

231st OAIP—in the western region of Cuba, designated as the main means to fire on the coast in the northeastern and northern sectors, and as a secondary mission in the direction of the Isle of Pines.

222nd OAIP—in the eastern part of the island. This regiment must be prepared, upon signal from the General Staff, in the main sector of the southeastern direction to strike the U.S. naval base at Guantanamo. Secondary firing sectors in the northeastern and southwestern directions.

The fighter aviation regiment armed with MiG-21 F-13 aircraft is included as a PVO division, but crews of all fighters will train also for operations in support of the Ground Forces and Navy.

3. Organize security and economy of missiles, warheads, and special technical equipment, and all combat equipment in the armament of the Group of Soviet Forces in Cuba.

4. Carry out daily cooperation and combat collaboration with the armed forces of the Republic of Cuba, and work together in instructing the personnel of the Cuban armed forces in maintaining the arms and combat equipment being transferred by the Soviet Union to the Republic of Cuba.

5. Deploy the rear units and offices and organize all-round material, technical, and medical support of the troops.

Rear area bases will be located in the regions as follows:

Main Base—comprising: the 758 th command base, separate service companies, the 3 rd automotive platoon, 784 th POL fuel station, the 860 th food supply depot, the 964 th warehouse, the 71 st bakery factory, the 176 th field technical medical detachment—Mariel, Artemisa, Guira de Melena, Rincon;

Separate rear base—comprising: 782 nd POL station, 883 rd food supply depot, a detachment of the 964 th warehouse, [the 1st] field medical detachment, a detachment of the 71 st bakery factory—Caibarien, Camajuani, Placetas;

Separate rear base—comprising: separate detachments of the 784 th POL station, the 883 rd food supply depot, the 964 th warehouse, [the 71 st bakery unit, and the 1st field medical detachment—Gibara, Holguin, Camasan.

Fuel stocks for the Navy will be:

Depot No. 4472—Mariel, a branch at Guanabacoa,

Depot No. 4465—vicinity of Banes.

Hospitals will be set up in the regions: Field hospitals No. 965 with blood transfusion unit—Guanajay; No. 121—Camajuani, Placetas; No. 50—Holguin.

The transport of material to be organized by troop transport means, and also do not use local rail or water transport.

6. The operational plan for the employment of the Group of Soviet Forces in Cuba should be worked out by 01 November 1962.

Attachments:

1. List of targets for missile forces and missile submarines for working out flight missions—attached separately.

2. List of the order of battle of the Group of Soviet Forces in Cuba in 3 pages, r r/t #164

3. List of launchers, missiles and nuclear warheads possessed by the Group of Forces, on 2 pages r r/t #164.

USSR Minister of Defense [signature]
Marshal of the Soviet Union
R. Malinovsky

Chief of the General Staff [signature]
Marshal of the Soviet Union

M. Zakharov

No. 76438
Send in cipher

Soviet Memorandum

8 September 1962

To the Commander of the Group of Soviet Forces in Cuba

For the purpose of strengthening of the Group of Soviet Forces in Cuba and increasing capability to fight against the enemy landing, are sending you

additional means: − −squadron of plane-carriers IL-28 (6 planes and 6 nuclear bombs− −407 H) with PRTB

-−-three battalions of "Luna" (6 launchers, 12 missiles, 12 special warheads and 24 conventional missiles) with PTRB

In a situation of an enemy landing on the island of Cuba and of the concentration of enemy ships with amphibious forces off the coast of Cuba in its territorial waters, when the destruction of the enemy is delaying and there is no possibility of receiving instructions from the USSR Ministry of Defense, you are permitted to make your own decision and to use the nuclear means of the "Luna," IL-28 or PKR-1 as instruments of local warfare for the destruction of the enemy on land and along the coast in order to achieve the complete destruction of the invaders on the Cuban territory and to defend the Republic of Cuba.

USSR Minister of Defense [signature]
Marshal of the Soviet Union R. Malinovsky
P.P.

Chief of the General Staff [signature]
Marshal of the Soviet Union M. Zakharov
8 September 1962

/ Signed
S. P. lvanov

Statement By Soviet Union

September 11, 1962

The Soviet Government has stated more than once that, carrying through a policy of peaceful coexistence with all countries irrespective of their socio-political order, it has exerted and does exert all efforts to safeguard peace for all the peoples of the world, to secure agreement on general and complete disarmament under strict international control.

The Government of the U.S.S.R. deems it necessary to draw the attention of the governments of all countries and world opinion to the provocations the United States Government is now staging, provocations which might plunge the world into the disaster if a universal world war with the use of thermonuclear weapons.

Bellicose-minded reactionary elements of the United States have long since been conducting in the United States Congress and in the American press an unbridled propaganda campaign against the Cuban Republic, calling for an attack on Cuba, an attack on Soviet ships carrying the necessary commodities and food to the Cuban people, in one word, calling for war.

At first the Soviet Union did not pay special importance to this propaganda against peace, against humanity and humaneness, believing that this propaganda was conducted by irresponsible persons who do not represent or represent but do not heed the interests of the people and that all this provocative clamor was raised in the United States in connection with the preparation for the Congressional elections when the rival bourgeois parties, the Republicans and the Democrats, as usual in imperialist states, vie with each other in who can hurl more infamies against the peace forces. Unfortunately, there still are many people in the United States who were fooled by this vile propaganda. The United States monopoly capital owning the entire press of the country, radio and broadcasting, all means of influencing the minds of the peoples, keep the American people as captives of ignorance and take advantage of this in order to condition public opinion of the country in a direction that suits them. During the many years of coexistence with the United States we have already become accustomed to such kind of devil's Sabbath and therefore did not attach special importance to it.

Now, however, one cannot ignore this, because the President of the United States asked Congress to permit the call-up of 150,000 reservists to the armed forces of the United States. Motivating his request, the President said that the United States must have the possibility of rapidly and effectively reacting in case of need to a danger that might arise in any part of the free world, and that he was taking such a step in connection with the strengthening of the armed forces of Cuba, which, they say, aggravates tension and all but creates a threat to other countries.

Such a step by the United States Government cannot be assessed otherwise than a screen for aggressive plans and intentions of the United States itself and will inevitably lead to aggravating the international atmosphere. It is said that this step is allegedly designed to ease tension. But it has never been thought that a fire can be put out by kerosene or petrol. Each thoughtful person understands that such steps do not lead to the relaxation of tension, but on the contrary are a means of aggravating tension to the limit and creating such a situation when the disaster of a world thermonuclear war can be sparked off by some accident. Hence, this is a provocation against the peace, this is done in the interests of war, in the interests of aggression.

The United States leaders seek to explain this step by the aggravation of tension. But, compared with the situation a year or even two ago, no special change can be observed. Hence, such a step is not designed to ease tension, but on the contrary, this is done to aggravate tension in the international situation.

What then has now taken place which alarmed and impelled the United States Government to take such aggressive actions? Members of the United States Congress and the press are calling a spade a spade thus giving away the real inside story behind such United States steps.

The American imperialists have been alarmed by the failure of the United States-staged economic blockade of revolutionary Cuba. They would like to strangle the Cuban people, to make them their satellite to wipe out the achievements of the revolution, accomplished by the heroic people of Cuba. To attain these ends they refused to purchase Cuban sugar, refused to sell to her their goods including even medicine and food; they did not even stop at seeking to strangle children and old folk and adults by the raw-boned hand of starvation. And all this they call humaneness!

The Soviet Union, like the other Socialist countries, stretched out a hand of assistance to the Cuban people because we understand full well Cuba's situation. After the October Revolution, when the young Soviet state was in capitalist encirclement and the peoples of our country lived through tremendous difficulties caused by postwar destruction, the United States, instead of rendering assistance, staged armed intervention against the Soviet Republic. United States troops were landed in Murmansk, Archangel and in the Far East. British troops were landed at Archangel and occupied Baku. French troops were landed at Odessa and Japanese in the Primorye (Maritime) Territory. The imperialist powers set up counter-revolutionary armies under the leadership of Kolchak, Yudenich, Denikin, Vrangel, mobilized and armed the entire counter-revolutionary mob, this scum. The peoples of the Soviet

Union firmly resolved to establish at home their own order which would accord with their aspirations, exerted many efforts and sacrificed many lives to smash internal counter-revolution and expel the foreign invaders from the country.

The Soviet Union, in spite of tremendous difficulties, not only held out in the struggle for its independence but also demonstrated to the whole world the superiority of the people's Socialist order in which all means of production belong to the people, when everything is being done for the sake of the people. The whole world knows that the Soviet Union is the first Socialist country, which made a tremendous progress in the advance of the economy, science and culture, the first, that blazed a trail into outer space and successfully continues the exploration of outer space. The peaceful constructive labor of the Soviet people is yielding rich fruit. The flight of two Soviet spacemen side by side for three-four days and the simultaneous landing of their space ships indeed overwhelmed the minds of all honest people who rejoice in progress, rejoice in the successes of the Soviet Union, in the exploration of outer space for peaceful purposes. This has been a striking manifestation of the peace-loving policy of the Soviet Union, al whose efforts are aimed at safeguarding peace and the progress of mankind.

The United States now wants to repeat against little heroic Cuba what they undertook at one time against our country. But one can say confidently that such plans are doomed to failure.

The Soviet Union could not fail to take account of the situation it which Cuba had found itself as a result of imperialist provocations am threats, and it went fraternally to the Cuban people's assistance. This is being done by the other Socialist countries, too, and also by other peace-loving states which maintain trade relations with Cuba. Soviet ships carry to Cuba the goods she needs and return with commodities she has in abundance, particularly sugar, which the United States— previously the main importer— has refused to buy in the hope of undermining the economy of the Cuban Republic. This is why the Soviet Union and other Socialist countries are buying this sugar— to support the economy of the Cuban state.

If one is honest and proceeds from the understanding of the nee of living in peace, declared by the United States President himself, i.e to safeguard peaceful coexistence between states irrespective of the socio-political order, what could have alarmed the American leader what is the reason for this devil's Sabbath raised in Congress and in the American press around Cuba?

To this one can say: Gentlemen, you are evidently so frightened that you are afraid of your own shadow and you do not believe in if strength of your ideas and your capitalist order. You have been much frightened by the October Socialist Revolution and the success of the Soviet Union, achieved and developed on the basis of this revolution, that it seems to you some hordes are supposedly moving to Cuba when potatoes or oil, tractors, harvesters combines and other farming and industrial machinery are carried to Cuba to maintain the Cuban economy.

We can say to these people that these are our ships, and that what we carry in them is no business of theirs. It is the internal affair of the sides engaged in this commercial transaction. We can say, quoting the popular saying: "Don't butt your noses where you oughtn't."

But we do not hide from the world public that we really are supplying Cuba with industrial equipment and goods which are helping to strengthen her economy and raise the well-being of the Cuban people.

At the request of the Cuban Government, we also send Soviet agronomists, machine-operators, tractor-drivers and livestock experts to Cuba to share their experience and knowledge with their Cuban friends in order to help them raise the country's economy. We also send rank-and-file state and collective farm workers to Cuba, and accept thousands of Cubans to the Soviet Union to exchange experience and teach them the more progressive methods of agriculture, to help them master the Soviet farm machinery which is being supplied to Cuba.

It will be recalled that a certain amount of armaments is also being shipped from the Soviet Union to Cuba at the request of the Cuban Government in connection with the threats by aggressive imperialist circles. The Cuban statesmen also requested the Soviet Government to send to Cuba Soviet military specialists, technicians who would train the Cubans in handling up-to-date weapons, because up-to-date weapons now call for high skill and much knowledge. It is but natural that Cuba does not yet have such specialists. That is why we considered this request. It must, however, be said that the number of soviet military specialists sent to Cuba can in no way be compared to the number of workers in agriculture and industry sent there. The armaments and military equipment sent to Cuba are designed ex-clusively for defensive purposes and the President of the United States and the American military just as the military of any country know what means of defense are. How can these means threaten the United States?

No, gentlemen, it is not this that alarms you. You yourselves realize the absurdity of your claims that there is some threat to the United States emerging on the part of Cuba. You have invented this threat yourselves, and you now want to persuade others of its existence. It is the revolutionary spirit that you fear, and not the military equipment received by the Cubans for their own defense. And why should this alarm you if the statement by the President of the United States that the United States is not preparing an aggression against Cuba, is not contemplating an attack against her, accords with the intentions of the American Government? If this is an honest statement, and the Government of the United States abides by it in its policy, then the means of defense which Cuba is getting will not be used because the need to use them will arise only in the event of aggression against Cuba.

The Government of the Soviet Union also authorized Tass to state that there is no need for the Soviet Union to shift its weapons for the repulsion of aggression, for a retaliatory blow, to any other country, instance Cuba. Our nuclear weapons are so powerful in their explosive force and the Soviet Union has so powerful rockets to carry these nuclear warheads, that there is no need to search for sites for them beyond the boundaries of the Soviet Union. We have said and we do repeat that if war is unleashed, if the aggressor makes an attack on one state or another and this state asks for assistance, the Soviet Union has the possibility from its own territory to render assist-ance to any peace-loving state and not only to Cuba. And let no one doubt that the Soviet Union will render such assistance just as it was ready in 1956 to render military assistance to Egypt at the time of the Anglo-French-Israeli aggression in the Suez Canal region.

We do not say this to frighten someone. Intimidation is alien to the foreign policy of the Soviet State. Threats and blackmail are an integral part of the imperialist states. The Soviet Union stands for peace and wants no war.

The Soviet Government calls the attention of the world public and the governments of all countries which stand on positions of peaceful coexistence to the fact that even now, when the United States of America is preparing an act of aggression and is increasing its armed forces for this purpose by calling up 150,000 reservists, into the army, when the President of the United States is asking Congress for permis-sion to do this, the U.S.S.R. Minister of Defense, Marshal Malinovsky, has ordered the discharge into reserve of the service men who have completed their term. Trained soldiers are being released from the armed forces of the U.S.S.R. and recruits are being called up to replenish the units. This alone is a clear enough indication of our peaceful intentions. No Government would take such a measure if it contemplated any action of a military nature. One must realize what it means when trained soldiers are being released from the army and recruits called up who must yet be trained — and this is not so easy to do considering the complex equipment of the army which requires a great amount of knowledge not only from the commander but also from every private. In taking this step we realize measures in our day-by-day life which confirm that the Soviet Union is following a policy of insuring peace and friendship with all peoples.

The Soviet Union will not take any similar retaliatory actions to the call-up of 150,000 reservists in the United States, the more so that this cannot be of any serious military importance, given up-to-date means of nuclear rocket warfare. If in the past the yardsticks for armies of the belligerents were mainly the number of soldiers, sabers and bayonets, in our time the might of these armies is deter-mined by a different yardstick — nuclear rocket weapons.

But at a moment when the United States is taking measures to mobilize its armed forces and is preparing for aggression against Cuba and other peace-loving states, the Soviet Government would like to draw attention to the fact that one cannot now attack Cuba and expect that the aggressor will be free from punishment for this attack. If this attack is made, this will be the beginning of the unleashing of war.

How are the preparations for aggression against Cuba being motivated? By saying that Soviet merchant ships carry cargoes to Cuba, and the United States considers them to be military cargoes. But this is a purely internal matter of the states which send these cargoes and those which buy and receive them.

The whole world knows that the United States of America has ringed the Soviet Union and other Socialist countries with bases. What have they stationed there—tractors? Are they perhaps growing rice, wheat, potatoes, or some other farm crops there? No, they have brought armaments there in their ships, and these armaments, sta-tioned along the frontiers of the Soviet Union—in Turkey, Iran, Greece, Italy, Britain, Holland, Pakistan and other countries belong-ing to the military blocs of NATO, CENTO and SEATO—are said to be there lawfully, by right. They consider this their right! But to others the United States does not permit this even for defense, and even measures are nevertheless taken to strengthen the defenses of or that country the United States raises an outcry and declares t an attack, if you please, is being prepared against them. What conceit! The United States apparently believes that in the present conditions one can proceed to aggression with impunity.

Equal rights and equal opportunities must be recognized for all tries of the world. This is not only in conformity with the recognized standards of the international law which have already taken shape. This should be strictly adhered to in practical life and activity And what happens in fact? The United States, for instance, is now mobilizing allegedly because our merchant ships are proceeding to Cuba. At the same time United States ships, not merchant ships, it is not a question of merchant ships, but warships, the entire Sixth Fleet of the United States are in the Mediterranean. How many kilometers, what distance is this from the United States? The Seventh United States Fleet is in the Taiwan Strait. By how many thousands of kilometers is this fleet separated from the shores of the United States? It is even said in the United States that they have the right to be there.

What are the aims of the presence of these fleets in the Mediterranean and in the Taiwan Strait? They are not peaceful aims. That much is certain. They are aggressive military aims. And can it conduce to normal relations when United States warships cruise off shores of other states while American admirals and generals, as if competing with each other, prattle in the press and radio from time to time about the Sixth and Seventh Fleets being designed for attack, for destroying the Socialist countries?

So long as this madness continues, this policy will not contribute the strengthening of peace but will, on the contrary, always be a source which might at any moment produce a military conflict with all attendant consequences.

A vile campaign against the Soviet Union is now being conducted in the United States. It is shouted from the housetops that since a merchant fleet is plying between the U.S.S.R. and Cuba, carrying freight, this gives the United States the right to attack Cuba and the Soviet Union. But what purpose serves the stay of United States warships in Turkish ports, and by what right is their stay there regarded as lawful and normal? What do they want—to obtain for themselves some exclusion from the general rules? What is declared a violation of standards for one, is regarded as normal for others.

We warn that given present conditions the Socialist camp has no fewer forces and opportunities than the United States and its allies in war blocs. This must be taken into consideration. One must be guided by this in politics so that it does not prejudice one side or the other. Only under these conditions can one avoid a military conflict, safeguard peace. Resort to provocations, guided by the absurd expectation to frighten the other side, this means irresponsible playing with the destinies of the world. Such a policy can but lead to dismal results.

It should be remembered that the times have gone forever when the United States had the monopoly of nuclear weapons. Today the Soviet Union has these weapons in sufficient quantities and of a higher quality. It should be known therefore that he who starts a war, he who sows the winds, will reap a hurricane. In digging an abyss for its opponents an aggressor will inevitably fall into it himself. Only a madman can think now that a war started by him will be a calamity only for the people against which it is unleashed. No, already Hitler's experience should have taught something to those who contemplate aggression in our days. Hitler, who started war together with Mussolini, himself perished in it, and brought disaster to all the peoples of the world. A war now would be a hundredfold more terrible, and it would bring calamities to both the peoples against which the United States is preparing aggression now, and to the people of the United States itself, and probably bigger, not lesser calamities than this will be even truer of those states, allies of the United States, who border on the Soviet Union, and also of its other Allies in Europe and Asia.

But those quarters that determine the policy of the United States do not take this into consideration, they set up military bases on territories of the United States allies, build up nuclear weapons stores there, install rockets, for instance, in Turkey, Italy and Japan. It is not difficult to understand what destiny they are preparing for these their allies in case of war. For all this is done to attack the Soviet Union, the People's Republic and other Socialist states. This is well understood by the people in those very countries where United States military bases are being established, for instance, in Japan whose peo-ple are resolutely protesting against these bases.

In the light of the latest events, in the light of the request of the United States President to Congress for the permission to call up 150,000 reservists, the Soviet Government also assesses differently the flight of the American U-2 reconnaissance plane over Soviet territory in the region of Sakhalin on August 30 this year. Reports have ap-peared to the effect that U-2 planes are being based in Britain, Japan, Turkey, the Federal Republic of Germany and are making flights from American bases in those countries. These flights are explained by alleging that they have peaceful purposes—they take samples of air, study cloud movements. But today it is still clearly visible what samples they are taking and for what purposes these flights are under-taken.

That is why the Soviet Government appeals to the peoples urging them to raise a voice of denouncing aggressive schemes, not to allow the American aggressors to unleash war, to safeguard world peace.

The Government of the U.S.S.R. appeals to the Soviet people urging them to continue working as successfully as they are working now. The Government of the Soviet Union will do its utmost to safeguard peace and peaceful coexistence with all countries. But this does not always depend on us. The Soviet Union did not want the second World War, but Hitler imposed it upon us and we were forced to wage war. That is why we must do everything to be prepared, to see to it that our armed forces—the strategic rocket forces and the ground forces, the anti-aircraft defense, the navy and especially the submarine fleet of the Soviet Union—be able to cope with their tasks. If the aggressors unleash war our armed forces must be ready to strike a crushing retaliatory blow at the aggressor.

The Soviet Government will not follow the way of the United States which is calling up 150,000 reservists. If we repeated this action of the United States we would do what apparently is wanted by certain American circles—we would help them inflame the situation. But neither can we disregard the aggressive preparations of the United States. The Soviet Government considers it its duty in this situation to display vigilance and to instruct the Minister of Defense of the Soviet Union, the command of the Soviet Army, to take all measures to raise our armed forces to peak military preparedness.

But these are exclusively precautionary measures. We shall do everything on our part so that peace is not disturbed.

The Soviet Government appeals to the government of the United States urging it to display common sense, not to lose self-control and to soberly assess what its actions might lead to if it unleashes war.

Instead of aggravating the atmosphere by such actions as the mobilization of reservists, which is tantamount to the threat of starting war, it would be more sensible if the Government of the United States, displaying wisdom, would offer a kind gesture— would establish diplomatic and trade relations with Cuba. The desirability of which has been recently declared by the Cuban Government. If the American Government displayed this wisdom, the peoples would assess this properly as a realistic contribution of the United States to the relaxation of international tension, the strengthening of world peace.

If normal diplomatic and trade relations were established between the United States of America and Cuba, there would be no need for Cuba to strengthen her defenses, her armed forces. For then nobody would menace Cuba with war or other aggressive actions, and the situation would become normal.

Thus stand matters now, such is the situation at the present moment.

The Soviet Government has declared more than once and declares now: We are stretching out a hand of friendship to the people and Government of the United States. We would like to pool our efforts with the Governments of the United States and other countries to solve all ripe international problems, to safeguard peace on earth. To do so one must agree, above all, on the first step which might be a solution of the problem of ending nuclear weapons tests. We are ready to reach agreement on general and complete disarmament under strict international control.

The Soviet Government expresses the hope that the Government of the United States will at last draw sober conclusions concerning the need for a peace treaty with Germany. There have been many negotiations on this question, but no progress has thus far been made. A pause has now been reached in the talks on a German peace treaty. But the issue remains as sharp as ever before, and is felt even more acutely now in view of the provocations by revanchists in West Berlin against the German Democratic Republic. It is said that it is difficult for the United States to negotiate on the German peace treaty now as elections to the American Congress are due in November. Well, the Soviet Government is prepared to reckon with this. But one cannot link the solution of the question of a German peace treaty all the time to elections in this or that country. Elections are held often — now here, now there, and further delay in settling the question of a German peace treaty can only produce fresh difficulties and fresh dangers. The Soviet Government, as before, stands for the earliest conclusion of a German peace treaty and the adjustment of the situation in West Berlin on its basis.

This task must be accomplished and it will be accomplished. The sovereignty of the German Democratic Republic must be protected and it will be protected. The vestiges of World War II in Europe, including the occupation regime in West Berlin, must be liquidated and they will be liquidated. This accords not only with the interests of the Soviet Union and the German Democratic Republic, it accords with the vital interests of all states, all peoples.

The Soviet Union is stretching out a hand of friendship to all peoples of the world, in order to achieve by common effort the establishment of an enduring, inviolable peace on our planet. As regards questions of the internal, socio-political order of states, they must be settled by each people independently, without any outside interven-tion. Peace can be safeguarded only if one respects the inalienable right of each people to independence, if one strictly observes the principle of non-intervention by some states in the domestic affairs of other states. That is precisely the meaning of peaceful coexistence, underlying the peaceable policy of the Soviet state.

Briefing Paper

Washington, October 1, 1962.
SUBJECT
Analysis of SAM Sites

1. The intelligence community has now identified and confirmed a total of 15 SA-2 SAM sites. From the location of these sites, a discernible pattern is developing:

a. In the Oriente Province, the identified sites (3) form a triangular pattern around the new military airfield at Holguin. This field is probably not yet operational, but soon could be. At the present time, there are no MIG-type aircraft stationed at this field. The MIGs believed to be assigned to the operational control of the Commander, Eastern Army, are stationed at the airfield at Camaguey, in the Central Army area. When Holguin becomes operational, these aircraft will probably be moved to that location. There are no SA-2 sites identified in the vicinity of Camaguey.

b. In the Central Army area, 4 SA-2 sites form a rectangular pattern around the military airfield near Santa Clara. This airfield has had MIGs for several months and is also the field upon which the first MIG 21 was identified.

c. In the Western Army area, there are 3 and possibly 4 SA-2 sites forming a liner pattern to provide defense for the military airfield at San Antonia de los Banos and coincidentally for the defense of the Havana-Mariel complex. San Antonio de los Banos is the headquarters for the Cuban revolutionary Air Force and the assembly point for all MIGs, except the MIG-21, which have previously been received in Cuba.

2. Further west in the Pinar del Rio Province a triangular pattern of 3 SA-2 sites cannot be connected with any significant military installation. The only known installation within this triangle are 2 underground facilities whose use and purpose are unknown. The only other military installation in this particular area is the military air base at San Julian near the western tip of Cuba. However, 1 of the 3 SA-2 sites is located at or very near this military airfield, a most unlikely spot to place SA-2s for the defense of this particular air base. Therefore, curiosity is immediately aroused to the purpose of this triangular pattern on the far western tip of Cuba.

3. In the north central portion of the Pinar del Rio Province is a large trapazoid-shaped restricted area controlled by the Soviet military personnel recently introduced into Cuba, measuring 15-20 miles on a side. There are no known military installations in this rough and sparsely populated area. According to reports from refugees arriving in Miami, all Cubans have been evacuated from this restricted area. The purpose of this restricted area is not currently known.

4. Information concerning the deployment of Soviet military personnel and "technicians" recently arriving in Cuba is derived from unevaluated refugee sources, however, an attempt has been made to plot all reported locations to determine whether there is any correlation between the location of Soviet personnel and missiles or missile activity. So far, the pattern indicates that there is a definite correlation, but significantly the greatest concentration of Soviet personnel, activity and camps is in the western end of the Island of Cuba. This would indicate a greater interest on the part of the Soviets in Pinar del Rio than in the other provinces.

5. A single unevaluated report states that the Soviet "SS-4 Shyster" missile may have been delivered to Cuba on or about 11 September. Some confusion is apparent in this report. The SS-4 missile is nicknamed "Sandal," while the "Shyster" carriers a designation of SS-3. This confusion was caused by the

interrogators of the source using a recognition manual which designated the SS-4 as the Shyster. However, the description of the missiles reportedly observed by the source could have applied equally to either the Shyster or the Sandal. Both missiles have essentially the same outward appearance except that the Sandal is about 5 feet longer. In all other respects, including the missile carrier, the two appear identical. The source of this report stated that on 12 September he had personally seen some 20 such missiles in the vicinity of Campo Libertad, a small airfield on the western edge of Havana. While this report is still unconfirmed and there are no other reports concerning the presence of either SS-3 or SS-4 missiles, it is significant to note that by using the approximate center of the restricted area referred to above as a point of origin and with a radius of 1100 nm, the accepted range of the SS-4 missile, the arc includes the cities of Philadelphia, Pittsburgh, St. Louis, Oklahoma City, Fort Worth-Dallas, Houston, San Antonio, Mexico City, all of the capitals of the Central American nations, the Panama Canal, and the oil fields in Maricaibo, Venezuela. The presence of operational SS-4 missiles in this location would give the Soviets a great military asset.

Memorandum

Washington, October 4, 1962.
SUBJECT
Presidential Interest in SA-2 Missile System and Contingency Planning for Cuba

1. In your memorandum of 21 September 1962, you noted an apparent lack of unanimity between General LeMay and Admiral Anderson with respect to aircraft losses that might occur in attacking an SA-2 site. You further requested assurance as to the currency of contingency planning for Cuba.

2. I have discussed with General LeMay and Admiral Anderson their estimate of aircraft losses in attacking SA-2

missile sites. Admiral Anderson agrees with General LeMay's point that no losses would be suffered from the SA-2 missile since the attacking aircraft would fly below the effective minimum altitude of the SA-2. General LeMay shares Admiral Anderson's estimate that attacking aircraft might suffer some loss to antiaircraft artillery defenses of the SA-2 site. The National Intelligence Estimate credits the SA-2 missile system with a minimum effective altitude of 3000 feet due to inherent radar limitations.

3. If antiaircraft artillery is employed in direct support of the missile site, losses may be expected. World War II and Korean experience, updated to reflect current antiaircraft artillery capabilities against modern aircraft, indicates that low level attack forces would incur some combat losses from antiaircraft artillery fire; however, numbers cannot be predicted accurately. There are currently no known antiaircraft artillery defenses of SA-2 sites in Cuba. Attack plans can be amended to take the antiaircraft weapons under fire during the attack if reconnaissance shows such defenses and if analysis shows such fire suppression necessary. Korean experience proved that such fire suppression was unnecessary when surprise could be achieved.

4. In my opinion and that of the Joint Chiefs, it is not necessary to build a model of an SA-2 site for training purposes. However, the aircraft revetment of the type found at Santa Clara and Camaguey is a more difficult target than the SA-2 site. Therefore, the Air Force has found it desirable to reproduce that type aircraft revetment to aid in the selection of weapons, method of delivery and to assist in training crews. The target was completed at Nellis AFB, Nevada, on 30 September 1962, at an approximate cost of $28,000. Initial tests indicate that the GAM 83, 20 mm cannon, and napalm is the most effective weapons mix against aircraft in such revetments.

5. I have taken steps to insure that our contingency plans for Cuba are kept up to date.

6. The Navy plans to attack SA-2 targets at low level using 4 divisions of A-4D's (4 aircraft per division) armed with 250#,

500#, and 2000# low drag bombs and napalm. All crews are proficient in the delivery techniques planned. Similarly, the Air Force plans primary use of napalm and 20 mm cannon delivered at low level, and crews are proficient. Both have made detailed target studies; target folders are in the hands of crews; and crews are familiar with their assigned targets. As new missile sites are located, they are picked up in the target and attack plans within a few hours of receipt of photographs.

Robert S. McNamara

Memorandum

Washington, October 5, 1962, 5:15 p.m.

1. McCone reviewed details of the Donovan negotiations, discussions with the President, Attorney General, Eisenhower, the decisions not to approach Congressional leadership, the discussion with Senator Javits, and the final report from Donovan. Bundy expressed general agreement.

2. At the October 4th meeting of the Special Group Mongoose was discussed in some detail as was the meeting with Carter, Lansdale, et al. in DCI's office on that day. McCone stated there was a feeling in CIA and Defense that the "activist policy" which founded the Mongoose operation was gone and that while no specific operational activities had been (refused) the amount of "noise"from minor incidents such as the sugar, the students firing on the Havana Hotel and other matters and the extreme caution expressed by State had led to this conclusion. More importantly, however, the decisions to restrict U-2 flights had placed the United States Intelligence Community in a position where it could not report with assurance the development of offensive capabilities in Cuba. McCone stated he felt it most probable that Soviet-Castro operations would end up with an established offensive capability in Cuba including

MRBMs. McCone stated he thought this a probability rather than a mere possibility. Bundy took issue stating that he felt the Soviets would not go that far, that he was satisfied that no offensive capability would be installed in Cuba because of its world-wide effects and therefore seemed relaxed over the fact that the Intelligence Community cannot produce hard information on this important subject. McCone said that Bundy's viewpoint was reflected by many in the Intelligence Community, perhaps a majority, but he just did not agree and furthermore did not think the United States could afford to take such a risk.

3. Bundy then philosophized on Cuba stating that he felt that our policy was not clear, our objectives not determined and therefore our efforts were not productive. He discussed both the Mongoose operations and the Rostow "Track Two". Bundy was not critical of either or of the Lansdale operations. It was obvious that he was not in sympathy with a more active role such as those discussed at 5412 on Thursday as he felt none of them would bring Castro down nor would they particularly enhance U.S. position of world leadership. Bundy seemed inclined to support the Track Two idea and also inclined (though he was not specific) to play down the more active Lansdale operation. Bundy had not talked to Lansdale but obviously had received some of the "static" that is being passed around in Washington. (Before) McCone in reporting on the discussions at Thursday's 5412 meeting repeated the views of the President and expressed by the Attorney General it was agreed that the whole Government policy with reference to Cuba must be resolved promptly as basic to further actions on our part. In general, Bundy's views were that we should either make a judgment that we would have to go in militarily (which seemed to him intolerable) or alternatively we would have to learn to live with Castro, and his Cuba and adjust our policies accordingly.

4. McCone then elaborated on his views of the evolution of Soviet-Castro military capability stating he felt defense was just phase one, phase two would be followed by various offensive

capabilities and indeed the existing defensive capabilities such as the (MIG) 21s a very definite offensive capability against nearby American cities and installations. McCone stated that he thought that the establishment of a very expensive defensive mechanism could not be the ultimate objective of the Soviets or Castro and therefore the objective was (a) to establish an offensive base or (b) to insert sufficient Soviet specialists and military leaders to take Cuba away from Castro and establish it as a true Soviet controlled satellite. McCone stated that he felt there were only two courses open—one was to take military action at the appropriate time or secondly to pursue an effort to split Castro off from the Communists and for this reason he, McCone, had vigorously supported the Donovan mission as it is the only link that we have to the Castro hierarchy at the present time. Note in this connection it might be well to study the evolution of the Toure experience in Guinea when the Communists moved in and captured all elements of the Government and economy and forced Toure to expel the Ambassador and try to rectify the situation. There may be a parallel here.

5. McCone reviewed the Eisenhower discussions. Bundy read the memorandum covering these discussions. Bundy stated that Adenauer did not express the concern of the U.S. policy reflected by Eisenhower and reported in the memorandum.

6. Bundy rejected the idea of regular NSC meetings stating that every President has to organize his Government as he desires and that the Eisenhower pattern was not necessarily adaptable to the Kennedy type of administration. McCone stated that if this is the case he intended to request occasional NSC meetings to review specific estimates or other intelligence situations and the next one would be a report and discussion of the estimate of Soviet air defense capabilities. Bundy agreed.

7. Bundy rejected the idea (calling) the several Special Groups 5412, CIA, Mongoose, and North Vietnam together feeling it was better to keep them separated. He also rejected the idea that the visiting commissions such as the Byroade Team

and the Draper Team should report back to the Special Group (CI) feeling it was appropriate that they report to the President, (through) the Secretary of State, with consultation with the Special Group (CI). It was agreed that we would have a further discussion over the weekend.

John A. McCone
Director

Memorandum

MEMORANDUM ON DONOVAN PROJECT
Meeting 10 Oct 62
Immediately after my discussion with the Cannon Committee (including Taber, Ford and Mahon), I went to the White House and explained to the President and McGeorge Bundy the positions taken by Ford and Mahon, as covered in separate memorandum prepared by Mr. Warner. The President made the judgment that we should proceed with the negotiations, recognizing there would be some political consequences and criticisms, but he, the President, was willing to accept this as a fact.

I then showed the President photographs of the crates which presumably would carry, or were carrying, IL 28s, Soviet medium bombers, and were deck loaded on a ship which had arrived in Havana in the early days of October. The President requested that such information be withheld at least until after elections as if the information got into the press, a new and more violent Cuban issue would be injected into the campaign and this would seriously affect his independence of action.

McCone stated that these particular photographs could not be restricted as they had been disseminated to the Intelligence Community and several joint and specified commands, such as CINCLANT, SAC, NORAD, and others and would be reported in the CIA Bulletin on Thursday morning. The President then requested that the report be worded to indicate a probability rather than an actuality because in the final analysis we only saw crates, not the bombers themselves. DCI agreed. The President further requested that all future information be suppressed. DCI stated that this was extremely dangerous.

It was then agreed that future information would be disseminated to members of USIB, with appropriate instructions that only those responsible for giving the President advice be given the information. Furthermore, that within CIA circles a minimum number of experts be informed. McCone stated there was no problem in CIA, that it was secure. It was therefore agreed that the USIB members would be instructed to restrict the information to their personal offices and fully and currently inform the Chiefs of Staff, the Chairman, the Service Secretaries and the Secretary of Defense. Similar restrictive action would be taken in State. Therefore all those involved in "giving advice to the President" would be fully informed. However operational divisions and the joint and specified commands would not be informed at this time, except at the direction of the above people who are receiving the information.

At this point the President mentioned that "we'll have to do something drastic about Cuba" and I am anxiously looking forward to the JCS operational plan which is to be presented to me next week.

McCone effected the above instructions by calling Mr. Cline, who was unavailable, and then Mr. Sheldon who agreed to prepare a procedure for review on Thursday morning.

McCone then called the Attorney General and advised him of his talk with the Cannon Committee. The Attorney General had no particular comment.

At six o'clock McCone received a report from Houston that Donovan had gone into a meeting at five o'clock. At eleven o'clock Houston reported the meeting was still in progress. At seven o'clock on Thursday morning Donovan still had no report.

At 11:15 General Eisenhower called McCone stating he was sorry a meeting could not be arranged, he was leaving very early the following morning for Gettysburg. McCone reported that negotiations were in progress and he also reported objections stated by several members of Congress. Eisenhower advised that the negotiations be pursued, indicating his support of it and furthermore stated that if the negotiations were satisfactorily concluded the complaints and objections would, in his words, disappear.

McCone told General Eisenhower there were some defendable evidences of shipments of twin-engined light jet bombers. Eisenhower responded the situation must be watched very carefully. Positive action might be indicated and then he said there had been two instances where action was warranted but had not been taken. Eisenhower did not elaborate; however, I know from previous discussions he feels that when Castro embraced Communism publicly and announced publicly his allegiance to Moscow, we had then a reason to act militarily and if we had chosen to so act, such action would have been defendable.

On Thursday morning McCone reported by telephone to Mr. Kennedy, reviewing the Eisenhower discussion and stating that he, McCone, was concerned over Donovan's safety in view of the rash of publicity, most particularly the Herald Tribune article, and that he had instructed that contact be made with Donovan and that if things were not proceeding satisfactorily and a conclusion to the negotiations along the lines agreed in sight, then Donovan should come out. The Attorney General stated that he had no concern over Donovan's personal safety, that "they will not do anything to him". McCone stated he was not so sure and that he therefore concluded to bring Donovan out unless things were going well.

With reference to the political implications, McCone recalled that he had told the President and the AG that he would take all, or his full share of responsibility, that he wished the AG to bear this in mind as the position taken in this respect by Mr. McCone in the first conversation after his return from Europe still stood. AG expressed appreciation for this statement.

John A. McCone

Memorandum

REPORT OF CONVERSATION WITH AMBASSADOR DOBRYNIN ON SATURDAY, OCTOBER 13th, REGARDING CUBA AND OTHER SUBJECTS

A week ago Ambassador Dobrynin called my office to say that he understood I was leaving for Africa and would like to have our "long postponed luncheon" before my departure.

I met him at the U.S.S.R. Embassy on 16th Street at 1 p.m. on October 13th. With the exception of an occasional exchange of courtesies at diplomatic functions, this was the first time I had talked with him.

It was a frank, free-wheeling discussion, lasting more than an hour and a half. Dobrynin's manner was pleasant, with a show of reasonableness and concern about the current drift in Soviet-American relations.

At my first opportunity, I expressed deep disappointment that no more progress had been made in reducing tensions, and concern over the consequences of a further decline. I said that since I was speaking wholly unofficially, he should not attempt to read anything into my remarks. I would like to be utterly frank with him.

Almost immediately Dobrynin brought up the question of Cuba and expressed worry and surprise at the intensity of U.S. public reaction.

In response to his question as to why we attached such importance to a relatively small island, I outlined the history of U.S.-Cuban relations and drew a parallel to the situation in 1898, the presence of Spanish misrule, and the U.S. public agitation that abetted the outbreak of war.

When he protested that the Soviet presence in Cuba was no greater provocation than the U.S. presence in Turkey, I pointed out that the present Administration had inherited a status quo that had grown up since the war. In some areas the advantage in this status quo had been with us, in others with Moscow; in still others it was a stand-off.

Our presence in Greece and Turkey, for instance, represented our reaction to Stalin's military and political pressures against these two countries following the war. It had become part of a status quo which in all its complexity could safely be changed only by negotiation with reciprocal benefits to each side.

The Kennedy Administration had hoped and expected that we could in fact negotiate a more rational set of relationships, easing the various danger points on a basis of reciprocal action to everyone's benefit.

However, in Cuba the U.S.S.R. had unilaterally altered this status quo by introducing a wholly new element. Our reaction, in these circumstances, should have been foreseeable.

Moreover, many U.S. students of Soviet affairs were soberly convinced that the U.S.S.R. had made this move deliberately to provoke a U.S. military response against Cuba on the theory that this would divert our energies from Berlin, and elsewhere, and enable Soviet spokesmen to charge us with aggression in the UN.

If this kind of thinking had in fact played a part in the Soviet analysis, it was extremely dangerous. If we did move into Cuba in response to some overt act or offensive build-up by the U.S.S.R., a global chain of events might be set in motion which could have catastrophic consequences.

For instance, the Soviets might then be tempted to take what they would term "counter-action" in Berlin and perhaps Turkey; and the United States, by that time in an extremely tense mood, would react with vigor.

The U.S.S.R., in turn, would feel pressed by the Chinese and other extremists to counter our moves, and we would be on our way together down the long slippery slide.

I asked Dobrynin if he had read The Guns of August. He said "only a three-page summary."

I urged him to read at least the first few chapters in which he would see a pattern of politico-military action and counter-action that could be repeated in the next six months.

In July 1914, men of intelligence in Russia, Germany, Austria-Hungary, France and England, all quite conscious of the forces which were feeding the approaching holocaust, found themselves enmeshed in internal pressures, commitments and precedents which left them powerless to avoid the inevitable. It would be the greatest folly in history if we were to repeat this insane process in the nuclear age.

Dobrynin asked me what, in the circumstances, I thought could be done in regard to Cuba. Stressing that I was speaking solely as an individual, I suggested three moves that the U.S.S.R. could sponsor to ease the situation.

1. Dobrynin should remind his government of President Kennedy's sharp distinction between defensive and offensive weapons in his recent statement. I was particularly concerned on this point because current reports indicated that Soviet shipments were in fact beginning to include weapons which had a clearly offensive capacity.

If this continued, it could produce—with the help of some incident perpetrated perhaps by individuals striving to provoke another "Remember the Maine" incident—the very conflict which the Administration is anxious to avoid. President Kennedy had committed himself to act under certain specific circumstances. This was a clear commitment, and the U.S.S.R. should not take it lightly.

2. From many reports, Castro now had ample defensive arms with which to protect himself from casual landings. The U.S.S.R. should tell him that under present circumstances no more arms will be shipped. The U.S.S.R. should then ask Castro himself to make a statement announcing that the defense of Cuba was assured and that no more arms were needed. Moscow could then inform us that no more arms would be shipped.

3. Castro should be asked by Moscow to state that he has no design on his neighbors, that his entire energies would henceforth be devoted to the economic development of Cuba, and that he sought only peaceful competition with other Latin American nations. His decision not to indulge in further

subversion, propaganda, and expansion in neighboring Latin American countries would, of course, have to be confirmed by deeds. However, Soviet assurances on this point would serve to reduce some of the current tensions and give us all a breathing spell.

If some progress along these lines were not possible, I had deep forebodings about the weeks ahead.

To all of this Dobrynin appeared to listen intently. I believe he was impressed.

He answered that in spite of our worries, the U.S.S.R. was not shipping offensive weapons and well understood the dangers of doing so. Moreover, it was unreasonable for the U.S., as a major power, to expect a small, weak country such as Cuba to make such public concessions to U.S. public opinion even though both the U.S.S.R. and Cuba might accept all three points in principle.

Why, he asked repeatedly, do we get so excited about so small a nation? Although the U.S.S.R. could not let Cuba down, they had no desire to complicate the situation further. Was it not possible for us to negotiate a modus vivendi with Castro directly?

I commented that Cuba had initiated the current conflict. Indeed, in 1959 most Americans had strongly applauded Castro's revolution. If Dobrynin were misinformed about the types of weapons now arriving in Cuba, it would not be the first time in diplomatic history that this had occurred. As long as Soviet weapons flowed into Cuba and Cuban money was used to subvert Latin American countries which we were striving to assist into the 20th century, the situation would remain dangerously explosive.

I hoped that his government would see the danger and act accordingly to help ease the tensions.

Without directly responding to my remarks, Dobrynin referred to Max Frankel's story in the morning Times which cited agitation by various private agencies, Cuban and American, to provoke a "Maine incident" with the connivance of U.S. official groups. I replied that our government would have no part in such an operation, that we were genuinely worried, and that his government should view the situation with serious concern.

Telegram from US Embassy

Moscow, October 16, 1962, 7 p.m.

978. Policy. Khrushchev-Kohler — Part III — Cuba.
Parts I, II, and IV of Kohler's conversation with Khrushchev on October 15, transmitted in telegrams 973, 974, and 979 from Moscow, October 16, are in volume V; Part V, transmitted in telegram 981 from Moscow, October 16, is in vol. XV, pp. 359-362.

Khrushchev said he wanted to express his disappointment at one thing that adds fuel to fire of the cold war, namely, that US now is trying to stop Soviet airplanes from flying to Cuba. After I interjected confirmation, he said they regard this as unfriendly act. This is not wartime. We should be developing trade and culture between our countries. He could not understand why we were acting this way. Perhaps we were frightened and our leaders' nerves were bad. If we were going to start a war, then he could understand it. US was boycotting trade with Cuba and appealing to all countries to stop their ships from going there. US is great country with population 183 million, while Cuba has only seven million. Could it really be that US was afraid of Cuba? Who would believe that Cuba was a nightmare for US? It was too small; even if it wanted to gobble up US, it couldn't. (There followed some good-natured byplay about census figures.) Khrushchev said that what US was doing complicated life of simple people and did not simplify it. Result was to make Cuban people go hungry. What did US want? To start war? If not, what was happening? "Are you too afraid? Do you want to commit suicide?" When last war started in USSR, on third or fourth day, a certain General came to him, where he was serving as member of military council of front, and said everything was lost, just as in France. General said command must be changed. General went to sleep that night and next morning came into peasant hut in which Khrushchev was staying and shot himself. He was a coward, lost his self-control, and let his nerves dominate his mind. Had US become a coward? Such people end by shooting themselves. Did US want to commit suicide? Is this the state in which American imperialism now finds itself?

I said I should of course report his remarks to President. At Vienna, President had spoken very frankly to him about Cuba. Chairman was misinterpreting Castro regime. Not only US, but all Western Hemisphere countries, feel Castro has let Cuban people down. US and other Western Hemisphere states are not going to help Cuba. We are certainly not afraid of them but we don't intend to help them. Of course, we have different views than Chairman about situation. Speaking as frankly as he had, I felt I must add that size of Soviet shipments to Cuba has increased feeling in US on this problem.

Khrushchev said we must be responsible, since our countries are great powers. We cannot demand that other countries live as we like or there would be war. US has bases in countries neighboring USSR, such as Turkey, as well as in Greece, Italy, France, West Germany and Pakistan. But USSR does not attack these countries. If US thinks it has right to do as it likes about Cuba, why hasn't USSR right to do as it likes about these countries? If we acted that way, might would make right. UN Charter would lose its force. That would be policy of banditry. Cuba is small; US is big. "You are so afraid of Cuba, you almost lost your pants." US is located in Western Hemisphere; what is it doing in Eastern Hemisphere? USSR does not recognize right of US to be everywhere in world and to rule everywhere. It was one thing when US was very powerful, but now there is a force as great as yours. We will never agree to your capitalistic way of thinking. Our policy is, let us live in peace. Let us have our socialism and you can have your capitalism. Let's respect internal affairs of other countries and not interfere with life of other countries. Take, for example, Shah of Iran, whom we don't like. But we have no intention of attacking him. Or take Afghanistan, country with monarchical government. Its King recently visited me here and I entertained him. He is a nice fellow. We have good relations with him and this is the way it should be.

I said I took note of Chairman's remarks. President has made it clear we are not going to interfere in Cuba by force. But we are not going to help Cuba, which does not mean we intend to interfere there.

Khrushchev accepted this, saying he also understood President that way but must still express his disappointment about blockade, which is inimical action. Let the people choose their own system. As a result of blockade, Cuban people are suffering and will become more embittered against US. You should trade with Cuba, as we do with Turkey and other of your allies. Why are you not trading with us? You want to strangle us. But you've lost any real understanding of history.

Transcript

Washington, October 16, 1962, 11:50 a.m.

JFK: Secretary Rusk?

Rusk: Yes. Mr. President, this is a, of course, a (*inaudible*) serious development. It's one that we, all of us, had not really believed the Soviets could, uh, carry this far. Uh, they, uh, seemed to be denying that they were going to establish bases of their own (*inaudible*) with a Soviet base, thus making it essential to Cuban point of view. The Cubans couldn't (*unintelligible*) with it anyhow, so. . . . Now, um, I do think we have to set in motion a chain of events that will eliminate this base. I don't think we can sit still. The questioning becomes whether we do it by sudden, unannounced strike of some sort, or we, uh, build up the crisis to the point where the other side has to consider very seriously about giving in, or, or even the Cubans themselves, uh, take some, take some action on this. The thing that I'm, of course, very conscious of is that there is no such thing, I think, as unilateral action by the United States. It's so (inaudible) involved with 42 allies and confrontation in many places, that any action that we take, uh, will greatly increase the risks of direct action involving, uh, our other alliances and our other forces in other parts of the world. Um, so I think we, we have to think very hard about two major, uh, courses of action as alternatives. One is the quick strike. The point where we think, that is the, uh, overwhelming, overriding necessity to take all the risks that are involved doing that. I don't think this in itself would require an invasion of Cuba. I think that with or without such an invasion, in other words if we make it clear that, uh, what we're doing is eliminating this particular base or any other such base that is established. We ourselves are not moved to general war, we're simply doing what we said we would do if they took certain action. Uh, or we're going to decide that this is the time to eliminate the Cuban problem by actually eliminating the island.

The other would be, if we have a few days—from the military point of view, if we have the whole time—uh, then I would think that, uh, there would be another course of action, a combination of things that, uh, we might wish to consider. Um, first, uh, that we, uh, stimulate the OAS procedure immediately for prompt action to make it quite clear that the entire hemisphere considers that the Rio Pact has been violated (and actually?) what acts should (we take or be taken?) in, under the terms of the Rio Pact. The OAS could constitute itself an organ of consultation promptly, although maybe, it may take two or three days to get, uh, instructions from governments and things of that sort. The OAS could, I suppose, at any moment, uh, take action to insist to the Cubans that an OAS inspection, uh, team be permitted to come and, itself, look directly at these sites, provide assurance(s?) to the hemisphere. That will undoubtedly be turned down, but it will be another step in building up the, uh, building a position.

I think also that we ought to consider getting some word to Castro, perhaps through the Canadian ambassador in Havana or through, uh, his representative at the U.N. Uh, I think perhaps the Canadian ambassador would be the best, the better channel to get to Castro (apart?) privately and tell him that, uh, this is no longer support for Cuba, that Cuba is being victimized here, and that, uh, the Soviets are preparing Cuba for destruction or betrayal.

You saw the Times story yesterday morning that high Soviet officials were saying, "We'll trade Cuba for Berlin." This ought to be brought to Castro's attention. It ought to be said to Castro that, uh, uh, this kind of a base is intolerable and not acceptable. The time has now come when he must take the interests of the Cuban people, must now break clearly with the Soviet Union, prevent this missile base from becoming operational.

And I think there are certain military, um, uh, actions that we could, we might well want to take straight away. First, to, uh, to call up, uh, highly selective units (no more than?) 150,000. Unless we feel that it's better, more desirable to go to a general national emergency so that we have complete freedom of action. If we announce, at the time that we announce this development—and I think we do have to announce this development some time this week—uh, we announce that, uh, we are conducting a surveillance of Cuba, over Cuba, and we will enforce our right to do so. We reject the mission of secrecy in this hemisphere in any matters of this sort. We, we reinforce our forces in Guantanamo. We reinforce our forces in the southeastern part of the United States—whatever is necessary from the military point of view to be able to give, to deliver an overwhelming strike at any of these installations, including the SAM sites. And, uh, also to take care of any, uh, MIGs or bombers that might make a pass at Miami or at the United States. Build up heavy forces, uh, if those are not already in position.

That, uh, we then would move openly and vigorously into the, into the guerrilla field, and, uh, create maximum confusion on the island. (You know?) won't be too squeemish at this point about the overtness, covert (counter?) (*unintelligible*) of what is being done.

We review our attitude on, an alternative Cuban government. We get Miro Cardona and his group in, Manuel Rey and his group, and see if they won't get together on a progressive junta. Uh, that would pretty well combine all principal elements, other than the Batista group, as the leaders of Cuba. And, uh, have them, give them more of a status, whether we proceed to full recognition or not is something else, but get, get the Cuban elements highly organized on this matter.

I think also that we need a few days, um, to alert our other allies, for consultation with NATO. I'll assume that we can move on this line at the same time to interrupt all air traffic from free world countries going into Cuba, insist to the Mexicans, the Dutch, that they stop their planes from coming in. Tell the British, who, and anyone else who's involved at this point, that, uh, if they're interested in peace, they've got to stop their ships from Cuban trade at this point. Uh, in other words, isolate Cuba completely without at this particular moment a, uh, a forceful blockade.

I think it would be important to use the, uh, consider, uh, calling in General Eisenhower, giving him a full briefing before a public announcement is made as to the situation and the (forcible?) action which you might determine upon.

But I think that, by and large, there are, there are these two broad alternatives: one, the quick strike; the other, to alert our allies and Mr. Khrushchev that there is utterly serious crisis in the making here, and that, uh . . . Mr. Khrushchev may not himself really understand that or believe that at this point. I think we'll be facing a situation that could well lead to general war; that we have an obligation to do what has to be done but do it in a way that gives, uh, everybody a chance to, uh, put the (word unintelligible) down before it gets too hard. Those are my, my reactions of this morning, Mr. President. I naturally need to think about this very hard for the next several hours, uh, what I and what my colleagues at the State Department can do about it.

McNamara: Mr. President, there are a number of unknowns in this situation I want to comment upon, and, in relation to them, I would like to outline very briefly some possible military alternatives and ask General Taylor to expand upon them.

But before commenting on either the unknowns or outlining some military alternatives, there are two propositions I would suggest that we ought to accept as, uh, foundations for our further thinking. My first is that if we are to conduct an air strike against these installations, or against any part of Cuba, we must agree now that we will schedule that prior to the time these missile sites become operational. I'm not prepared to say when that will be, but I think it is extremely important that our talk and our discussion be founded on this premise: that any air strike will be planned to take place prior to the time they become operational. Because, if they become operational before the air strike, I do not believe we can state we can knock them out before they can be launched; and if they're launched there is almost certain to be, uh, chaos in part of the east coast or the area, uh, in a radius of six hundred to a thousand miles from Cuba.

Uh, secondly, I, I would submit the proposition that any air strike must be directed not solely against the missile sites, but against the missile sites plus the airfields plus the aircraft which may not be on the airfields but hidden by that time plus all potential nuclear storage sites. Now, this is a fairly extensive air strike. It is not just a strike against the missile sites; and there would be associated with it potential casualties of Cubans, not of U.S. citizens, but potential casualties of Cubans in, at least in the hundreds, more likely in the low thousands, say two or three thousand. It seems to me these two propositions, uh, should underlie our, our discussion.

Now, what kinds of military action are we capable of carrying out and what may be some of the consequences? Uh, we could carry out an air strike within a matter of days. We would be ready for the start of such an air strike within, within a matter of days. If it were absolutely essential, it could be done almost literally within a matter of hours. I believe the chiefs would prefer that it be deferred for a matter of days, but we are prepared for that quickly. The air strike could continue for a matter of days following the initial day, if necessary. Uh, presumably there would be some political discussions taking place either just before the air strike or both before and during. In any event, we would be prepared, following the air strike, for an air, invasion, both by air and by sea. Approximately seven days after the start of the air strike, that would be possible if the political environment made it desirable or necessary at that time. (Fine?) Associated with this air strike undoubtedly should be some degree of mobilization. Uh, I would think of the mobilization coming not before the air strike but either concurrently with or somewhat following, say possibly five days afterwards, depending upon the possible invasion requirements. The character of the mobilization would be such that it could be carried out in its first phase at least within the limits of the authority granted by Congress. There might have to be a second phase, and then it would require a declaration of a national emergency.

Now, this is very sketchily the military, uh, capabilities, and I think you may wish to hear General Taylor, uh, outline his choice.

Speaker?: Almost too (words unintelligible) to Cuba.

Speaker?: Yes.

Taylor: Uh, we're impressed, Mr. President, with the great importance of getting a, a strike with all the benefit of surprise, uh, which would mean ideally that we would have all the missiles that are in Cuba above ground where we can take them out. Uh, that, that desire runs counter to the strong point the Secretary made if the other optimum would be to get every missile before it could, becomes operational. Uh, practically, I think the, our knowledge of the timing of the readiness is going to be so, so, uh, difficult that we'll never have the, the exact permanent, uh, the perfect timing. What we'd like to do is to look at this new photography, I think—and take any additional—and try to get the, the layout of the targets in as near an optimum, uh, position as possible, and then take 'em out without any warning whatsoever. That does not preclude, I don't think, Mr. Secretary, some of the things you've been talking about. It's a little hard to say in terms of time how much I'm discussing. But we must do a good job the first time we go in there, uh, pushing a 100 percent just as far, as closely as we can with our, with our strike. I'm having all the responsible planners in this afternoon, Mr. President, at four o'clock, to talk this out with 'em and get their best judgment.

I would also mention among the, the military actions we should take that once we have destroyed as many of these offensive weapons as possible, we should, should prevent any more coming in, which means a naval blockade. So I suppose that all . . . . And also a reinforcement of Guantanamo and evacuation of dependents. So, really, the, in point of time, I'm, I'm thinking in terms of three phases.

One, a, an initial pause of some sort while we get completely ready and get, get the right posture on the part of the target, so we can do the best job. Then, virtually concurrently, an air strike against, as the Secretary said, missiles, airfields, uh, unclear sites that we know of. At the same time, naval blockade. At the same time, reinforce Guantanamo and evacuate the dependents. I'd then start this continuous reconnaissance, the list that you had, continue over Cuba.

Then, then the decision can be made as we, as we're mobilizing, uh, with the air strike as to whether we invade or not. I think that's the hardest question militarily in the whole business—one which we should look at very closely before we get our feet in that deep mud in Cuba.

Rusk: There are st-, one or two things, Mr. President, uh. Gromyko asked to see you Thursday. Uh, it may be of some interest to know what he says about this, if he says anything. He may be bringing a message on this subject. Uh, but that. . . . I just want to remind you that you are seeing him and that may be relevant to this (topic?). I might say incidentally, sir, that you delay anything else you have to do at this point.

Secondly, I don't believe, myself, that the critical question is whether you get a particular missile before it goes off because if they shoot those missiles we are in general nuclear war. In other words, the Soviet Union has got quite a different decision to make. If they, if they shoot those missiles, want to shoot 'em off before they get knocked out by aircraft. . . . So, I'm not sure that this is, uh, necessarily the precise (critical?) element, Bob.

McNamara: Well, I would strongly emphasize that I think our time should be based on the assumption it is, Dean. We don't know what kinds of communications the Soviets have with those sites. We don't know what kinds of control they have over the warheads.

Rusk: Yes, (words unintelligible) . . .

McNamara: If we saw a warhead on the site and we knew that that launcher was capable of launching that warhead, I would . . . . Frankly, I would strongly urge against the air attack, to be quite frank about it, because I think the danger to this country in relation to the gain that would accrue with the excessive (time?). . . . This is why I suggest that if we're talking about an air attack, I believe we should consider it only on the assumption that we can carry if off before these become operational.

JFK: What is the, uh, advant- . . . . Must be some major reason for the Russians to, uh, set this up as a . . . . Must be that they're not satisfied with their ICBMs. What'd be the reason that they would, uh . . . .

Taylor: What it'd give 'em is primary, it makes the launching base, uh, for short range missiles against the United States to supplement their rather (deceptive?) ICBM system, for example. There's one reason.

JFK: Of course, I don't see how we could prevent further ones from coming in by submarine.

Taylor: Well, I think that that thing is all over . . .

JFK: I mean if we let 'em blockade the thing, they come in by submarine.

McNamara: Well, I think the only way to prevent them coming in, quite frankly, is to say you'll take them out the moment they come in. You'll take them out and you'll carry on open surveillance and you'll have a policy to take them out if they come in. I think it's really rather unrealistic to think that we could carry out an air attack of the kind we're talking about. We're talking about an air attack of several hundred sorties because we don't know where these airplanes are.

Bundy: Are you absolutely clear of your premise that an air strike must go to the whole air complex?

McNamara: Well, we are, Mac . . .

Bundy: . . . air complex? (Appears to be a repeat of the words above.)

McNamara: . . . because we are fearful of these MIG 21s. We don't know where they are. We don't know what they're capable of. If there are nuclear warheads associated with the launchers, you must assume there will be nuclear warheads associated with aircraft. Even if there are not nuclear warheads associated with aircraft, you must assume that those aircraft have high explosive potential. We have a serious air defense problem. We're not prepared to report to you exactly, uh, what the Cuban air force is capable of; but I think we must assume that the Cuban air force is definitely capable of penetrating, in small numbers, our coastal air defense by coming in low over the water. And I would think that we would not dare go in against the missile sites, knock those out leaving intact Castro's air force, and run the risk that he would use part or all of that air force against our coastal areas—either with or without nuclear weapons. It would be a, a very heavy price to pay in U.S. lives for the, the damage we did to Cuba.

Rusk: Still, about why the Soviets are doing this, um, Mr. McCone suggested some weeks ago that one thing Mr. Khrushchev may have in mind is that, uh, uh, he knows that we have a substantial nuclear superiority, but he also knows that we don't really live under fear of his nuclear weapons to the extent that, uh, he has to live under fear of ours. Also we have nuclear weapons nearby, in Turkey and places like that. Um. . . .

JFK: How many weapons do we have in Turkey?

Taylor?: We have Jupiter missiles . . .

Bundy?: Yeah. We have how many?

McNamara?: About fifteen, I believe it is.

Bundy?: I think that's right. I think that's right.

Speaker?: (Words unintelligible)

Rusk: But then there are also delivery vehicles that are, could easily . . .

McNamara: Aircraft.

Rusk: . . . be moved through the air, aircraft and so forth.

Speaker?: Route 'em through Turkey.

Rusk: Um, and that Mr. McCone expresses the view that Khrushchev may feel that it's important for us to learn about living under medium-range missiles, and he's doing that to sort of balance that, uh, that political, psychological (plank?). I think also that, uh, Berlin is, uh, very much involved in this. Um, for the first time, I'm beginning really to wonder whether maybe Mr. Khrushchev is entirely rational about Berlin. We've (hardly?) talked about his obsession with it. And I think we have to, uh, keep our eye on that element. But, uh, they may be thinking that they can either bargain Berlin and Cuba against each other, or that they could provoke us into a kind of action in Cuba which would give an umbrella for them to take action with respect to Berlin. In other words like the Suez-Hungary combination. If they could provoke us into taking the first overt action, then the world would be confused and they would have, uh, what they would consider to be justification for making a move somewhere else. But, uh, I must say I don't really see the rationality of, uh, the Soviets pushing it this far unless they grossly misunderstand the importance of Cuba to this country.

Bundy: It's important, I think, to recognize that they did make this decision, as far as our estimates now go, in early summer, and, this has been happening since August. Their TASS statement of September 12, which the experts, I think, attribute very strongly to Khrushchev himself, is all mixed up on this point. It has a rather explicit statement, "The harmless military equipment sent to Cuba designed exclusively for defense, defensive purposes. The President of the United States and the American military, the military of any country know what means of defense are. How can these means threaten United States?"

Now there, it's very hard to reconcile that with what has happened. The rest, as the Secretary says, has many comparisons between Cuba and Italy, Turkey and Japan. We have other evidence that Khrushchev is, honestly believes, or, or at least affects to believe that we have nuclear weapons in, in Japan, that combination, (word unintelligible) . . .

Rusk: Gromyko stated that in his press conference the other day, too.

Bundy: Yeah. They may mean Okinawa.

Speaker?: Right.

McNamara: It's not likely, but it's conceivable the nuclear warheads for these launchers are not yet on Cuban soil.

Bundy: Now that seems to me that's . . . . It's perfectly possible that this, that they are in that sense a bluff. That doesn't make them any less offensive to us . . .

McNamara: No.

Bundy: . . . because we can't have proof about it.

McNamara: No, but it does possibly indicate a different course of action . . .

Bundy: Yeah.

McNamara: . . . and therefore, while I'm not suggesting how we should handle this, I think this is one of the most important actions we should take: to ascertain the location of the nuclear warheads for these missiles. Later in the discussion we can revert back to this. There are several alternative ways of approaching it.

JFK: Doug, do you have any . . . .

Dillon: No. The only thing I'd, would say is that, uh, this alternative course of, of warning, getting, uh, public opinion, uh, OAS action and telling people in NATO and everything like that, would appear to me to have the danger of, uh, getting us wide out in the open and forcing the Russians to, uh, Soviets to take a, a position that if anything was done, uh, they would, uh, have to retaliate. Whereas, uh, a, a quick action, uh, with a statement at the same time saying this is all there is to it, might give them a chance to, uh, back off and not do anything. Meanwhile, I think that the chance of getting through this thing without a Russian reaction is greater under a quick, uh, strike than, uh, building the whole thing up to a, a climax then going through. . . . (It will be a lot of debate on it?)

Rusk: That is, of course, a possibility, but, uh. . . .

Bundy: The difficulties—I, I share the Secretary of the Treasury's feeling a little bit—the difficulties of organizing the OAS and NATO; the amount of noise we would get from our allies saying that, uh, they can live with Soviet MRBMs, why can't we; uh, the division in the alliance; the certainty that the Germans would feel that we were jeopardizing Berlin because of our concern over Cuba. The prospect of that pattern is not an appetizing one . . .

Rusk: Yes, but you see . . .

Bundy: . . . (Words unintelligible)

Rusk: . . . uh, uh, everything turns crucially on what happens.

Bundy: I agree, Mr. Secretary.

Rusk: And if we go with the quick strike, then, in fact, they do back it up, then you've exposed all of your allies (word unintelligible), ourselves to all these great dangers without . . .

Bundy: You get all these noises again.

Rusk: . . . without, uh, the slightest consultation or, or warning or preparation.

JFK: But, of course, warning them, uh, it seems to me, is warning everybody. And I, I, obviously you can't sort of announce that in four days from now you're going to take them out. They may announce within three days they're going to have warheads on 'em; if we come and attack, they're going to fire them. Then what'll, what'll we do? Then we don't take 'em out. Of course, we then announce, well, if they do that, then we're going to attack with nuclear weapons.

Dillon: Yes, sir, that's the question that nobody, I didn't understand, nobody had mentioned, is whether this s-, uh, "take-out," this mission, uh, was (word unintelligible) to deal with . . .

Speaker?: I don't know.

Dillon: . . . high explosives?

Speaker?: High explosives, yes.

JFK: How effective can the take-out be, do they think?

Taylor?: It'll never be a 100 percent, Mr. President, we know. Uh, we hope to take out a vast majority in the first strike, but this is not just one thing, one strike, one day, but continuous air attack for whenever necessary, whenever we di-, discover a target.

Bundy: They're now talking about taking out the air force as well. . . .

Speaker?: I (could tell you that in the staff?).

Speaker?: (Words unintelligible)

Bundy: I do raise again the question whether, uh, whether we (words unintelligible) the problem, military problem, but there is, I would think, a substantial political advantage in limiting the strike in surgical terms to the thing that is in fact the cause of action.

McNamara?: I suggest, Mr. President, that if you're involved in several hundred strikes, this is what you would — and against airfields — this is what you would do, pre-invade. And, uh, it would be very difficult to convince anybody that this was not a pre-invasion strike. I think also once you get this volume of attack that public opinion reaction, uh, to this, as distinct from the reaction to an invasion, uh, there's (word unintelligible) little difference. And, uh, from both standpoints, it would seem to me that if you're talking about a, a general air attack program, you might as well think about whether we can eradicate the whole problem by an invasion just as simply with as little chance of reaction.

Taylor: Well, I would think we would have, should be in a position to invade at any time if we so desired. Hence that, uh, in this preliminary, we should be, uh, it's all bonus if we are indeed taking out weapons (word unintelligible) . . .

JFK: Well, let's say we just take out the missile bases, then, uh, they have some more there. Obviously they can get 'em in by submarine and so on, I don't know whether you, you just can't keep high strikes on.

Taylor: I suspect, Mr. President, we'd have to take out the surface-to-air missiles in order to get in, to get in, take some of them out. Maybe (words unintelligible).

JFK: How long will, do we estimate this will remain secure, this, uh, information, uh, people have it?

Bundy: In terms of the tightness of our intelligence control, Mr. President, I think we are in unusually and fortunately good position. We set up a, uh, new security classification governing precisely the field of offensive capability in Cuba just five days ago, four days ago, under General Carter. That, uh, limits this, uh, to people who have an immediate, operational necessity in intelligence terms to work on the data and the people who have . . .

JFK: How many would that be, about?

Bundy: Oh, that will be a very large number, but that's not generally where leaks come from. Uh, the more (important?) limitation is that only officers with the policy responsibility for advice directly to you'll receive this . . .

JFK: How many would get it over in the Defense Department, General, with your meeting this afternoon?

Taylor: Well, I was going to mention that. We'd have to ask for relaxation of the ground rules, uh, that, that Mac has just enunciated, so that I can, uh, give it to the senior commanders who are involved in the plans.

JFK: Would that be about fifty?

Taylor: By then. . . . No, sir. I would say that, uh, within, at this stage ten more.

McNamara: Well, Mr. President, I, I think, to be realistic, we should assume that this will become fairly widely known, if not in the newspapers, at least by political representatives of both parties within—I would, I'm just picking a figure—I'd say a week.

(Several speakers speak at once and none of the words are intelligible.)

McNamara: And I say that because we have, we have taken action already that is raising questions in people's minds. Normally, when a U-2 comes back, we duplicate the films. The duplicated copies go to a series of commands. A copy goes to SAC. A copy goes to CINCLANT. A copy goes to CIA. And normally, uh, the photo interpreters and the, and the operational officers in these commands are looking forward to these. We have stopped all that, and this, this type of information is going on throughout the department. And I, I doubt very much that we can keep this out of the hands of, uh, of members of Congress, for example, for more than a week.

Rusk: Well, Senator Keating has already, in effect, announced it on the floor of the Senate.

Bundy: Senator Keating said this on the floor of the Senate on the tenth of October . . .

Rusk: (That's correct?)

Bundy: . . . "Construction has begun on at least a half-dozen launching sites for intermediate range tactical missiles."

Rusk: Well, that's, that's the way that (words unintelligible). I think we can count on announcing it not later than Thursday or Friday of this week.

Taylor?: There is a refugee who's a major source of intelligence on this, of course, who has described one of these missiles in terms which we can recognize, who is now in this country.

JFK: Is he the one who's giving Keating his stuff?

Taylor?: We don't know.

Bundy: My question, Mr. President, is whether as a matter of, uh, tactics we ought not to interview Senator Keating and check out his data. Seems to me that that ought to be done in a routine sort of way by an open officer of the intelligence agency.

Speaker?: I think that's (right?).

JFK: You have any thoughts, Mr. Vice President?

Johnson: I agree with Mac that that ought to be done. I think that, uh, we're committed at any time that we feel that there's a build up that in any way endangers to take whatever action we must take to assure our security. I would think the Secretary's evaluation of this thing being around all over the lot is a pretty accurate one, I would think it'd take a week to do it. Maybe a little before then.

I would, uh, like to hear what the responsible commanders have to say this afternoon. I think the question with the base is whether we take it out or whether we talk about it, and, uh, both, either alternative is a very distressing one, but of the two, I would take it out.

JFK: Well, uh, the, uh . . .

Johnson: Assuming these commanders felt that way. I'm fearful if we . . . . I spent the weekend with the ambassadors of the Organization of American States. I think this organization is fine, but I don't think, I don't rely on 'em much for any strength in anything like this. And, I, the fact that we're talking about our other allies, uh, I take the position that Mr. Bundy says, We ought to be living all these years with (words unintelligible) get your blood pressure up. But the fact is the country's blood pressure is up and they are fearful, and they're insecure, and we're getting divided, and, uh, I don't think that, uh . . . . I take this little State Department Bulletin that you sent out to all the congressmen. One, one of the points you make — that any time the build up endangers or threatens our security in any way, we're going to do whatever must be done immediately to protect our own security. And when you say that, why the, give unanimous support. People are really concerned about this, in my opinion. Uh, I think we have to be prudent and cautious, talk to the commanders and see what they say, what they're . . . . (I'm) not much for circularizing it over the Hill or our allies, even though I realize it's a breach of faith. It's the one not to confer with them. We're not going to get much help out of them.

Bundy: There is an intermediate position. There are perhaps two or three of our principal allies or heads of government we could communicate, at least on a 24-hour notice basis. Certainly ease, ease the . . .

Johnson: (Take a large?) (words unintelligible) (to?) stop the planes, stop the ships, stop the submarines and everything else from (sending?). Just not going to permit it. And then stop them from coming in.

Speaker?: Yeah.

JFK: Uh, eh, well, this, which . . . . What you're really talking about are two or three different, uh, (tense?) operations. One is the strike just on this, these three bases. One, the second is the broader one that Secretary McNamara was talking about, which is on the airfields and on the SAM sites and on anything else connected with, uh, missiles. Third is doing both of those things and also at the same time launching a blockade, which requires really the, uh, the, uh, third and which is a larger step. And then, as I take it, the fourth question is the, uh, degree of consultation. *[censored]*

Speaker?: Um.

JFK: Just have to (words unintelligible) and do it. Probably ought to tell them, though, the night before.

RFK: Mr. President.

JFK: Yes.

RFK: We have the fifth one, really, which is the invasion. I would say that, uh, you're dropping bombs all over Cuba if you do the second, uh, air, the airports, knocking out their planes, dropping it on all their missiles. You're covering most of Cuba. You're going to kill an awful lot of people, and, uh, we're going to take an awful lot of heat on it . . .

Speaker?: Yeah.

RFK: . . . and, uh, and then, uh, you know, the heat, you're going to announce the reason that you're doing it is because, uh, they're sending in these kind of missiles. Well, I would think it's almost incumbent upon the Russians, then, to say, Well, we're going to send them in again, and if you do it again, we're going to do, we're going to do the same thing to Turkey, or We're going to do the same thing to Iran.

(Here follow 5 pages of discussion of which targets might be attacked.)

JFK: I think we ought to, what we ought to do is, is, uh, after this meeting this afternoon, we ought to meet tonight again at six, consider these various, uh, proposals. In the meanwhile, we'll go ahead with this maximum, whatever is needed from the flights, and, in addition, we will . . . . I don't think we got much time on these missiles. They may be . . . . So it may be that we just have to, we can't wait two weeks while we're getting ready to, to roll. Maybe just have to just take them out, and continue our other preparations if we decide to do that. That may be where we end up. I think we ought to, beginning right now, be preparing to. . . . Because that's what we're going to do anyway. We're certainly going to do number one; we're going to take out these, uh, missiles. Uh, the questions will be whether, which, what I would describe as number two, which would be a general air strike. That we're not ready to say, but we should be in preparation for it. The third is the, is the, uh, the general invasion. At least we're going to do number one, so it seems to me that we don't have to wait very long. We, we ought to be making those preparations.

Bundy: You want to be clear, Mr. President, whether we have definitely decided against a political track. I, myself, think we ought . . .

Taylor?: Well, we'll have . . .

Bundy: . . . to work out a contingency on that.

Taylor?: We, we'll develop both tracks.

JFK: [censored] We ought to just decide who we talk to and how long ahead and how many people, really, in the government. There's going to be a difference between those who know that—this will leak out in the next few days—there are these, uh, uh, bases, until we say or the Pentagon or State won't be harsh. We've already said it on the (words unintelligible). So we, let's say, we've got two or three days.

Bundy: Well, let's play it, shall we play it still harder and, uh, simply say that there's no evidence and that we have to . . .

JFK: We ought to stick the battle till we want to do something.

Bundy: . . . (words unintelligible) the alliance (words unintelligible).

JFK: Otherwise we give ourselves away, so let's . . .

Bundy: May I make one other cover plan suggestion . . .

JFK: Yes.

Bundy: . . . Mr. President? There will be meetings in the White House. I think the best we can do is to keep the people with a specific Latin American business black and describe the rest as "intensive budget review sessions," but I haven't been able to think of any other . . .

JFK: Nobody, it seems to me, in the State Department. I discussed the matter with, uh, Bohlen of the Soviet bloc and told him he could talk to Thompson. So that's those two. It seems to me that there's no one else in the State Department that ought to be talked to about it . . .

Speaker?: (Words unintelligible) in the department.

JFK: . . . in any level at all, and, uh, until we know a little more. And then, as I say, in Defense we've got to keep it as tight as possible . . .

Speaker?: (Words unintelligible)

JFK: . . . particularly what we're going to do about it. Maybe a lot of people know about what's there, but what we're going to do about it really ought to be, you know, the tightest of all because otherwise we botch it up.

McNamara: Mr. President, may I suggest that we come back this afternoon prepared to, to answer three questions. First, should we surface our surveillance? I think this is a very important . . .

Speaker?: Very important point.

McNamara: . . . question at the moment. We ought to try to decide today either yes or no.

JFK: By "surface our" . . .

McNamara: I mean should we state publicly . . .

JFK?: Oh.

McNamara: . . . that, that you have stated we will, we'll act to take out any offensive weapons. In order to be certain as to whether there are or are not offensive weapons, we are scheduling U-2 flights or other surveillance . .

Carter?: What's the (skull number, commissar?). (Laughs)

McNamara: . . . or reconnaissance flights to, uh, to obtain this information. We'll make the information, uh, public.

JFK: There may not be one. All right, why not?

McNamara: This is one question. A second question is: Should we precede the military action with political action? If so, on what, uh, timing? I would think the answer's almost certainly, yes. And I wouldn't, I would think particularly of the contacts with Khrushchev. And I would think that if these are to be done, they must be scheduled in terms of time very, very carefully in relation to a potential military action. There must be a very, very precise series of, of contacts with him, and indications of what we'll do at certain times following that. And, thirdly, we should be prepared to answer your questions regarding the, the effect of these strikes and the time required to carry them off. I think . . .

JFK: How long would it take to get 'em organized.

McNamara: E-, e-, exactly. We'll be prepared . . .

JFK: In other words, how many days from tomorrow morning would it . . . . How many mornings from tomorrow morning would it take to get the, to take out just these missile (sites) . . .

Transcript
Washington, October 16, 1962, 6:30-7:55 p.m.

JFK: Uh, anything in 'em?

Carter: Nothing on the additional film, sir. We have a much better read-out on what we had initially. There's good evidence of their back-up missiles for each of the four launchers at each of the three sites, so that there would be twice the number for a total of eight which could eventually be erected. This would mean a capability of from sixteen or possibly twenty-four missiles. We feel, on the basis of information that we presently have, that these are solid propellant, inertial guidance missiles with eleven-hundred-mile range rather than the oxygen propellant, uh, radar-controlled. Primarily because we have no indication of any radar or any indication of any oxygen equipment. And it would appear to be logical from an intelligence estimate viewpoint that if they are going to this much trouble that they would go ahead and put in the eleven hundred miles because of the tremendously increased threat coverage. Let me see that (words unintelligible).

JFK: What is this map?

Carter: That's, shows the circular range . . .

JFK: When was this drawn?

Carter: . . . capability.

JFK: Is this drawn in relation to this information?

Carter: Uh, no, sir. It was drawn in, uh, some time ago, I believe, but the ranges there are the nominal ranges of the missiles rather than the maximum.

Speaker ?: The circles (around, or are added?) . . .

Carter: That's a ten hundred and twenty circle, as against eleven hundred.

JFK: Well, I was just wondering, uh, whether, uh, San Diego de los Banos is where these missiles are?

Carter: Uh, yes, sir. Well, the . . .

JFK: Well, I wonder how many of these have been printed out.

Bundy: Yeah, well, the circle is drawn in red ink on the map, Mr. President.

Carter: The circle is . . .

JFK: Oh, I see. It was never printed?

Carter: No, that's on top.

JFK: I see. It isn't printed.

Carter: It would appear that with this type of missile, with the solid propellant and inertial guidance system, that they could well be operational within two weeks as we look at the pictures now. And once operational, uh, they could fire on very little notice. They'll have a refire rate of from four to six hours over each launcher.

JFK: What about the vulnerability of such a missile to a, t-, uh, bullets?

Speaker ?: Highly vulnerable, (Mr. President?).

Carter: Uh, they're vulnerable. They're not nearly as vulnerable as the oxygen propellant, but they are vulnerable to ordinary rifle fire. We have no evidence whatsoever of any nuclear warhead storage near the field launchers. However, ever since last February we have been observing an unusual facility which now has automatic anti-aircraft weapon protection. This is at (Bahu?). There are some similarities, but also many points of dissim-, similarity between this particular facility and the national storage sites in the Soviet Union. It's the best candidate for a site, and we have that marked for further surveillance. However, there is really totally inadequate evidence to say that there is a nuclear storage capability now. These are field-type launchers. They have mobile support, erection and check-out equipment. And they have a four-in-line deployment pattern in launchers which is identical — complexes about five miles apart — representative of the deployments that we note in the Soviet Union for similar missiles.

JFK: Uh, General, how long would you say we had, uh, before these — at least to the best of your ability for the ones we now know — will be ready to fire?

Carter: Well, our people estimate that these could be fully operational within two weeks. Uh, this would be the total complex. If they're the oxygen type, uh, we have no. . . . It would be considerably longer since we don't have any indication of, uh, oxygen refueling there nor any radars.

Speaker ?: This wouldn't rule out the possibility that one of them might be operational very much sooner.

Carter: (Well, or No?), one of 'em, uh, one of them could be operational much sooner. Our people feel that this has been, being put in since probably early September. We have had two visits of a Soviet ship that has an eight-foot-hold capacity sideways. And this about, so far, is the only delivery vehicle that we would have any suspicion that they came in on. And that came in late August, and one in early September. (Uh. . . .)

Speaker ?: Why would they have to be sideways (though?)?

Carter: Well, it's just easier to get 'em in, I guess.

Speaker ?: (Well?), this way it sets down on (words unintelligible).

Speaker ?: Well, all right.

Speaker ?: Fine.

Rusk: Uh, the, the, the total readout on the, uh, flights yesterday will be ready tonight, you think?

Carter: It should be, uh, finished pretty well by midnight.

JFK: Now what, that was supposed to have covered the whole island, was it, uh?

Carter: Uh, yes, sir.

JFK: Except for . . .

Carter: In two throws. But, uh, part of the central and, in fact, much of the central and part of the eastern was cloud covering. The western half was, uh, in real good shape.

JFK: I see. Now what have we got laying on for tomorrow?

Carter: There are seven, six or seven . . .

McNamara: I just left (word unintelligible) (equipment?). We're having ready seven U-2 aircraft: two high-altitude U-2s, five lesser-altitude U-2s; six equipped with an old type film, one equipped with a new type, experimental film which hopefully will increase the resolution. We only need two aircraft flying tomorrow if the weather is good. We will put up only two if the weather is good. If the weather is not good, we'll start off with two and we'll have the others ready to go during the day as the weather improves. We have weather aircraft surrounding the periphery of Cuba, and we'll be able to keep track of the weather during the day over all parts of the island. Hopefully, this will give us complete coverage tomorrow. We are planning to do this, or have the capability to do this, every day thereafter for an indefinite period.

Carter: This is a field-type missile, and from collateral evidence, not direct, that we have with the Soviet Union, it's designed to be fielded, placed and fired in six hours. Uh, it would appear that we have caught this in a very early stage of deployment. It would also appear that there does not seem to be the degree of urgency in getting them immediately into position. This could be because they have not been surveyed. Or it could be because it is the shorter-range missile and the radars and the oxygen has not yet arrived.

JFK: There isn't any question in your mind, however, uh, that it is an intermediate-range missile?

Carter: No, there's no question in our minds at all. These are . . .

JFK: Just (word unintelligible) . . .

Carter: . . . all the characteristics that we have seen, (live ones?).

Rusk: You've seen actual missiles themselves and not just the boxes have you?

Carter: No, we've seen. . . . In the picture there is an actual missile.

Rusk: Yeah. Sure there is.

Carter: Yes. There's no question in our mind, sir. And they are genuine. They are not, uh, a camouflage or covert attempt to fool us.

Bundy: How much do we know, uh, (Pat?)? I don't mean to go behind your judgment here, except that there's one thing that would be really catastrophic would be to make a judgment here on, on a bad guess as to whether these things are. We mustn't do that.

Carter: Well . . .

Bundy: How do we really know what these missiles are and what their range is?

Carter: Only that from the read-out that we have now and in the judgment of our analysts and of the guided missile and astronautics committee, which has been convening all afternoon, these signatures are identical with those that we have clearly earmarked in the Soviet Union, and have fully verified.

Bundy: What (made?) the verification? That's really my question. How do we know what a given Soviet missile will do?

Carter: We, uh, know something from the range firings that we have vetted for the past two years. And we know also from comparison with the characteristics of our own missiles as to size and length and diameter. Uh, as to these particular missiles, we have a family of Soviet missiles for which we have all accepted the, uh, specifications.

Bundy: I know that we have accepted them . . .

Carter: This is . . .

Bundy: . . . and I know that we've had these things in charts for years, but I don't know how we know.

Carter: Well, we know from a number of sources, including our Ironbark sources, as well as from range firings, which we have been vetting for several years, as to the capabilities. But, uh, I would have to get the analysts in here to give you the play-by-play account.

Rusk: Pat, we don't know of any sixty-five-foot Soviet missile that has a range of, say, fifteen miles, do we?

Carter: Fifteen miles? No, we certainly don't.

Rusk: In other words, if they are missiles this size, they are missiles of considerable range, I think.

McNamara: I tried to prove today—I am, I'm satisfied—that these were not MRBMs. And I worked long on it. I got our experts out, and I could not find evidence that would support any conclusion other than that they are MRBMs. Now, whether they're eleven-hundred miles, six-hundred mile, nine-hundred mile is still a guess in my opinion. But that they are MRBMs seems the most probable assumption at the moment.

Speaker ?: I would apparently agree, uh, given the weight of it.

JFK: Is General Taylor coming over?

McNamara: He is, uh, Mr. President.

JFK: Have you finished, General?

Carter: Yes, sir. That, I think that's at, uh, (word unintelligible) . . .

Rusk: (Because?) we've had some further discussion meetings this afternoon and we'll be working on it (presently?) this evening, but, um, I might mention certain points that are, some of us are concerned about. The one is, um, the chance that, uh, this might be the issue on which, uh, Castro would elect to break with Moscow if he knew that he were in deadly jeopardy. Now, this is one chance in a hundred, possibly. But, in any event, um, we, we're very much, uh, interested in the possibility of a direct message to Castro, uh, as well as Khrushchev, might make some sense here before an actual strike is put on. Uh, Mr. Martin will present you with outline, uh, the kind of, uh, message to Castro that, uh, we had in mind.

Martin: This would be an oral note, message through a third party. Uh, first, uh, describing just what we know about what exists in th-, the missile sites, so that he knows that we are informed about what's going on. Uh, second, to point out that the issues this raises as far as the U.S. security is concerned, it's a breach of two of the points that you have made public. Uh, first, the ground-to-ground missile, and, second, obviously, it's a Soviet-operated base in Cuba. Uh, thirdly, this raises the greatest problems for Castro, as we see it. In the first place, uh, by this action the Soviets have, uh, threatened him with attack from the United States, and, uh, therefore the overthrow of his regime; used his territory to, uh, make this, uh, to put him in this jeopardy. And, secondly, the Soviets are talking to other people about the possibility of bargaining this support and these missiles, uh, against concessions in Berlin and elsewhere, and therefore are threatening to, to bargain him away. Uh, in these circumstances, we wonder whether he, uh, realizes the, the position that, uh, he's been put in and the way the Soviets are using him.

Then go on to say that, uh, we will have to inform our people of the threat that exists here, and we mean to take action about it in the next day or so. And we'll have to do this unless we receive word from him that he is prepared to take action to get the Soviets out of the site. Uh, he will have to show us that not only by statements, privately or publicly, but, uh, by action; that we intend to, uh, keep close surveillance by overflights of the site to make su-, to know what is being done. But we will have to know that he is doing something to remove this threat, uh, in order to withhold the action that we intend to, we will be compelled to take.

Uh, if, uh, Castro feels that an attempt by him to take the kind of action that we're suggesting to him, uh, would result in serious difficulties for him within Cuba, we at least want him to know that, uh, er, to, and to convey to him and remind him of the statement that you, Mr. President, made a year and a half ago in effect that there are two points that are non-negotiable. One is the Soviet tie and presence, and the second is aggression in Latin America. This is a, a hint, but no more than that, that, uh, we might have sympathy and help for him in case he ran into trouble trying to throw the old-line Communists and the Soviets out.

Rusk: Yes.

Martin: We'll give him twenty-four hours to respond.

Rusk: The disadvantage in that is, of course, the, uh, the advance notice if he judges that we, we would not in this, in such approach here say exactly what we would do, but, uh, it might, of course, lead him to bring up mobile anti-aircraft weapons around these, uh, missiles themselves, uh, or, uh, take some other action that will make the strike that more difficult. Um, but there is that, there is that (move that?).

There are two other problems that we are concerned about. Uh, if we strike these missiles, we would expect, I think, uh, maximum Communist reaction in Latin America. In the case of about six of those governments, unless the heads of government had some intimation, uh, requiring some preparatory steps from the security point of view, uh, one or another of those governments could easi-, uh, could easily be overthrown—they, Venezuela for example or Guatemala, Bolivia, Chile, possibly even Mexico—uh, and therefore, uh, uh, the question will arise as to whether we should not somehow, uh, indicate to them in some way the seriousness of the situation so they can take precautionary steps, whether we tell them exactly what we have in mind or, or not.

The other is the NATO problem. Um, we, uh, we would estimate that the Soviets, uh, would almost certainly take, uh, some kind of action somewhere. Um, for us to, to take an action of this sort without letting, uh, our closer allies know of a matter which could subject them to very great, uh, danger, uh, is a very, uh, far-reaching decision to make. And, uh, we could find ourselves, uh, isolated and the alliance crumbling, very much as it did for a period during the Suez affair, but at a moment of much greater danger over an issue of much greater danger than the Suez affair, for the alliance. I think that these are matters that we'll be working on very hard this evening, but I think I ought to mention them because it's, uh, necessarily a part of this problem.

JFK: Can we get a little idea about what the military thing is? Well, of course, one, would you suggest taking these out?

McNamara: Yes, Mr. President. Uh, General Taylor has just been with the Chiefs, and the unified commanders went through this, uh, in detail. Uh, to take out only the missiles, uh, or to take out the missiles and the MIG aircraft and the associated nuclear storage facilities if we locate them, uh, could be done in twenty-four-hours' warning. That is to say, twenty-four hours between the time of decision and the time of strike, uh, starting with a decision no later than, no earlier than this coming Friday and with the strike therefore on Saturday, or anytime thereafter with twenty-four hours between the decision and time of strike. Uh, General Taylor will wish to comment on this, but the Chiefs are strong in their recommendation against that kind of an attack, believing that it would leave, uh, too great a capability in Cuba undestroyed. The specific number of sorties required to, to accomplish this end has not been worked out in detail. The capability is for something in excess of seven hundred sorties per day. Uh, it seems highly unlikely that that number would be required to carry out that limited an objective, but at least that capability is available in the air force alone, and the navy sorties would rise on top of that number. The Chiefs have also considered other alternatives extending into the full invasion, uh, you may wish to discuss later. But that's the answer to your first question.

JFK: That would be taking out these three missile sites, uh, plus all the MIGs?

McNamara: Well, you can go from the three missile sites to the three missile sites plus the MIGs, to the three missile sites plus MIGs plus nuclear storage plus airfields and so on up through the offensive, potential offensive (words unintelligible) . . .

JFK: Just the three missiles, however, would be?

McNamara: Could be done with twenty-four-hours' notice and would require, uh, a relatively small number of sorties, less than a day's air attack, in other words.

JFK: Of course, all you'd really get there would be. . . . What would you get there? You'd get the, probably you'd get the missiles themselves that are, have to be on the . . .

McNamara: You'd get the launchers . . .

JFK: . . . (Words unintelligible).

McNamara: . . . the launchers and the missiles on the (words unintelligible) . . .

JFK: The launchers are just what? They, they're not much are they?

McNamara: No, they're simply a mobile launchers, uh, device.

Taylor: This is a point target, Mr., uh, President. You're never sure of having, absolutely of getting everything down there. We intend to do a great deal of damage because we can (words unintelligible). But, as the Secretary says here, there was unanimity among all the commanders involved in the Joint Chiefs, uh, that in our judgment, it would be a mistake to take this very narrow, selective target because it invited reprisal attacks and it may be detrimental. Now if the, uh, Soviets have been willing to give, uh, nuclear warheads to these missiles, there is every, just as good reason for them to give nuclear capability to these bases. We don't think we'd ever have a chance to take 'em again, so that we lose this, the first strike surprise capability. Our recommendation would be to get complete intelligence, get all the photography we need, the next two or three days, no, no hurry in our book. Then look at this target system. If it really threatens the United States, then take it right out with one hard crack.

JFK: That would be taking out the, uh, some of those fighters, bombers and . . .

Taylor: Fighters, the bombers, uh, IL-28s may turn up in this photography. It's not that all unlikely there're some there.

JFK: Think you could do that in one day?

Taylor: Uh, we think that the first strike, we'd get a great majority of this. We'll never get it all, Mr. President. But we then have to come back day after day for several days—we said, uh, five days perhaps—to do the complete job. Uh, meanwhile, we could then be making up our mind as to whether or not to go on and invade the island. I'm very much impressed with the need for a time something like five to seven days for this air purpose because of the parachute aspect of the in-, proposed invasion. You can't take parachute formations, close formations of, uh, troop carrier planes in in the face of any air opposition really. So the first job, before the, any land, uh, attack, including (parachutes or paratroops?), is really cleaning out the, the MIGs and the, uh, the accompanying aircraft.

McNamara: Mr. President, could I outline three courses . . .

JFK?: (Yes?).

McNamara: . . . of action we have considered and speak very briefly on each one? The first is what I would call the political course of action, in which we, uh, follow some of the possibilities that Secretary Rusk mentioned this morning by approaching Castro, by approaching Khrushchev, by discussing with our allies. An overt and open approach politically to the problem (attempting, or in order?) to solve it. This seemed to me likely to lead to no satisfactory result, and it almost stops subsequent military action. Because the danger of starting military action after they acquire a nuclear capability is so great I believe we would decide against it, particularly if that nuclear capability included aircraft as well as, as, uh, uh, missiles, as it well might at that point.

A second course of action we haven't discussed but lies in between the military course we began discussing a moment ago and the political course of action is a course of action that would involve declaration of open surveillance; a statement that we would immediately impose an, uh, a blockade against offensive weapons entering Cuba in the future; and an indication that with our open-surveillance reconnaissance, which we would plan to maintain indefinitely for the future, we would be prepared to immediately attack the Soviet Union in the event that Cuba made any offensive move against this country . . .

Bundy: Attack who?

McNamara: The Soviet Union. In the event that Cuba made any offensive move against this country. Now this lies short of military action against Cuba, direct military action against Cuba. It has some, some major defects.

But the third course of action is any one of these variants of military action directed against Cuba, starting with an air attack against the missiles. The Chiefs are strongly opposed to so limited an air attack. But even so limited an air attack is a very extensive air attack. It's not twenty sorties or fifty sorties or a hundred sorties, but probably several hundred sorties. Uh, we haven't worked out the details. It's very difficult to do so when we lack certain intelligence that we hope to have tomorrow or the next day. But it's a substantial air attack. And to move from that into the more extensive air attacks against the MIGs, against the airfields, against the potential nuclear storage sites, against the radar installations, against the SAM sites means, as, as Max suggested, possibly seven hundred to a thousand sorties per day for five days. This is the very, very rough plan that the Chiefs have outlined, and it is their judgment that that is the type of air attack that should be carried out. To move beyond that into an invasion following the air attack means the application of tens of thousands, between ninety and, and, uh, over a hundred and fifty thousand men to the invasion forces. It seems to me almost certain that any one of these forms of direct military action will lead to a Soviet military response of some type some place in the world. It may well be worth the price. Perhaps we should pay that. But I think we should recognize that possibility, and, moreover, we must recognize it in a variety of ways. We must recognize it by trying to deter it, which means we probably should alert SAC, probably put on an airborne alert, perhaps take other s-, alert measures. These bring risks of their own, associated with them. It means we should recognize that by mobilization. Almost certainly, we should accompany the initial air strike with at least a partial mobilization. We should accompany an, an invasion following an air strike with a large-scale mobilization, a very large-scale mobilization, certainly exceeding the limits of the authority we have from Congress requiring a declaration therefore of a national emergency. We should be prepared, in the event of even a small air strike and certainly in the event of a larger air strike, for the possibility of a Cuban uprising, which would force our hand in some way. Either force u-, us to accept a, a, uh, an unsatisfactory uprising, with all of the adverse comment that result; or would, would force an invasion to support the uprising.

Rusk: Mr. President, may I make a very brief comment on that? I think that, um, uh, any course of action involves heavy political involvement. Um, it's going to affect all sorts of policies, positions, uh, as well as the strategic situation. So I don't think there's any such thing as a nonpolitical course of action. I think also that, um, uh, we have to consider what political preparation, if any, is to occur before an air strike or in connection with any military action. And when I was talking this morning, I was talking about some steps which would put us in the best position to crack the . . .

JFK: I think the difficulty . . .

Rusk: . . . the strength of Cuba.

JFK: . . . it seems to me, is. . . . I completely agree that there isn't any doubt that if we announced that there were MRBM sites going up that that would change, uh, we would secure a good deal of political support, uh, after my statement; and, uh, the fact that we indicated our desire to restrain, this really would put the burden on the Soviet. On the other hand, the very fact of doing that makes the military. . . . We lose all the advantages of our strike. Because if we announce that it's there, then it's quite obvious to them that we're gonna probably do something about it. I would assume. Now, I don't know, that, it seems to me what we ought to be thinking about tonight is if we made an announcement that the intelligence has revealed that there are, and if we (did the note?) message to Khrushchev. . . . I don't think, uh, that Castro has to know we've been paying much attention to it any more than. . . . Over a period of time, it might have some effect, (have settled?) back down, change. I don't think he plays it that way. So (have?) a note to Khrushchev. . . . I don't. . . . It seems to me, uh, my press statement was so clear about how we wouldn't do anything under these conditions and under the conditions that we would. He must know that we're going to find out, so it seems to me he just, uh . . .

Bundy: That's, of course, why he's been very, very explicit with us in communications to us about how dangerous this is, and . . .

JFK: That's right, but he's . . .

Bundy: . . . the TASS statement and his other messages.

JFK: He's initiated the danger really, hasn't he? He's the one that's playing (his card, or God?), not us. So we could, uh . . .

Rusk: And his statement to Kohler on the subject of his visit and so forth, completely hypocritical.

(Reel 1 ends.)

(Reel 2 begins mid-conversation.)

McNamara: . . . Cuba. Is a great possibility they can place them in operational condition quickly. Unless, as General Carter said, the system may have a, a normal reaction time, set-up time of six hours. Whether it has six hours or two weeks, we don't know how much time has started, nor do we know what air-launch capabilities they have for warheads. We don't know what air-launch capability they have for high explosives. It's almost certainly, uh, a, a substantial high-explosive capability in the sense that they could drop one or two or ten high-explosive bombs some place along the East Coast. And that's the minimum risk to this country we run as a result of advance warning, too.

Taylor: I'd like to stress this last point, Mr. President. We are very vulnerable to conventional bombing attack, low-level bombing attacks in the Florida area. Our whole, uh, air defense has been oriented in other directions. We've never had low-level defenses prepared for this country. So it would be entirely possible for MIGs to come through with conventional weapons and do some amount, some damage.

JFK: Yeah. Not, uh, talking overall, not a great deal of damage . . .

Taylor: No, but it certainly is fair to . . .

JFK: . . . if they get one strike.

Dillon: What if they carry a nuclear weapon?

JFK: Well, if they carry a nuclear weapon. . . . You assume they wouldn't do that.

Taylor: (Words unintelligible) I think we would expect some conventional weapon.

Rusk: I would not think that they would use a nuclear weapon unless they're prepared to (join?) a nuclear war, I don't think. I just don't s-, don't, don't see that possibility.

Speaker ?: I would agree.

Bundy?: I agree.

Rusk: That would mean that, uh, we could be just utterly wrong, but, uh, we've never really believed that, that Khrushchev would take on a general nuclear war over Cuba.

Bundy: May I ask a question in that context?

JFK: We certainly have been wrong about what he's trying to do in Cuba. There isn't any doubt about that (possibly a word unintellig-ible) . . .

Bundy: (Words unintelligible) that we've been wrong.

JFK: . . . many of us thought that he was going to put MRBMs on Cuba.

Bundy: Yeah. Except John McCone.

Carter: Mr. McCone.

JFK: Yeah.

Bundy: But, the, uh, question that I would like to ask is, quite aside from what we've said—and we're very hard-locked onto it, I know—What is the strategic impact on the position of the United States of MRBMs in Cuba? How gravely does this change the strategic balance?

McNamara: Mac, I asked the Chiefs that this afternoon, in effect. And they said, substantially. My own personal view is, not at all.

Bundy: Not so much.

McNamara: And, and I think this is an important element here. But it's all very . . .

Carter: The reason our estimators didn't think that they'd put them in there because of . . .

McNamara: That's what they said themselves . . .

Bundy: That's what they said themselves. . . .

McNamara: . . . in TASS statement.

Bundy: Yeah.

Carter: But then, going behind that . . .

JFK: (But why? Did it indicate? Being?) valuable enough?

Bundy: Doesn't prove anything in the strategic balance (overall?).

Carter: Doesn't prove anything. That was what the estimators felt, and that the Soviets would not take the risk. Mr. McCone's reasoning, however, was if this is so, then what possible reason have they got for going into Cuba in the manner in which they are with surface-to-air, uh, missiles and cruise-type missiles. He just couldn't understand while their, why the Soviets were so heavily bol-, bolstering Cuba's defensive posture. There must be something behind it, which led him then to the belief that they must be coming in with MRBMs.

Taylor: I think it was (cold-blooded?) . . .

Carter: (Words unintelligible)

Taylor: . . . point of view, Mr. President. You're quite right in saying that these, these are just a few more missiles, uh, targeted on the United States. Uh, however, they can become a, a very, a rather important adjunct and reinforcement to the, to the strike capability of the Soviet Union. We have no idea how far they will go. But more than that, these are, uh, uh, to our nation it means, it means a great deal more. You all are aware of that, in Cuba and not over in the Soviet Union.

Bundy: Well, I ask the question . . .

Taylor: Yeah.

Bundy: . . . with an awareness (laughter?) of the political . . .

JFK: I will say, my understanding's that . . .

Bundy: (Words unintelligible)

JFK: . . . let's just say that, uh, they get, they get these in there and then you can't, uh, they get sufficient capacity so we can't, uh, with warheads. Then you don't want to knock 'em out ('cause?), uh, there's too much of a gamble. Then they just begin to build up those air bases there and then put more and more. I suppose they really. . . . Then they start getting ready to squeeze us in Berlin, doesn't that. . . . You may say it doesn't make any difference if you get blown up by an ICBM flying from the Soviet Union or one that was ninety miles away. Geography doesn't mean that much.

Taylor: We'd have to target them with our missiles and have the same kind of, of pistol-pointed-at-the-head situation as we have in the Soviet Union at the present time.

Bundy: No question, if this thing goes on, an attack on Cuba becomes general war. And that's really the question whether . . .

JFK: That's why it shows the Bay of Pigs was really right. (We've, or We'd?) got it right. That was better and better and worse and worse.

Taylor: I'm (a pessimist,?) Mr. President. We have a war plan over there for you, calls for a, uh, for a quarter of a million Americans—soldiers, marines and airmen—to take an island we launched eighteen hundred Cubans against a year and a half ago.

(Faint laughter)

Taylor: (We've changed?) our evaluations well.

RFK: Of course, the other problem is, uh, in South America a year from now. And the fact that you got, uh, these things in the hands of Cubans, here, and then you, say your, some problem arises in Venezuela, er, you've got Castro saying, You move troops down into that part of Venezuela, we're going to fire these missiles.

Taylor: Well, I think you've (words unintelligible).

RFK: I think that's the difficulty . . .

Speaker ?: (Words unintelligible).

RFK: . . . rather than the (words unintelligible).

Speaker ?: (Words unintelligible).

RFK: I think it gives the (word unintelligible) image.

JFK: It makes them look like they're coequal with us and that
. . .

Dillon: We're scared of the Cubans.

RFK: We let the, uh. . . . I mean like we'd hate to have it in
the hands of the Chinese. (Possibly words unintelligible)

Dillon: (Right?) I agree with that sort of thing very strongly.

Martin: It's a psychological factor. It won't reach as far as
Venezuela is concerned.

Dillon: Well, that's . . .

McNamara: It'll reach the U.S. though. This is the point.

Speaker ?: That's the point.

Dillon: Yeah. That is the point.

Martin: Yeah. The psychological factor of our having taken
it.

Dillon: Taken it, that's the best.

RFK: Well, and the fact that if you go there, we're gonna fire
it.

JFK: What's that again, Ed? What are you saying?

Martin: Well, it's a psychological factor that we have sat
back and let 'em do it to us, that is more important than the
direct threat. Uh, it is a threat in the Caribbean . . .

JFK: (Words unintelligible) I said we weren't going to.

Martin: . . . (Words unintelligible).

Bundy?: That's something we could manage.

JFK: Last month I said we weren't going to.

(Laughter)

JFK: Last month I should have said we're . . .

Speaker ?: Well . . .

JFK: . . . that we don't care. But when we said we're not
going to and then they go ahead and do it, and then we do
nothing, then . . .

Speaker ?: That's right.

JFK: . . . I would think that our risks increase. Uh, I agree. What difference does it make? They've got enough to blow us up now anyway. I think it's just a question of. . . . After all this is a political struggle as much as military. Well, uh, so where are we now? Where is the. . . . Don't think the message to Castro's got much in it. Uh, let's just, uh, let's try to get an answer to this question. How much. . . . It's quite obviously to our advantage to surface this thing to a degree before. . . . First to inform these governments in Latin America, as the Secretary suggests; secondly to, uh, the rest of NATO [censored]. Uh, how much does this diminish. . . . Not that we're going to do anything, but the existence of them, without any say about what we're gonna do. Let's say we, twenty-four hours ahead of our doing something about it, [censored] we make a public statement that these have been found on the island. That would, that would be notification in a sense that, uh, of their existence, and everybody could draw whatever conclusion they wanted to.

Martin?: I would say this, Mr. President, that I would, that if you've made a public statement, you've got to move immediately, or they, you're going to have a . . .

JFK: Oh, I . . .

Martin?: . . . a (words unintelligible) in this country.

JFK: . . . oh, I understand that. We'll be talking about. . . . Say, say we're going to move on a Saturday and we would say on Friday that these MRBMs, that the existence of this presents the gravest threat to our security and that appropriate action must be taken.

RFK: Could you stick planes over them, until you made the announcement at six o'clock Saturday morning? And at the same time or simultaneously put planes over to make sure that they weren't taking any action or movement, and that you could move in if they started moving in the missiles in place or something, you would move in and knock, that would be the trigger that you would move your planes in and knock them out. Otherwise you'd wait until six o'clock or five o'clock that night. I don't, is that, uh, is that. . . .

Taylor: I don't think anything like that. . . . I can't visualize doing it, uh, doing it successfully that way. I think that, uh, uh, anything that shows, uh, our intent to strike is going to place the airplanes and, and the missiles into, these are por-, really mobile missiles. They can be . . .

RFK: (You mean they can just?) . . .

Taylor: They can pull in under trees and forest and disappear almost at once, as I visualize.

McNamara: And they can also be readied, perhaps, between the time we, in effect, say we're going to come in and the time we do come in. This, this is a very, very great danger to this, this coast. I don't know exactly how to appraise it because . . .

Speaker ?: I don't know.

McNamara: . . . of the readiness period, but it is possible that these are field missiles, and then in that case they can be readied very promptly if they choose to do so.

Carter: These are field missiles, sir. They are mobile-support-type missiles.

Taylor: About a forty-minute countdown, something like that's been estimated.

Ball?: So you would say that, uh, the strike should precede any public discussion?

McNamara: I believe so, yes, if you're going to strike. I think before you make any announcements, you should decide whether you're going to strike. If you are going to strike, you shouldn't make an announcement.

Bundy: That's right.

Dillon: What is the advantage of the announcement earlier? Because it's, it's to build up sympathy or something for doing it; but you get the simultaneous announcement of what was there and why you struck, with pictures and all, I (believe?) would serve the same . . .

Ball?: Well, the only announ-, the only advantage is, it's a kind of ultimatum, it's, there is an opportunity of a response that, which would preclude it. I mean it's, it's more, a more, for, for the appearance than as for the reality. 'Cause obviously you're not going to get that kind of response. But I would suppose that there is a course which is a little different, which is a private message from the President to *[censored]* . . .

Martin?: *[censored]*

Ball?: Uh, and, uh, that this is, you're going to have to do this, you're compelled and you've gotta move quickly and you want them to know it. Maybe two hours before the strike, something like that . . .

Dillon: Well, that's it, that's different.

Ball?: . . . even the night before. Uh, but you. . . . But it has to be kept on that basis of total secrecy. And then the question of what you do with these Latin American governments is another matter. I think if you, if you notify them in advance . . .

JFK: That's right. (Indicated?)

Ball?: . . . it may be all over.

JFK: Then you just have to, uh, Congress would, take Congress along . . .

Bundy: I can't. . . . I think that's just not, not right.

Speaker ?: (Words unintelligible)

JFK: I'm not completely, uh, I don't think we ought to abandon just knocking out these missile bases as opposed to, that's much more, uh, defensible, explicable, politically or satisfactory-in-every-way action than the general strike which takes us . . .

Speaker ?: Move down . . .

JFK: . . . us into the city of Havana . . .

Speaker ?: . . . those two.

JFK: . . . and (it is plain to me?) takes us into much more . . .

Speaker ?: (Words unintelligible)

JFK: . . . hazardous, shot down. Now I know the Chiefs say, Well, that means their bombers can take off against us, uh, but, uh . . .

Bundy: Their bombers take off against us, then they have made a general war against Cuba of it, which is a, it then becomes much more their decision. We move this way. . . . The political advantages are, are very strong, it seems to me, of the small strike. Uh, it corresponds to the, the punishment fits the crime in political terms, that we are doing only what we warned repeatedly and publicly we would have to do. Uh, we are not generalizing the attack. The things that we've already recognized and said that we have not found it necessary to attack and said we would not find it necessary to attack . . .

JFK: Well, here's. . . . Let's, look, let's, let's, tonight, it seems to me we ought to go on the assumption that we're going to have the general—number two we've called it . . .

Bundy: Uh-huh.

JFK: . . . course number two, which would be a general strike—that you ought to be in position to do that . . .

Bundy: I agree.

JFK: . . . then if you decide you'd like to do number one.

RFK: How does that in. . .

JFK: What?

RFK: Does that encompass, uh, an invasion?

JFK: Uh, no, I'd say that's the third course. Let's first start with. . . . I'd have to say first find out, uh, the air, so that I would think that we ought to be in position to do one and two. Which would be. . . . One would be just taking out these missiles, if there were others we'd find in the next twenty-four hours. Number two would be to take out all the airplanes, and number three is invade (here?).

Speaker ?: Well, they'd have to take out the SAM sites . . .

Dillon ?: (Words unintelligible) also, Mr. President.

JFK: (Okay?) but that's in, that would be in two, included in number two . . .

Speaker ?: Well . . .

Speaker ?: That's the, that's a terrifically difficult . . .

Dillon: That's a, I mean that's just (words unintelligible) . . .

Speaker ?: (Words unintelligible) that may be three, and invasion four.

Taylor: In order to get in to get the airfields, there's a good number we'd have to (get out?).

Gilpatric?: Well, isn't there a question whether any of the SAM sites are operational?

Taylor?: We're not sure yet.

JFK: Okay, well, let's say we've decided, uh, we've gotta go in the whole way. So let's say that number two is the SAM site plus the air . . .

Bundy: It's actually to clear the air . . .

JFK: Yeah. Well, whatever it is . . .

Bundy: . . . to win the air battle.

JFK: . . . (words unintelligible) (to talk over?). Yeah. Now, it seems to me we ought to be preparing now in the most covered (covert?) way to do one and two, with the freedom to make the choice about number one depending on what information we have on it, uh, what (word unintelligible) moves that requires, and how much is that gonna . . .

McNamara: Mr. President, it requires no action other than what's been started, and you can make a decision prior to the start Saturday or any time thereafter.

Speaker ?: (Words unintelligible)

JFK: Well, where do we put all these planes?

Taylor: You recall, uh, we have . . .

Speaker ?: (Words unintelligible)

Taylor: . . . this problem, Mr. President. We're going to get new intelligence that will be coming in from these flights . . .

JFK: Right.

Taylor: . . . and that's gonna be, have to be cranked into the, any strike plans we're preparing, so there is that factor of time. The Secretary has given you the, the time, the minimum time is to make a decision, uh, now to, so that we can brief the pilots and then crank in the new intelligence. I would point out that, well . . .

McNamara: (The main fact?), to answer the question you asked, we don't have to decide how we're gonna do it. All we have to decide is if we want . . .

Taylor: No.

McNamara: . . . Sweeney to be prepared to do it.

Taylor: That's correct, the (words unintelligible) . . .

McNamara: And Sweeney has said that he will take the tape that comes in tomorrow and process it Thursday and Friday and prepare the mission folders for (word unintelligible) strikes on Saturday or earl-, every day thereafter.

Taylor: Yes. The point is that we'll have to brief pilots. We're, we're . . .

McNamara: Right.

Taylor: . . . holding, uh, holding that back. And there'll be, oh, would say four hundred pilots will have to go, to be briefed in the course of this. So I'm just saying this is widening the, the whole military scope of this thing very materially, if that's what we're, we're supposed to do at this time.

JFK: Well, now when do we start briefing the pilots?

Taylor: They'll need at least twenty-four hours on that . . .

JFK: They will.

Taylor: . . . when this new intelligence comes in and it's, uh . . .

JFK: In other words, then, until tomorrow. . . . All I was thinking of at least until . . .

Bundy: Can they be briefed in such a way that they're secure . . .

Taylor: (Words unintelligible) . . .

McNamara: (Words unintelligible) . . .

Bundy: . . . they have no access to (words unintelligible) . . .

McNamara: . . . (words unintelligible) now. You don't have to s-. . . . The President does not have to make any decision until twenty-four hours before the strike, except the decision to be prepared.

Speaker ?: Uh-huh.

McNamara: And the process of preparation will not in itself run the risk of overt disclosure of the preparation.

Bundy? Doesn't imply briefing, the preparation?

Taylor: Uh, it does but . . .

McNamara: It implies the preparation of mission folders.

Taylor: . . . uh, say twenty-four hours before they, before they go, they start a briefing. I'd like to say this, Mr. President, the more time you can give, the better. Because they can then do a lot more rehearsing and checking out of all the pilots, so, uh, while I accept the, the, uh, the time cycle, I . . .

JFK: Well, now let's say you give a pilot, uh. . . . I mean, how does he find his way down to, uh, a SAM site off of one of these things?

Taylor: Well, they'll give him a target folder with all, all the possible, uh . . .

JFK: They know how to do that, do they?

Taylor: . . . uh, guidance and so on to hit the target. Yes, sir, they're well-trained in that, that procedure.

McNamara: Mission folders have already been prepared on all the known targets. The problem is that we don't have the unknown targets, specifically these, these, uh, missile-launchers and the nuclear storage, and we won't have that until tomorrow night at the earliest, and it'll be processed photographically on Thursday, interpreted Thursday night, turned into target folders on Friday, and the mission could go Saturday. This is Sweeney's estimate of the earliest possible time for a spare strike against the missiles. Decision by the President on Friday, strike on Saturday. As General Taylor pointed out, if, if we could have either another day of preparation, which means no strike till Saturday, or al-, and/or alternatively . . .

Speaker: (Words unintelligible)

McNamara: . . . more than twenty-four hours between the time of decision and the first strike, it will run more smoothly.

JFK: Right. Well, now, what is it, in other, the next twenty-four hours, what is it we need to do in order, if we're going to do, well, let's first say, one and two by S-, S-, Saturday or Sunday? You're doing everything that is . . .

McNamara: Mr. President, we need to do two things, it seems to me. First, we need to develop a specific strike plan limited to the missiles and the nuclear storage sites, which we have not done. This would be a part of the broader plan . . .

JFK: Yeah.

McNamara: . . . but I think we ought to estimate the minimum number of sorties. Since you've indicated some interest in that possibility, we ought to provide you that option. We haven't done this.

JFK: Okay.

McNamara: But that's an easy job to do. The second thing we ought to do, it seems to me as a government, is to consider the consequences. I don't believe we have considered the consequences . . .

Speaker ?: (Words unintelligible)

McNamara: . . . of any of these actions satisfactorily, and because we haven't considered the consequences, I'm not sure we're taking all the action we ought to take now to minimize those. I, I don't know quite what kind of a world we live in after we've struck Cuba, and we, we've started it. We've put let's say a hundred sorties in, just for purposes of illustration, I don't think you dare start with less than a hundred. You have, you have, uh, uh, twenty-four objects. Well, you have twenty-four, you have twenty-four, uh, laun-, uh, vehicles, plus, uh, sixteen launchers, plus a possible nuclear storage site, but there's the absolute minimum that you would wish to kill. And you couldn't possibly go in after those with less than, I would think, uh, fifty to a hundred sorties.

Taylor: And you'll miss some.

McNamara: And you'll miss some. That's right. Now after we've launched fifty to a hundred sorties, what kind of a world do we live in? How, how do we stop at that point? I don't know the answer to this. I think tonight State and we ought to work on the consequences of any one of these courses of actions, consequences which I don't believe are entirely clear . . .

Ball: With . . .

McNamara: . . . to any of us.

Ball: . . . at any place in the world.

McNamara: At any place in the world, George. That's right. I agree with you.

Taylor: Uh, Mr. President, I should say that the, the Chiefs and the commanders feel so strongly about the, the dangers inherent in the limited strike, that they would prefer taking no military action rather than to take (that limited?) strike. They feel that the, it's opening up the United States to attacks which they can't prevent if we don't take advantage of . . .

JFK: Yeah, but I, I think the only thing is the, the, uh, chances of it becoming a much broader struggle are increased as you step up the, uh. . . . Talk about the dangers to the United States, uh . . .

Bundy: Yeah.

JFK: . . . once you get into, uh, beginning to shoot up those airports, then you get in, you get a lot of anti-aircraft, and you got a lot of, I mean you're running a much more major operation, therefore the dangers of the world-wide effects are substantial to the United States are increased. That's the only argument for it. I quite agree that the, if (you're? or we're?) just thinking about Cuba, the best thing to do is to be bold if you're thinking about trying to get this thing under some degree of, uh, control.

Rusk?: In that regard, Mr. President, there is a combination of the plans which might be considered, namely the limited strike and then the messages, or simultaneously the messages to Khrushchev and Castro, which would indicate to them that this was none other than simply the, fulfilling the statements we've made all along.

JFK: Well, I think we. . . . In other words, that's a matter we've gotta think about tonight.

Speaker ?: Well . . .

JFK: I don't. . . . Let's not let the Chiefs knock us out on this one . . .

(Laughter)

JFK: . . . uh, General, because I think that, uh, uh, what we gotta be thinking about is if you go into Cuba in the way we're talking about and taking out all the planes and all the rest, then you really haven't got much of an argument against invading it.

Martin?: It seems to me a limited strike plus planning for invasion five days afterwards, to be taken unless something untoward occurs, makes much more sense.

Taylor: Well, I would be. . . . First thing, Mr. President, my, my inclination all against, against the invasion, but none the less trying to eliminate as effectively as possible every weapon that can strike the United States.

JFK: But you're not for the invasion?

Taylor: I would not at this moment (words unintelligible).

McNamara: This is why . . .

Taylor: (Words unintelligible) we get committed to the, to the degree that shackles us with West Berlin.

McNamara: This is why I say I, I think we have to think of the consequences here. I, I would think an, a forced invasion, uh, associated with assisting an uprising, following an extensive air strike, is, is a highly probable set of circumstances. I don't know whether you could carry out an extensive air strike of, let's say, the kind we were talking about a moment ago—seven hundred sorties a day for five days—without an uprising in Cuba. I, I just don't . . .

Martin: (Well?) in this morning's discussion we went into this, talked to some of your people, I believe, a little bit, and we felt an air strike, even of several days, against any military targets primarily, would not result in any substantial unrest. People would just stay home and try to keep out of trouble.

McNamara: Well, when you're talking about military targets, we have seven hundred targets here we're talking about. It, this is a very . . .

JFK: (Words unintelligible)

McNamara: . . . a damned expensive target system.

Taylor: That was in number (word unintelligible), Mr. Secretary . . .

McNamara: Yeah.

Taylor: . . . but that's not the one I recommended.

McNamara: Well, neither is the one I'd recommend.

JFK: What does that include, every anti-aircraft gun, or what does that include?

McNamara: Yeah, uh . . .

Taylor: This includes (related?) defenses, all sorts of things.

McNamara: . . . radar, radar sites, uh, SAM sites, and so on. But whether it's seven hundred or two hundred, uh, and it's at least two hundred, I think . . .

Taylor: More in the order of two hundred, I'd say.

McNamara: It's at least two hundred. You can't carry that out without the danger of an uprising.

RFK: Mr. President, while we're considering this problem tonight, I think that we should also consider what, uh, Cuba's going to be a year from now, or two years from now. Assume that we go in and knock these sites out, uh, I don't know what's gonna stop them from saying, We're gonna build the sites six months from now, bring 'em in . . .

Taylor: Noth-, nothing permanent about it.

RFK: Uh, the, what, where are we six months from now? Or that we're in any better position, or aren't we in worse position if we go in and knock 'em out and say, uh . . .

Speaker ?: (We sure are?)

RFK: . . . Don't do it. Uh, I mean, obviously they're gonna have to do it then.

McNamara: You have to put a blockade in following any . . .

Speaker ?: Sure.

McNamara: . . . limited action.

RFK: Then we're gonna have to sink Russian ships.

McNamara ?: Right.

RFK: Then we're gonna have to sink . . .

McNamara ?: Right.

RFK: . . . Russian submarines. Now whether it wouldn't be, uh, the argument, if you're going to get into it at all, uh, whether we should just get into it and get it over with and say that, uh, take our losses, and if we're gonna. . . . If he wants to get into a war over this, uh. . . . Hell, if it's war that's gonna come on this thing, or if he sticks those kinds of missiles in, it's after the warning, and he's gonna, and he's gonna get into a war for, six months from now or a year from now, so. . . .

McNamara: Mr. President, this is why I think tonight we ought to put on paper the alternative plans and the probable, possible consequences thereof in a way that State and Defense could agree on, even if we, uh, disagree and put in both views. Because the consequences of these actions have not been thought through clearly. The one that the Attorney General just mentioned is illustrative of that.

JFK: If the, uh, it doesn't increase very much their strategic, uh, strength, why is it, uh, can any Russian expert tell us why they. . . . After all Khrushchev demonstrated a sense of caution (thousands?) . . .

Speaker ?: Well, there are several, several possible . . .

JFK: . . . Berlin, he's been cautious, I mean, he hasn't been, uh . . .

Ball?: Several possibilities, Mr. President. One of them is that he has given us word now that he's coming over in November to, to the UN. If, he may be proceeding on the assumption, and this lack of a sense of apparent urgency would seem to, to support this, that this isn't going to be discovered at the moment and that, uh, when he comes over this is something he can do, a ploy. That here is Cuba armed against the United States, or possibly use it to try to trade something in Berlin, saying he'll disarm Cuba if, uh, if we'll, uh, yield some of our interests in Berlin and some arrangement for it. I mean, that this is a, it's a trading ploy.

Bundy: I would think one thing that I would still cling to is that he's not likely to give Fidel Castro nuclear warheads. I don't believe that has happened or is likely to happen.

JFK: Why does he put these in there though?

Bundy: Soviet-controlled nuclear warheads (of the kind?) . . .

JFK: That's right, but what is the advantage of that? It's just as if we suddenly began to put a major number of MRBMs in Turkey. Now that'd be goddam dangerous, I would think.

Bundy?: Well, we did, Mr. President.

U.A. Johnson?: We did it. We . . .

JFK: Yeah, but that was five years ago.

U.A. Johnson?: . . . did it in England; that's why we were short.

JFK: What?

U.A. Johnson?: We gave England two when we were short of ICBMs.

JFK: Yeah, but that's, uh . . .

U.A. Johnson?: (Testing?)

JFK: . . . that was during a different period then.

U.A. Johnson?: But doesn't he realize he has a deficiency of ICBMs, needs a PR capacity perhaps, in view of. . . . He's got lots of MRBMs and this is a way to balance it out a bit?

Bundy?: I'm sure his generals have been telling him for a year and a half that he had, was missing a golden opportunity to add to his strategic capability.

Ball?: Yes, I think, I think you, you look at this possibility that this is an attempt to, to add to his strategic capabilities. A second consideration is that it is simply a trading ploy, that he, he wants this in so that he could, he could (words unintelligible) . . .

Bundy?: (A prime consistent to his?) (words unintelligible) . . .

Speaker ?: (Words unintelligible) it means if he can't trade, he's still got the other.

(Several speakers speak at once and only a few words are intelligible.)

Speaker ?: And so . . .

Speaker ?: But (words unintelligible) . . .

Speaker ?: . . . the political impact in Latin America.

Speaker ?: (Words unintelligible) the source (words unintelligible).

Speaker ?: (Words unintelligible) up front?

Speaker ?: Sure. Sure.

U.A. Johnson?: We are now considering these then Soviet missiles, a Soviet . . .

Speaker ?: I think we ought to.

U.A. Johnson?: . . . offensive capability.

Taylor?: You have to consider them Soviet missiles.

U.A. Johnson?: It seems to me if we go in there, lock-stock-and-barrel, we can consider them entirely Cuban.

Bundy: Ah, well, what we say for political purposes and what we think are not identical here.

Speaker ?: But, I mean, any, any rational approach to this must be that they are Soviet missiles, because I think . . .

Speaker ?: You mean . . .

Speaker ?: . . . Khrushchev himself would never, would never risk a major war on, on a fellow as obviously erratic, uh, and foolish as, as Castro.

Speaker ?: (A sub-lieutenant?)

JFK: Well, now let's say . . .

RFK: Let me say, of course . . .

JFK: Yeah.

RFK: . . . one other thing is whether, uh, we should also think of, uh, uh, whether there is some other way we can get involved in this through, uh, Guantanamo Bay, or something, er, or whether there's some ship that, you know, sink the Maine again or something.

Taylor: We think, Mr. President, that under any of these plans we will probably get an attack on, on Guantanamo, at least by, by fire. They have artillery and mortars in the, easily within range, and, uh, any of these actions we take we'll have to give air support to Guantanamo and probably reinforce the garrison.

JFK: Well, that's why, uh, it seems to me that, uh, this, if we decide that we are going to be in a position to do this, either one and two Saturday or Sunday, then I would think we would also want to be in a position, depending on (really?) what happens, either because of an invasion, attack on Guantanamo or some other reason to do the inva-, uh, to, to do the eviction.

Taylor: Mr. President, I personally would just urge you not to set a schedule such as Saturday or Sunday . . .

JFK: No, I haven't.

Taylor: . . . until all the intelligence that could be . . .

JFK: That's right. I just wanted, I just wanted, I thought we ought to be moving, I don't want to waste any time though if we decide that, uh, time is not particularly with us. I just think we ought to be ready to do something, even if we decide not to do it. I'm not saying . . .

Taylor: All . . .

JFK: . . . we should do it.

Taylor: . . . all of this is moving, short of the briefing. We've held back, uh . . .

JFK: I understand.

Taylor: . . . we've restricted people to . . .

JFK: What about, now, this invasion? If we were going to launch that, what do you have, what do we have to be doing now so that wh-, ten days from now we're in a position to invade if that was immediate?

Taylor: I would say that my answer would be largely planning, particularly in the field of mobilization, just what we wan-, uh, what we will, uh, want to recreate after we, uh, (words unintelligible) these forces to Cuba.

Speaker ?: This is (perhaps?) (words unintelligible).

Taylor: I might say that air defense measures we're going to, we're started to take already. We moved more fighters into the southeastern United States and gradually improving some of our, our patrol procedures, uh, under the general guise of, uh, of preparations for that part of the country. We don't think there'd be any, any leaks there that might react against our military targets. I, I'd repeat that our defenses have always been weak in that part of the country.

JFK: Uh, Mr. Secretary, is there anything that, or any of these contingencies if we go ahead that, uh, the next twenty-four hours—we're going to meet again tomorrow (for this?) in the afternoon—is there anything (words unintelligible) . . .

McNamara: No, sir, I believe that the military planning has been carried on for a considerable period of time, is well under way. And I believe that all the preparations that we could take without the risk of preparations causing discussion and knowledge of this, either among our public or in Cuba, have been taken and are authorized; all the necessary reconnaissance measures are being taken and are authorized. The only thing we haven't done, really, is to consider fully these alternatives.

Bundy: Our principal problem is to try and imaginatively to think . . .

McNamara: Yes.

Bundy: . . . what the world would be like if we do this . . .

McNamara: (I know?)

Bundy: . . . and what it will be like if we don't . . .

McNamara: That's exactly right.

Bundy: . . . if we fail if we do.

McNamara: We ought to work on that tonight.

Ball?: This may be incidental, Mr. President, but if we're going to get the prisoners out this would be a good time to get them out.

JFK: I guess they're not gonna get. . . . Well. . . .

Bundy: You mean take 'em out.

Ball?: No, what I meant was . . .

(Laughter)

Ball?: . . . if we're gonna trade 'em (word unintelligible) . . .

JFK: They're on the Isles of Pines? These prisoners?

RFK: No. Some of them . . .

Speaker ?: (Yes?) sir.

RFK: . . . are. They're split up.

Bundy: (If you can?) get them out alive, I'd make that choice.

JFK: There's no sign of their getting out now, is there? The exchange?

RFK: No, but they will take a few weeks.

JFK: A few weeks.

RFK: (Yeah?). You know they're having that struggle between the young Cuban leaders and the (words unintelligible) . . .

Bundy: We have a list of the sabotage options, Mr. President, and I. . . . It's not a very loud noise to raise at a meeting of this sort, but I think it would need your approval. I take it you are in favor of sabotage. The one question which rises is whether we wish to do this in, uh, naval area, (getting in?) international waters, or in positions which may. . . . Mining international waters or mining Cuban waters, may hit. . . . Mines are very indiscriminate. Uh. . . .

JFK: Is that what they're talking about? Mining?

Bundy: That's one of the items. There are, uh, there. . . . Most of them relate to infiltration of raiders, and will simply be deniable internal Cuban activities. The question that we need guidance from you on is whether you now wish to authorize sabotage which might have its impact on neutrals or even friendly ships.

JFK: I don't think we want to put mines out right now, do we? (Make use of the nets?)

McNamara: Shouldn't wait for twenty-four hours at least before any (words unintelligible) . . .

RFK: (Words unintelligible)

Bundy: Well, let's put the others into action then in Cuba, the internal ones, not . . .

Speaker ?: Huh?

Bundy: . . . the other ones.

JFK: Mr. Vice President, do you have any thoughts? Between one and two?

L.B. Johnson: I don't think I can add anything (that is essential?).

JFK: The, uh . . .

Speaker ?: There's a . . .

JFK: . . . the, uh, let's see, what time we gonna meet then tomorrow? What is it we want to have by tomorrow from the. . . . We want to have from the department tomorrow in a little bit more concise form whether there is any kind of a (words unintelligible) we have to give. How much of a (words unintelligible) and, number two, what you think of these various alternatives we've been talking about, if you see there is any use bringing this to Khrushchev in the way of, (for?), for example, do we want to, for ex-, here is Dobrynin now, he's repeated. . . . Uh, I got to go to, uh, see Schroeder. Let's meet at, uh, eleven to twelve. What time do I get back tomorrow night?

Bundy?: Reasonably (early?).

JFK: Get back about 7:45.

JFK: We meet here by five. . . .

Bundy: Mr. Secretary, some of the staff are in trouble with the dinner for Schroeder tomorrow night.

JFK: Okay, well, now the. . . . I don't think, I don't know, think we'll have anything by noon tomorrow, do we?

Bundy: Would you want to wait until Thursday morning, Mr. President?

JFK: Looks to me like we might as well. I, I. . . . Uh. Everybody else can meet if they want to, if they need to. The Secretary of State, the Secretary of Defense can . . .

McNamara: I think it'd be very useful to meet or else stay afterwards tonight (words unintelligible) (for a while?).

Bundy: It would be a great improvement not to have any more intense White House meetings—trouble with all the (words unintelligible) if we could meet at the State Department tomorrow.

(Several speakers speak at once and none of the words are intelligible.)

JFK: All right, then I could meet you, Mac, when I get back tomorrow and just as well, whatever the thing is and then we can meet Thursday morning. I don't. . . . The question is whether, uh. . . . I'm going to see Gromyko Thursday and I think the question that I'd really like to have is some sort of a judgment on, is whether we ought to do anything with Gromyko. Whether we ought to say anything to him; whether we ought to, uh, indirectly give him sort of a, give him an ultimatum on this matter, or whether we just ought to go ahead without him. It seems to me that . . .

Speaker ?: In other words . . .

JFK: . . . he said we'd be. . . . The Attorney General, the ambassador told the Attorney General, as he told Bohlen the other day that they were not going to put these weapons there. Now either he's lying or doesn't know. Whether the Attorney General saw Dobrynin—not acting as if we had any information about 'em—said that, of course, that they must realize that if this ever does happen that this is going to cause this, give a very clear indication of what's going to happen. Now I don't know what would come out of that, I. . . . Possibly nothing. Possibly, uh, this'd alert them. Possibly they would reconsider their decision, but I don't think we've had any clear evidence of that, and it would give them. . . . We'd lose a week.

Ball?: You mean tell them that. . . .

JFK: Well, not tell them that we know that they've got it, but merely in the course of a conversation Dobrynin, having said that they would never do it, the Attorney General, who sees Dobrynin once in a while, would . . .

Ball?: How would we lose a week?

JFK: What?

Ball?: How would we lose a week?

JFK: Oh, we would be. . . . What we'd be, Bobby would be saying to them, in short, is if these ever come up that we're going to do, the present state would have to take action. And, uh, this (words unintelligible), uh, this could cause (words unintelligible) the most far-reaching consequences. On the possibility that that might cause them to reconsider their action. I don't know whether his, they're aware of what I sai-. . . . I can't understand their viewpoint, if they're aware of what we said at the press conferences. I say, I've never. . . . I don't think there's any record of the Soviets ever making this direct a challenge, ever, really . . .

Bundy: We have to be clear, Mr. President . . .

JFK: . . . since the Berlin blockade.

Bundy: . . . that they made this decision, in all probability, before you made your statements.

McNamara: Uh-huh.

Bundy: This is, uh, important element in the calendar.

Dillon: That didn't change it.

Bundy: No. Indeed, they didn't change it, but they, they. . . . It's quite a different thing. There was either a contravention on one . . .

Dillon: Yeah.

Bundy: My, I wouldn't bet a cookie that Dobrynin doesn't know a bean about . . .

Dillon?: Uh-huh.

Bundy: . . . this.

JFK: You think he does know?

RFK: He didn't know.

Bundy: I, I would (words unintelligible) . . .

RFK: He didn't even know that (words unintelligible) in my judgment.

Speaker ?: (Words unintelligible)

Taylor: Why it's, I mean there's evidence of sightings in late August, I think, and early September of, of some sort.

Speaker ?: It seems to me, Mr. President, there's, in your public presentation, simultaneous or subsequent to an action, your hand is strengthened somewhat if the Soviets have, uh, lied to you, either privately or in public.

Bundy?: I'll agree to that.

Speaker ?: And then if, or if you, uh, without knowing, if you ask Gromyko, or if Bobby asks Dobrynin again, or if some other country could get the Soviets to say publicly in the UN, No, we have no offensive . . .

RFK: TASS, of course, said they're gonna. . . .

JFK: When did TASS say that?

Speaker ?: A while back.

RFK: . . . said they would send offensive weapons to Cuba.

Bundy: Yeah. The TASS . . .

JFK: Khrushchev say that?

Bundy: . . . statement I read this morning.

RFK?: (Yes?)

Bundy: No, the TASS statement. It's . . .

Speaker ?: We don't know if Khrushchev under control yet.

Speaker ?: Uh.

Bundy: Uh, no, we don't have any detail on that. Soviet . . .

JFK: Well, what about my. . . . What question would be there for what I might say to Gromyko about this matter, if you want me just get in the record . . .

Speaker ?: Uh-huh.

JFK: . . . like asking him whether they plan to do it.

Speaker ?: Well, I think what you get is to . . .

Bundy: Putting it the other way around saying that we are . .
.

Speaker ?: . . . call his . . .

Bundy: . . . putting great weight upon the assurances of him .
. .

Speaker ?: . . . call the attention to the statement that you've made on this . . .

Speaker ?: Yup.

Speaker ?: . . . this is your public commitment and that, uh, you, you are going to have to, you're gonna abide by this, and you just want assurances from him that, that, uh, they're, they're living up to what they've said, that they're not gonna . . .

JFK: Well, let's say he said, Well, we're not planning to.

Bundy: "The government of the Soviet Union also authorized TASS to state that there is no need for the Soviet Union to shift its weapons for the repulsion of aggression for a retaliatory blow to any other country, for instance, Cuba. Our nuclear weapons are so powerful in their explosive force, the Soviet Union has so powerful rockets to carry those nuclear warheads that there is no need to search for" . . .

JFK: (I see?)

Bundy: . . . "sites for them beyond the boundaries of the Soviet Union."

JFK: Well, what date was that?

Bundy: September eleventh.

Speaker ?: (Words unintelligible)

Dillon: When they were all there.

Speaker ?: (Words unintelligible) certainly on the way.

JFK: But isn't that. . . . but, as I say, we have to. . . . We never really ever had a case where it's been quite this, uh. . . . After all, they backed down in, uh, Chinese Communists in '58. They didn't go into Laos. Agreed to a ceasefire there.

(Several speakers speak at once and many of the words are unintelligible.)

Bundy: We had this trouble . . .

JFK?: They backed up . . .

Bundy: . . . at (words unintelligible) where they . . .

Speaker ?: (Words unintelligible)

JFK?: (What's?) . . .

Bundy: . . . nuclear storage site.

Speaker ?: At least.

Bundy: Yeah. It's very clear.

JFK: What?

Bundy: I'm as puzzled as Bob is by the absence of a nuclear storage site.

Taylor: We don't know enough about it yet and we (words unintelligible) . . .

Bundy: I understand that. We may learn a lot overnight.

Speaker ?: Isn't it puzzling, also, there is no evidence of any troops protecting the sites?

Taylor: Well, there're troops there. At least there're tents . . .

(Several speakers speak at once and many of the words are unintelligible.)

Speaker ?: (A few campers?) (words unintelligible).

Taylor: . . . (presumably they have some personnel?).

McNamara?: But they look like (words unintelligible). It's as if you could walk over the fields into those vans. (I agree?)

JFK: Well, it's a goddamn mystery to me.

McNamara?: (Words unintelligible)

JFK: I don't know enough about the Soviet Union, but if anybody can tell me any other time since the Berlin blockade where the Russians have given us so clear provocation, I don't know when it's been, because they've been awfully cautious really. The Russians, I never. . . . Now, maybe our mistake was in not saying some time before this summer that if they do this we're (word unintelligible) to act. Maybe they'd gone in so far (that?) it's. . . .

RFK: Yeah, but then why did they put that statement in it?

JFK: Perhaps it. . . .

Speaker ?: That's it (words unintelligible) . . .

JFK: This was following my statement, wasn't it?

RFK: September eleventh.

Taylor: Quick ground (words unintelligible).

JFK: When was my statement? What?

Taylor: Ground it up. Well, I was asking Pat if they had any way of getting quick intelligence, that means somebody in there and out of there so we can really take a look on the ground.

Speaker ?: No, this is two days before your statement.

Carter: Uh, we can try it, but your problems about exfiltration and your problems with training an individual as to what to look for are not handled in twenty-four hours.

McNamara: A better way would be to send in a low-flying airplane . . .

Carter: Yes.

McNamara: . . . and we have today put those on alert, but we would recommend against . . .

Speaker ?: (Words unintelligible)

McNamara: . . . using the low-flying planes until shortly before the intention to strike.

Taylor: This was considered by the, by the co-, commanders today, and they're all of that opinion that the, the loss of surprise would there, was more serious than the, the information we'd get from that.

Speaker ?: I would think it would be very valuable to have them go in shortly before the strike, just to build the evidence. I mean, when you've got pictures that really show what you were, what was there.

JFK: Now, with these great demono-, uh, uh, Bohlen and Thompson, did they have an explanation of why the Russians are sticking a (word unintelligible) by itself?

(Several conversations are going on at once and only the following fragments are intelligible.)

Speaker ?: Take them out . . .

JFK: (Words unintelligible) Acheson (words unintelligible).

Speaker ?: . . . a little bit later something (words unintelligible). Yeah.

JFK: What're we going to say up in Connecticut? You expected the (Bentley trial?).

(Laughter)

JFK: This is a jeer for the . . . .

Speaker ?: (Words unintelligible) President?

JFK: (Words unintelligible) eight or nine-thirty . . .

Bundy: The cabinet at ten.

JFK: Yeah. I'll just see Tom Mann at one.

Bundy: And that's Mann or Sato or both?

JFK: Sato.

Speaker ?: Japanese, uh . . .

JFK: Mann ought to know something. Let's have it here at eleven. Rusk at nine-thirty. In fact, they don't even have to come.

Speaker ?: No.

JFK: (Words unintelligible) the cabinet.

Speaker ?: You just. . . .

JFK: We're going to discuss the (words unintelligible) budget. What about Schroeder? Do I have anything we want to say to Schroeder?

Bundy: We, uh, have a lot on that to discuss which, uh, was halfway in early in the morning. I don't think it's very complicated. The big issue that has come up is Schroeder makes a very strong case for refusing visas on the grounds that he thinks that, uh, that would undermine morale in Berlin in a very dangerous way. I think that's the principal issue that's between us.

JFK: I wonder if we could get somebody to give me something about what our position . . .

Bundy: You want that?

JFK: . . . should be on that.

Bundy: Yeah. Very happy to. You want it tonight?

JFK: No, no. Just in the morning.

Speaker ?: Mr. President, at least they're setting up the time . . .

Speaker ?: Yes, Mr. President.

Speaker ?: (Words unintelligible)

JFK: That's very good, General, thank you.

Speaker ?: (Words unintelligible) (Thompson here?)

(Several conversations are going on at once and only the following fragments are intelligible.)

McNamara: Where is Reilly going to be?

Speaker ?: (Words unintelligible)

Carter: Mr. McCone is coming in tonight.

McNamara: . . . in Mac's office. I'll get you one. Did you see him?

Carter: Yes. (Words unintelligible)

McNamara: Yeah, I'll go down and see him (words unintelligible).

Carter: I would suggest that we get into this hot water partly because of this.

JFK: Yeah, I want to talk to him in the morning. I'd like to just be briefed (words unintelligible). Why is that? (Words unintelligible)

Bundy?: He won't be. . . . Does he get back tonight?

Carter: Coming in tonight. Yes, sir. I'm going to get . . .

Bundy?: Then could he come in in the morning?

Carter: (Words unintelligible)

(Several conversations continue at the same time and only the following fragments are intelligible.)

Bundy?: Could he come in then at nine-thirty?

Carter?: Sure.

Speaker ?: (Bob?), (words unintelligible).

McNamara: Could we agree to meet, uh, mid-afternoon?

Speaker ?: Any time you say, Bob.

McNamara: And then, uh, guide our work tonight and tomorrow on that (schedule?). Why, why don't we say three o'clock? This'll give us some time . . .

Speaker ?: (Words unintelligible)

McNamara: . . . to cover all we've done . . .

Bundy: Yeah.

McNamara: . . . and then do some more tomorrow night if necessary tomorrow afternoon.

Bundy: Would it be (word unintelligible) to make it a little earlier? I ought to get to a four o'clock meeting with Schroeder.

McNamara: (Word unintelligible) said two o'clock, I think, with Schroeder.

Dillon?: Two o'clock.

Bundy: Good.

McNamara: Really plenty of time between (words unintelligible).

Speaker ?: Two o'clock (words unintelligible).

McNamara: (Words unintelligible) At 2:00 P.M. we'll do it at State.

Speaker ?: All right.

McNamara: Now, could we agree what we're gonna do? I would suggest that we, and I don't expect, in fact I . . .

(McNamara and another speaker speak at the same time and none of the words are intelligible.)

McNamara: . . . I would suggest that we, uh, divide the, the, uh, series of targets up by, in effect, numbers of DGZs and, uh, and, uh, numbers of sorties required to take those out for a series of alternatives starting only with the missiles and working up through the nuclear storage sites and the MIGs and the, er, and the SAMs and so on. So we can say, This target system would take so many points, eighty points and so many objects would take so many sorties to knock out. The, the. . . . Not because I think that these are reasonable alternatives . . .

Bundy?: They're not really going to be realistic, even, but they give us (words unintelligible) . . .

McNamara: . . . but they give an order (words unintelligible) to the President to get some idea of this. And this we can do, and this can be done very easily. But the most important thing we need to do is this appraisal of the world after any one of these situations . . .

Bundy: Sure.

McNamara: . . . in great detail.

Bundy?: That's right.

McNamara: And, and I think probably this is something State would have to do . . .

Speaker ?: (Word unintelligible)

McNamara: . . . and I would strongly urge we put it on paper . . .

Speaker ?: That's right.

McNamara: . . . and we, I'll be happy to stay, or, how, or, uh, look at it early in the morning, or something like that if, in order that we may inject disagreement if we (words unintelligible) . . .

Bundy: What I would suggest is that someone be deputized to, to do a piece of paper which really is what happens. I think the margin is between whether we take out the (missile zone?, or missiles on?) strike or take a lot of air bases. This is tactical within a decision to take military action. Now, doesn't, overwhelmingly, it may substantially if it doesn't overwhelmingly change the world. I think any military action does change the world. And I think not taking action changes the world. And I think these are the two worlds that we need to look at.

McNamara: I'm very much inclined to agree, but I think we have to make that point . . .

Bundy: I agree.

McNamara: . . . within the military action . . .

Bundy: I agree.

McNamara: . . . a gradation . . .

Bundy: Oh, many gradations and they have major, it can have major effects.

McNamara: Yeah.

Bundy: I mean, I don't need to exaggerate that now. The question is how to get ahead with that, and whether, uh, I would think, myself, that it, it, it, the appropriate place to make this preliminary analysis is at the Department of State. I think the rest of us ought to spend the evening really to some advantage separately trying to have our own views of this. And I think we should meet in order, at least, to trade pieces of paper, before two o'clock, uh, tomorrow morning if that's agreeable.

McNamara: Why don't we meet tomorrow morning, and, and with pieces of paper, uh, from State, and this is a h- . . .

Speaker ?: No.

McNamara: . . . maybe you don't feel this is reasonable, but . . .

Speaker ?: No. (Words unintelligible)

McNamara: . . . I, I would strongly urge that tonight State (words unintelligible) . . .

Bundy: Well, who is State's de facto? Is, are, are you all tied up tonight? Or what?

Speaker ?: No, no.

Ball?: Uh, the situation is that the only one who's tied up tonight is, is the Secretary and he is coming down at eleven o'clock from his dinner to look at what we will have done in the meantime.

Speaker ?: Alex is back waiting for him.

Ball?: Oh, good, we'll have Alex, we'll have Tommy. Well, we've kept . . .

Bundy: Right.

Ball?: . . . this to our, this has, this has been . . .

Bundy: But you have Tommy? I . . .

Speaker ?: Talked to him this afternoon some.

Bundy: Then you're, do you have any, uh. . . . I'd be fascinated by this, the first sense of how he sees this.

Ball?: Well, the, the, the argument was really between, uh, Hilsman's demonologists, who were already cut in because they (word unintelligible) your boots, who thought this was a low-risk operation. Tommy thought it was a high-risk operation by the Soviets, in other words they were taking real chances. Other people rather thought that they, they probably had miscalculated us and thought this wasn't a risky operation. You know, on the way they were going at it . . .

Speaker ?: (Words unintelligible)

Ball?: . . . either impatient like the SAM sites hadn't been set up to protect it, the various factors which suggest to them that they didn't think anything was gonna happen. Tommy leaned the other way.

McNamara: Could I suggest that tonight we actually draft a paper and it start this way—just a paragraph or two of, of the knowns. Uh, we have to. . . . The knowns are that the SAMs that are here. Let's say the, the probable knowns, because we're not certain of any of them. The probabilities are the SAM system isn't working today. This is important. The probabilities are that these missiles are not operational today. The probabilities are that they won't be operational in less than X days, although we can't be certain. Pat said two weeks. I'm not so sure I'd put it that far. But I. . . . There's just two or three of these knowns. I would put in there, by the way . . .

Speaker ?: How . . .

McNamara: . . . the number of . . .

Speaker ?: Unprotected.

McNamara: Uh, they're unprotected. Another known I'd put in is that they have about fifty X, uh, MIGs,-15,-17 and-19s; that they have certain crated, uh, I've forgotten, say, ten, er, X crated MIG-21s, only one of which we believe to have been assembled. They have X crated IL-28s, none of which we believe to have been assembled. These, this is, in a sense, the problem we, we face there.

Bundy: Do you believe State or the agencies should state the military knowns?

McNamara: Well, this. . . . I can sta- . . .

Speaker ?: I think . . .

McNamara: . . . we can do this in just ten seconds . . .

Speaker ?: Yeah.

McNamara: . . . a very, very simple . . .

Speaker ?: Yeah.

McNamara: . . . statement I think. But then I would follow that by the, the alternatives of, not all of them but the more likely alternatives that we consider open to us. And would hope we could stay just a second here and see if we could sketch them out now. Like . . .

Bundy: I'd like to throw one in of a military kind, and what. . . . . Shall we get them in order and, uh, you move. . . . Well, we'll all (words unintelligible). I would like to throw one in that I do not think the army and the Chiefs would normally consider, and that is, uh, the possibility of genuinely making a quite large-scale, uh, strike, followed by a drop, followed by a recovery of the people dropped to get these things and not simply to increase the chance that we've hit most of them. There's always unc-, incompleteness in a military opera-, in an air operation. But if these things are what the pictures show, you could drop a batallion of paratroopers and get 'em. Now what you do with a batallion, I grant you, is a hell of a problem.

Speaker ?: Yeah.

Bundy: I think there's an enormous political advantage, myself, within these options, granting that all the Chiefs didn't fully agree, taking out the thing that gives the trouble and not the thing that doesn't give the trouble.

McNamara?: This, as opposed to, uh, is it an air attack on . . .

Bundy: Supplementary to an air attack. I mean, how're you gonna know that you've got 'em? And if you haven't got 'em, what've you done?

Taylor: Well, this, this, of course, raises the question of having gotten this set, what happens to the set that arrives next week?

McNamara: Oh, I, I think the ans- . . .

Taylor: Yeah.

McNamara: . . . I, let me answer Mac's question first. How do we know we've got them? We will have photo recon (militarily?) with the strike. Sweeney specifically plans this, and . . .

Bundy: Proving a negative is a hell of a job.

McNamara: Pardon me?

Bundy: Proving a negative is a hell of a job.

Taylor: Yeah, but Central's on the ground very well out of there, uh, Mac.

Bundy: That's true.

McNamara: Terrible risk to put them in there, uh. . . .

Bundy: I ag-, I think the (words unintelligible) is probably a bad idea, but it . . .

McNamara: I think the risk troubles me, it's too great in relation to the risk of not knowing whether we get them.

Bundy: Well . . .

McNamara: But, in any case, this is a small variant of one . . .

Bundy: That's right, it's a minor . . .

McNamara: . . . of the plans.

Bundy: . . . variant of one plan.

McNamara: It seems to me that there are some major alternatives here that I don't think we discussed them fully enough today, and I'd like to see them laid on the paper, if State agrees. The first is what I, I still call it the political approach. Uh, let me say it's a nonmilitary action.

(Laughter)

McNamara: It doesn't start with one and it isn't gonna end with one.

Speaker ?: Yeah.

McNamara: And I, for that reason I call it a political approach.

Speaker ?: Right . . .

McNamara: And I say it isn't gonna end with one because once you start this political approach, I don't think you're gonna have any opportunity for a military operation.

Speaker ?: I agree.

Taylor: It becomes very difficult.

McNamara: But at least I think we ought to put it down there, uh.

Taylor: Right.

Bundy: And it should be worked out. I mean what, what is the maximum . . .

Speaker ?: Your ride is waiting downstairs (words unintelligible).

Speaker ?: Very good, thank you (words unintelligible).

McNamara: Yeah, it should, should definitely be worked out. What, exactly what does it in-, involve, and what are the chances of success of it? They're not zero. They're plus I think.

Taylor?: We did an outline this morning along these lines.

McNamara: All right. That, that's (word unintelligible) anyway . . .

Bundy: Um, but, do you see, it's, it's not just the chances of success, it's the, it ought to be examined in terms of the pluses and minuses of, of nonsuccess . . .

McNamara: Yes. Yes.

Bundy: . . . because there is such a thing as making this thing pay off in ways that are . . .

McNamara: Yeah. Yeah.

Bundy: . . . are of some significance, even though we don't act . . .

McNamara: Yeah. I completely agree.

Bundy: . . . or go with that.

McNamara: And, and this is my second alternative in . . .

Bundy: Yeah.

McNamara: . . . particular and I want to come to that in a moment. But the first one I . . .

Bundy: Yeah.

McNamara: . . . I completely agree it isn't. I, I phrased it improperly. Not the chances of success. It's the results . . .

Speaker ?: (Words unintelligible)

McNamara: . . . that (we're calling? or causing?) . . .

Bundy: Yep.

McNamara: . . . for the mankind.

Bundy: Yep.

McNamara: Now, the second alternative, I, I'd like to discuss just a second, because we haven't discussed it fully today, and I alluded it to, to it a moment ago. I, I, I'll be quite frank. I don't think there is a military problem here. This is my answer to Mac's question . . .

Bundy: That's my honest (judgment?).

McNamara: . . . and therefore, and I've gone through this today, and I asked myself, Well, what is it then if it isn't a military problem? Well, it's just exactly this problem, that, that, uh, if Cuba should possess a capacity to carry out offensive actions against the U.S., the U.S. would act.

Speaker ?: That's right.

Speaker ?: That's right.

McNamara: Now, it's that problem, this . . .

Speaker ?: You can't get around that one.

McNamara: . . . this, this is a domestic, political problem. The announcement—we didn't say we'd go in and not, and kill them, we said we'd act. Well, how will we act? Well, we want to act to prevent their use, and it's really the . . .

Bundy: Yeah.

McNamara: . . . the act. Now, how do we pre-, act to prevent their use? Well, first place, we carry out open surveillance, so we know what they're doing. All times. Twenty-four hours a day from now and forever, in a sense indefinitely. What else do we do? We prevent any further offensive weapons coming in. In other words we blockade offensive weapons.

Bundy: How do we do that?

McNamara: We search every ship.

Taylor: There're two kinds of, of blockade: a blockade which stops ships from coming in and, and simply a seizure, I mean a, simply a search.

McNamara: A search, that's right . . .

Taylor?: Yeah.

McNamara: . . . and . . .

Speaker ?: Well, it would be a search and removal if found.

Bundy: You have to make the guy stop to search him, and if he won't stop, you have to shoot, right?

Speaker ?: All (word unintelligible) up . . .

Speaker ?: And you have to remove what you're looking for if you find it.

Speaker ?: That's right.

McNamara: Absolutely. Absolutely. And then an ul-, I call it an ultimatum associated with these two actions is a statement to the world, particularly to Khrushchev, that we have located these offensive weapons; we're maintaining a constant surveillance over them; if there is ever any indication that they're to be launched against this country, we will respond not only against Cuba, but we will respond directly against the Soviet Union with, with a full nuclear strike. Now this alternative doesn't seem to be a very acceptable one, but wait until you work on the others.

Bundy: That's right.

(Laughter)

McNamara: This is the, this is the problem, but I've thought something about the others this afternoon.

Speaker ?: He's right.

Ball?: Bob, let me ask you one thing that seems slightly irrelevant. What real utility would there be in the United States if we ever actually captured one of these things and could examine it and take it apart?

McNamara: Not very much. No. No.

Ball?: Would we learn anything about the . . .

McNamara: No. no.

Ball?: . . . technology that would be meaningful?

McNamara: I don't (words unintelligible). Pat may . . .

Carter: I don't think so.

McNamara: . . . disagree with (me?), but I. . . .

Speaker ?: Yeah.

McNamara: Well, in any case, that's an alternative. I'd like to see it expressed and discussed.

Ball?: Of course, if, if it takes two hours to screw a head on as a guy said this morning, two to four hours . . .

McNamara: Oh, by the way, that should be one of the knowns in this . . .

Ball?: Yeah.

McNamara: . . . initial paragraph.

Bundy?: That's right.

Ball?: . . . uh, they got all night. How're you gonna survey 'em during the night? Uh, I mean, it seems to me that they're some gaps in the surveillance.

McNamara: Oh, well, it's really the, yes, it isn't the surveillance, it's the ultimatum that is . . .

Ball?: Yeah.

McNamara: . . . the key part in this.

Ball?: Yeah.

McNamara: And really what I tried to do was develop a little package that meets the action requirement of that paragraph I read.

Speaker ?: Yeah.

McNamara: Because, as I suggested, I don't believe it's primarily a military problem. It's primarily a, a domestic, political problem.

Ball: Yeah, well, as far as the American people are concerned, action means military action, period.

McNamara: Well, we have a blockade. Search and, uh, removal of, of offensive weapons entering Cuba. Uh, (word unintelligible) again, I don't want to argue for this . . .

Ball: No, no, I . . .

McNamara: . . . because I, I don't think it's . . .

Ball: . . . I think it's an alternative.

McNamara: . . . a perfect solution by any means. I just want to . . .

Bundy: Which one are we (still on?) would you say?

McNamara: Still on the second one, uh . . .

Ball: Now, one of the things we look at is whether any, the actual operation of a blockade doesn't, isn't a greater involvement almost than a . . .

McNamara: Might well be, George.

Ball: . . . military action.

Speaker ?: I think so.

McNamara: It's, it's a search, not a, not an embargo, uh. . . .

Speaker ?: Yeah.

Ball: It's a series of single, unrelated acts, not by surprise. This, uh, come in there on Pearl Harbor just frightens the hell out of me as to what's going beyond. (Yeah, well, anyway?) the Board of National Estimates have been working on this ever since . . .

Bundy: What, what goes, what goes beyond what?

Ball: What happens beyond that. You go in there with a surprise attack. You put out all the missiles. This isn't the end. This is the beginning, I think. There's a whole hell of a lot of things . . .

Bundy: Are they all working on powerful reaction in your (word unintelligible)?

Carter: Yes, sir.

Bundy: Good.

Ball: . . . which goes back down to, uh, Mr. Secretary, is this the central . . .

Bundy: Yeah.

Ball: . . . point of, to connect . . .

(Two conversations are going on at once. Only these fragments are intelligible.)

McNamara: Well, that, that takes me into the third category of action. I'd lump them all in the third category. I call it overt military action of varying degrees of intensity, ranging. . . . And, if you feel there's any difference in them, in the kind of a world we have after the varying degrees of intensity . . .

Cuban leader Fidel Castro. Removing him was one of the chief priorities for the United States.

Soviet leader Nikita Kruschev and President John F Kennedy meet in Vienna in 1961. A year later, they would take the world to the very edge of nuclear destruction.

A U-2 spy plane preparing for takeoff.

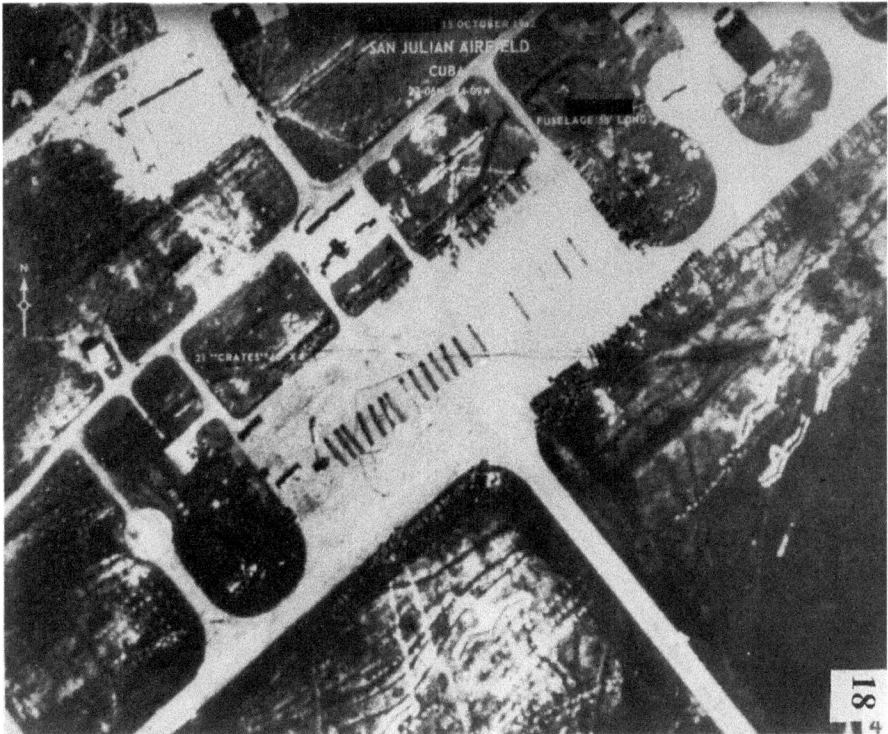

Since late summer 1962, the US had detected a buildup of Soviet-supplied weapons in Cuba. Here, crated Ilyushin IL-28 bombers are laid out on a runway awaiting assembly.

The IL-28. Although already obsolete in 1962, it was capable of carrying tactical nuclear weapons from Cuba to the United States.

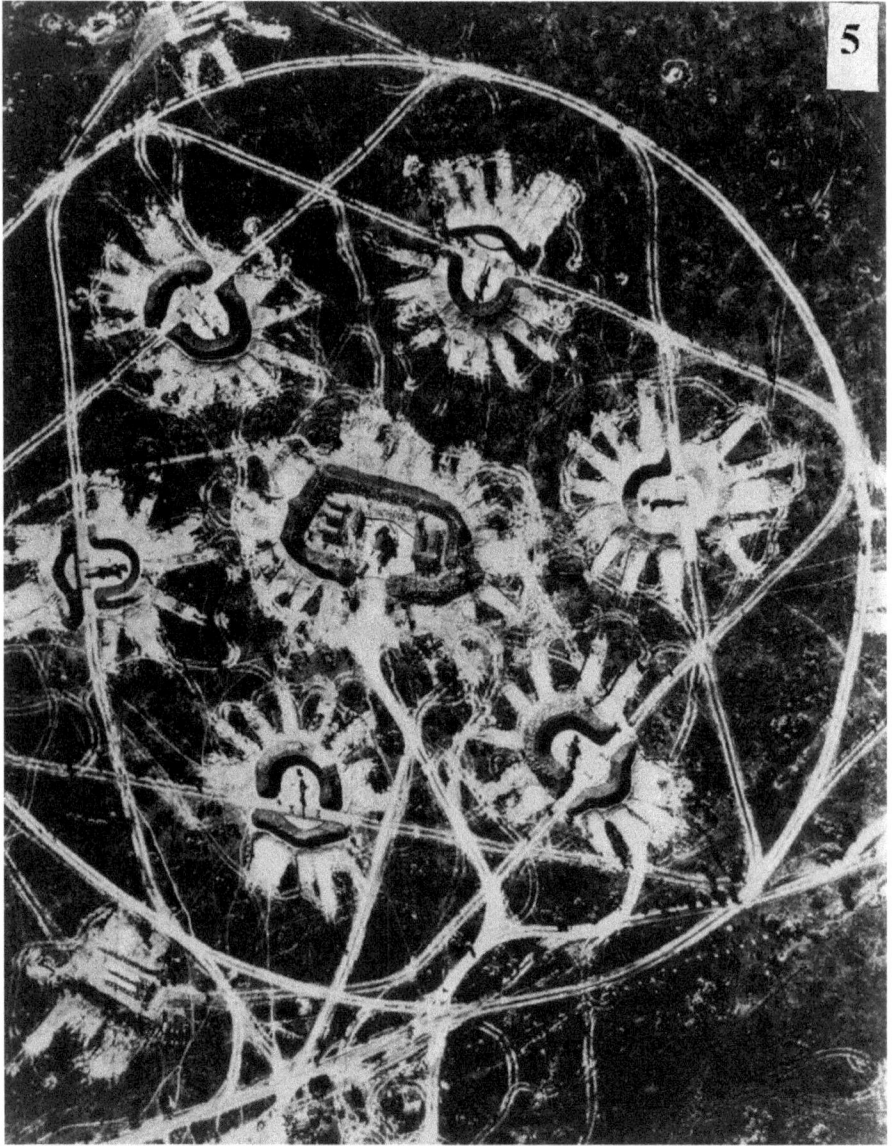

Aerial view of a completed SAM site. The first indications that something big was happening came when Soviet surface-to-air anti-aircraft missile sites began appearing in Cuba. Analysts knew they had to be protecting something important.

The Photo. The first U-2 photo in which Medium-Range Ballistic Missiles
were identified, taken October 14, 1962.

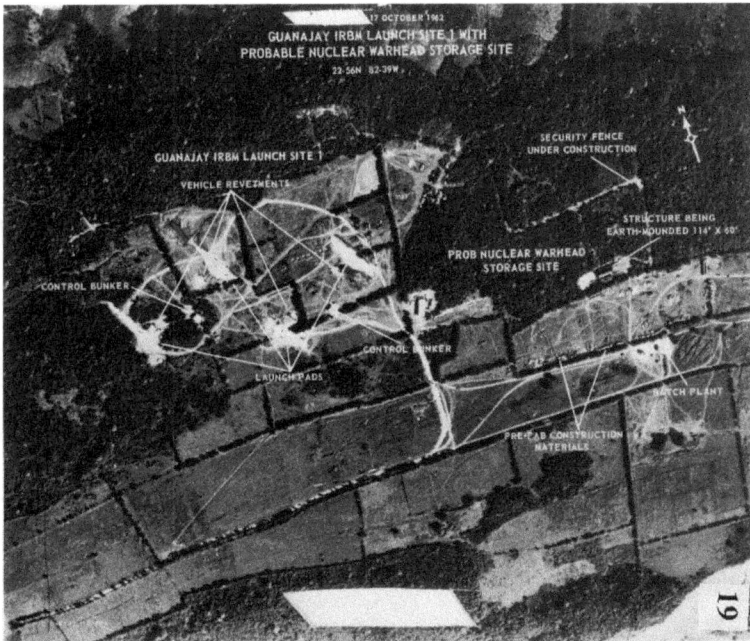

A short time later, this U-2 photo was taken, showing an Intermediate-Range
Ballistic Missile site under construction.

The SS-4 Medium-Range Ballistic Missile.

The SS-5 Intermediate-Range Ballistic Missile.

Map overlay showing the range of IL-28 bombers (inner circle), SS-4 MRBM's (middle circle) and SS-5 IRBM's (outer circle) launched from Cuba.

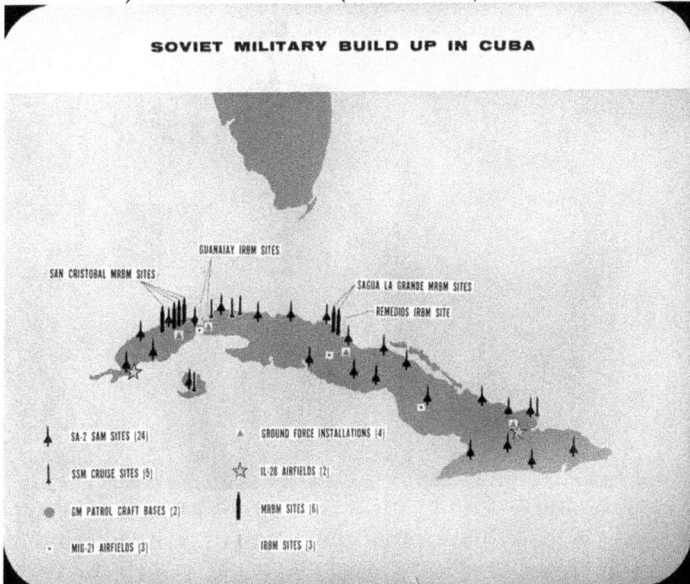

Briefing Chart showing locations of Soviet military forces in Cuba.

President Kennedy and his advisors meet to discuss the Cuban Missile Crisis. The entire matter was kept secret from the public for over a week after the missiles were discovered.

Soviet Foreign Minister Gromyko and Soviet Ambassador Dobrynin meet with Kennedy in the White House. Neither of them had been told by the Kremlin that missiles were being placed in Cuba, and Kennedy didn't tell them that he knew.

Briefing map showing locations of Soviet and American ships in the Caribbean.

October 23, 1962, President Kennedy signs the orders imposing a naval "quarantine" on all Soviet ships approaching Cuba.

Adlai Stevenson dramatically presents aerial photos of the Cuban missile sites to the United Nations Security Council.

One of the photos presented by Stevenson.

American reconnaissance planes begin to shadow Soviet ships approaching Cuba.

An American destroyer stops a Soviet cargo ship at the quarantine zone.

A NAVY HELICOPTER HOVERS OVER RUSSIAN SUBMARINE

A Soviet attack submarine is forced to the surface by American depth charges. Unbeknownst to the US, these subs carried nuclear-armed torpedos and were under orders to use them if attacked. Fortunately, the Captain of this sub chose to submit instead.

SOVIET SHIP POLTAVA ENROUTE TO CUBA

15 SEPTEMBER 1962

The Russian ship *Poltava* approaches the quarantine zone, carrying crated IRBM's on her deck.

The crisis ends. The *Poltava* reverses course and heads for home.

US low-level reconnaissance planes watch as the Cuban missiles are dismantled and crated aboard Russian ships for the return trip.

An American Jupiter IRBM. They were secretly removed from Turkey and Italy as part of the agreement that ended the Cuban Missile Crisis.

Speaker ?: Right.

McNamara: . . . you have to divide category three into subcategories by intensity and probable effect on the world thereafter. And I think there is, at least in the sense of the Cuban uprising, which I happen to believe is a most important element of category three, it applies to some elements in categ-, some categories of category three, but not all. But, in any event, what, what kind of a world do we live in? In Cuba what action do we take? What do we expect Castro will be doing after, uh, you attack these missiles? Does he survive as a, as a political leader? Is he overthrown? Uh, is he stronger, weaker? Uh, how will he react? How will the Soviets react? What can. . . . How, how could Khrushchev afford to accept this action without some kind of rebuttal? I don't think, he can't accept it without some rebuttal. It may not be a substantial rebuttal, but it's, gonna have to be some. Where? How do we react in relation to it? What happens when we do mobilize? How does this affect our allies' support of us in relation to Berlin? Well, you know far better than I the problems, uh, but it would seem to me if we could lay this out tonight and then meet at a reasonable time in the morning to go over a tentative draft, discuss it, and then have another draft for some time in the afternoon . . .

Gilpatric?: One kind of planning, Bob, that, uh, that, uh, we didn't explicitly talk about today, uh, which is to look at the points of vulnerability around the world, not only in Berlin . . .

McNamara: Sure.

Gilpatric?: . . . not only in Turkey . . .

McNamara: Sure. Iran.

Gilpatric?: Iran and all of them . . .

McNamara: And Korea.

Gilpatric?: What, what precautionary measures ought to be taken?

McNamara: Yes. Yes.

Gilpatric?: Well, these, this, these are, these are both military and political . . .

McNamara: Exactly. Well, uh, and we call it a world-wide alert . . .

Speaker ?: (Yeah?)

McNamara: . . . under that heading we've got a whole series of precautionary measures that we, we think, uh, should be taken. All of our forces should be put on alert, but beyond that, mobilization, redeployment, movement, and so on. . . . Well, would it be feasible to meet at some time in the morning, uh, that's . . .

Speaker ?: (Words unintelligible)

McNamara: . . . (words unintelligible)? Mac, what would you think?

Bundy: I ought to, uh, join the President for the meeting with Schroe-der and I'll be involved in getting some, started for that until ten o'-, uh, from about nine-thirty on. I could be, meet any time before that.

Speaker ?: Well, why don't we take the (words unintelligible)?

Carter: Well now, the President was going to see Mr. McCone at nine-thirty.

Bundy: That's right.

McNamara: Well, why don't we meet at eight-thirty? Is that . . .

Bundy: (Fine?)

McNamara: Let's, let's try that.

Bundy: Okay.

Speaker ?: Well you want. . . . Is (Halberstam?) coming?

McNamara: Now, there's not much we can do to help, uh, I'd be happy to, though . . .

Speaker ?: No. (Words unintelligible)

McNamara: . . . if you think of anything we can do. We'll, we'll go to work tonight and get these numbers of sorties by target systems laid out. I'll, Reilly's up in Mac's office and I'll go down there now and get them started on it.

Carter: I think Mr. McCone could be helpful to you all in the morning.

McNamara: Well, I think he should try to stay here at eight-thirty.

Speaker ?: Yeah.

Carter: He didn't worry about this for a heck of a long time .
. .

Bundy: Sure.

Carter: . . . (word unintelligible) some.

(Meeting appears to be breaking up. Only the following fragments of conversation are intelligible.)

McNamara: Yeah.

Speaker ?: We can meet while (words unintelligible).

Speaker ?: Yeah.

Speaker ?: Are you going to be dining tonight? Or whatever it was you (word unintelligible)?

Bundy: I'm at your service.

Speaker ?: (Words unintelligible) I thought I, we might be in touch with you . . .

Bundy: I'll be right there. I can come down, or at supper privately. Either way.

(Laughter)

Speaker ?: Well, uh, why don't we, why don't we see what it looks like . . .

Speaker ?: Yeah.

Speaker ?: . . . uh, (starting?) under way.

Ball?: We're trying to run this with a minimum of manpower and it must still (words unintelligible).

(Several speakers speak at once and only the following words are intelligible.)

Bundy: We must do.

Taylor?: Secretarial problems. This has been one of the problems.

Speaker ?: Well, I think I could bust out a staff . . .

Bundy: I have two, extremely, totally . . .

McNamara: I've got, I'd trust my staff anywhere, I mean, I. .
. . They (word unintelligible). . . . I've got my car out here, Admiral.

Speaker ?: Oh, it's out this way.

McNamara: Yeah. All right. Good night.

Bundy: Good night.

Speaker ?: (Words unintelligible)

(Conversations end. Room noises for almost four minutes. Telephone rings in the distance.)

Lincoln: Hello. (In the distance.)

(Footsteps)

Cleaning man: Yes, lady, I'm gonna bring this.

Lincoln: Hello, (words unintelligible) (left?)

Cleaning man: (Laughs) Here. There's just some stacks, that's all.

(Recording ends.)

Memorandum

MEMORANDUM OF MEETING ATTENDED IN SECRETARY BALL'S CONFERENCE ROOM BY SECRETARY MCNAMARA, BUNDY, GENERAL TAYLOR, ROBERT KENNEDY, MARTIN AND MCCONE AT 0830, 17 OCTOBER

1. Meeting involved an inclusive exploration of alternatives open to us in connection with the Cuban matter.

Ball seemed to feel military action would throw the NATO allies in disarray and permit Britain and France to separate from us on Berlin policy. Stated Kohler discussions with Khrushchev did not fit in with Soviet action in Cuba. Suggested Cuban situation might be by inadvertance. Suggested we might give Khrushchev an "out" on the grounds that he does not know what is going on in Cuba and discussed various types of action ranging from a limited military strike to minimize losses to the calling of a Summit conference.

2. During the discussion Taylor and Ball speculated as to whether this whole thing was not a "mock up" designed to draw out action by us, and that the war heads were not there. This view was not supported.

3. McNamara urged avoiding taking a position, considering all alternatives, with meetings this afternoon and this evening in preparation of final discussion with the President tomorrow.

4. Urged exploration of all facts and listed the following:

About 50 or 60 MIG 17s and 19s now in Cuba and these apparently have no offensive capability.

One MIG 21 has been seen and a number of suspicious crates also seen indicating some MIG 21 capability and we do not know whether the MIG 21 has an offensive capability.

IL 28's have been delivered.

Three MRBM sites under construction and can be ready in two weeks.

Warhead locations unknown; also unknown whether MRBM's are nuclear or conventional. Also feels that if nuclear warheads supplied them Soviet will also supply nuclear bombs for bombers with offensive capability.

Shiploads of boxes of unknown purpose reported by Lundahl to DCI on October 14th.

28 Soviet ships en route to Cuba at the present time.

Sited at Havana, mysterious excavations, revetments, covered buildings, railroad tracks through tunnels, etc., might be nuclear storage site.

Other facts should be developed today.

Note: McCone responded by reading numbered paragraphs 2, 3, and 4 of attached memorandum dated October 17th.

5. General Taylor and Thompson discussed political nature of problem including possibility of forcing settlement in Berlin and elsewhere—Khrushchev wished show down on Berlin and this gave a show down issue. Believes Khrushchev would be surprised to find we know about MRBMs. Thompson emphasized Khrushchev wants Berlin settlement but on his terms. And will probably deny knowledge of Cuban situation but at any event would justify actions because of our missiles in Italy and Turkey. Also Khrushchev recognizes that action by us would be devisive among our allies.

6. McCone emphasized his views on political objectives as stated in paragraph 5 of the attached memorandum, and also repeated paragraph 2-C. Also made the point in paragraph 6.

7. McNamara discussed many operational questions concerning the use of Soviet nuclear warheads in Cuba; how

communications could be arranged; what authority was in the field. Thompson believes Soviet nuclear warheads was under very tight control. McCone reviewed recent Chicadee reports, indicated considerable autonomy in hands of field commanders much more so than we have.

8. Bundy and McCone left for meeting with the President.

Memorandum

October 17, 1962.
SUBJECT

The Cuban Situation

1. The establishment of medium range strike capability in Cuba by the Soviets was predicted by me in at least a dozen reports since the Soviet buildup was noted in early August.

2. Purposes are to:

(a) Provide Cuba with an offensive or retaliatory power for use if attacked.

(b) Enhance Soviet strike capability against the United States.

(c) Establish a "hall mark" of accomplishment by other Latin American countries, most particularly Mexico, and other Central American countries within strike range of the United States.

3. The MRBM capability we have witnessed will expand and the defensive establishments to protect this capability likewise will be expanded. There appears to me to be no other explanation for the extensive and elaborate air defense establishment.

4. In my opinion the missiles are Soviet, they will remain under Soviet operational control as do ours, they will be equipped with nuclear warheads under Soviet control (because conventional warheads would be absolutely ineffective), Cubans will supply most of the manpower needs with the

Soviets permanently exercising operational command and control. Nevertheless, there will be a substantial number of Soviets on site at all times.

5. Soviet political objectives appears to me to be:

(a) The establishment of a "trading position" to force removal of U.S. overseas bases and Berlin.

(b) To satisfy their ambitions in Latin America by this show of determination and courage against the American Imperialist.

6. Consequences of action by the United States will be the inevitable "spilling of blood" of Soviet military personnel. This will increase tension everywhere and undoubtedly bring retaliation against U.S. foreign military installations, where substantial U.S. casualties would result, i.e., Tule, Spanish bases, Moroccan bases, and possibly SAC bases in Britain or Okinawa. Jupiter installations in Southern Italy, Turkey, and our facilities [*censored*] do not provide enough "American blood."

7. The situation cannot be tolerated. However, the United States should not act without warning and thus be forced to live with a "Pearl Harbor indictment" for the indefinite future. I would therefore:

(a) Notify Gromyko and Castro that we know all about this.

(b) Give them 24 hours to commence dismantling and removal of MRBMs, coastal defense missiles, surface to air missiles, IL 28s and all other aircraft which have a dual defensive-offensive capability, including MIG 21s.

(c) Notify the American public and the world of the situation created by the Soviets.

(d) If Khrushchev and Castro fail to act at once, we should make a massive surprise strike at air fields, MRBM sites and SAM sites concurrently.

John A. McCone
Director

Memorandum

Washington, October 18, 1962, 5 p.m.
SUBJECT
Cuba

PARTICIPANTS
US
The President
The Secretary
Ambassador Thompson
Mr. Hillenbrand
Mr. Akalovsky

USSR
Foreign Minister Gromyko
Mr. Semenov
Ambassador Dobrynin
Mr. Sukhodrev

After a discussion on Germany and Berlin, Mr. Gromyko stated he wished to set forth the Soviet position on Cuba and to voice the views of the Soviet Government with regard to US actions relating to Cuba. Continuing to read from his prepared text, he asserted that the Soviet Government stood for peaceful coexistence and was against interference by one state in the internal affairs of another state, and this also applied to relations between big and small states. This, he said, was the basic core, the credo of Soviet foreign policy, and it was not just a statement.

The President was surely fully familiar with the attitude of the Soviet Government, and of Mr. Khrushchev personally, toward recent developments and toward actions by the United States Government in relation to Cuba. For quite some time there had been an unabated anti-Cuban campaign in the United States, a campaign which was apparently backed by the United States Government. Now the United States Government wished to institute a blockade against trade with Cuba, and there had also been some talk of organized piracy under the aegis of the United States. All this could only lead to great misfortunes for mankind. The United States Government seemed to believe that the Cubans must settle their internal affairs not at their own discretion, but at the discretion of the United States. Yet Cuba belonged to Cubans and not to the United States. If this was so, why then were statements being made in the United States advocating invasion of Cuba? What did the United States want to do with Cuba? What could Cuba do to the United States? If one were to compare the human and material resources of Cuba and the United States, one would see immediately that the United States was a giant and Cuba only a baby. Cuba could not constitute a threat to any country in Latin America. It was strange to believe that small Cuba could encroach upon any Latin American country. Cuban leaders, including Castro personally, had stated for all the world to know and in the most solemn fashion that Cuba did not intend to impose its system and was in favor of peaceful coexistence. However, those who called for aggression against Cuba said that Cuban statements were insufficient, in spite of the fact that those statements were substantiated by deeds. If one were to approach problems this way, then it would be easy to justify any aggression. All international problems must be resolved by negotiation between the states concerned. After all, the US and USSR were now negotiating and making statements which should be given credence. Was it not sufficient for Cuba to state that it wished negotiations and a solution of existing problems on a mutually acceptable basis? The President was surely familiar with President Dorticos' speech at the General Assembly. What the Cubans wanted was to make their home and country secure. They appealed to reason and conscience and called upon the United States not to resort to encroachments. Thus the question arose of why it was necessary to fan this campaign, to organize hostile actions, and to take actions directed against those countries which were extending their hand of friendship to Cuba? This was a violation of international law, and how could the Soviet Government just sit by and observe this situation idly?

Mr. Gromyko said he knew that the President appreciated frankness. Mr. Khrushchev's conversation with the President at Vienna had been frank and therefore, with the President's permission, he himself wished to be frank, too. The situation today could not be compared to that obtaining in the middle of the 19th century. Modern times were not the same as those when colonies had been divided among colonial powers. Modern times could not be compared to those when it took weeks or months for the voice of the attacked to be heard. Statements had been made that the US was a powerful and great nation; this was true, but what kind of a nation was the USSR? Mr. Khrushchev had been favorably impressed with the President's statement at Vienna regarding the equality of forces of our two nations. Since this was so, i.e., since the USSR was also a great and strong nation, it could not stand by as a mere observer when aggression was planned and when a threat of war was looming. The US Government was surely aware of the Soviet Government's attitude toward the recent call-up of 150,000 Reservists in the United States. The Soviet Government believed that if both sides were for relaxation of international tensions and for solving the outstanding international problems, such demonstrations could be designed only for the purpose of increasing tensions and should therefore be avoided. If worse should come to worse and if war should occur, then surely 150,000 soldiers would be of no significance. As the President was surely aware, today was not 1812, when Napoleon had relied on the number of soldiers, sabres and rifles. Neither could today's situation be compared to 1941, when Hitler had relied on the number of tanks and guns. Today, life itself and military technology had created an entirely different situation, where it was better not to rely on arms. As to Soviet assistance to Cuba, Mr. Gromyko stated that he was instructed to make it clear, as the Soviet Government had already done, that such assistance, pursued solely for the purpose of contributing to the defense capabilities of Cuba and to the development of Cuba, toward the development of its agriculture and land amelioration, and training by Soviet specialists of Cuba nationals in handling defensive armaments were by no means offensive. If it were otherwise, the Soviet Government would have never become involved in rendering such assistance. This applied to any other country as well. Laos was a good and convincing illustration of this point. If the Soviet Government had pursued a different policy, the situation in that country today would be quite different. It was quite evident that the Soviet Union and its friends had broader opportunities of influencing the situation in that country than had the United States. However, the USSR had sought an understanding on that question, since it could not go back on the basic principle of its foreign policy, which was designed to alleviate tensions, to eliminate outstanding problems and to resolve them on a peaceful basis.

Such was the position of the Soviet Government with regard to Cuba. The Soviet Government and Mr. Khrushchev personally appealed to the President and the United States Government not to allow such steps as would be incompatible with peace, with relaxation of tensions, and with United Nations Charter under which both the US and the USSR had solemnly affixed their signatures. The Soviet Government addressed its appeal to the United States on this question because both our countries were major powers and should direct their efforts only to ensuring peace.

The President said he was glad that Mr. Gromyko had referred to Laos because he believed that the Soviet policy on that problem was as Mr. Gromyko had described it. So far the Soviet Union had apparently met its obligations just as the United States had met them. However, a most serious mistake had been made last summer with respect to Cuba. The US had not pressed the Cuban problem and had attempted to push it aside although of course a number of people in this country opposed the regime now prevailing in Cuba and there were many refugees coming to this country. However, there was no intention to invade Cuba. But then last July the USSR, without any communication from Mr. Khrushchev to the President, had embarked upon the policy of supplying arms to Cuba. The President said he did not know the reasons for that shift in Soviet policy, because there was no threat of invasion and he would have been glad to give appropriate assurances to that effect had Mr. Khrushchev communicated with him. Soviet arms supply had had a profound impact in the United States; Ambassador Dobrynin was surely aware of how the American people and the Congress felt on this matter. The administration had tried to calm this reaction and he, the President, had made a statement that in view of the nature of Soviet assistance to Cuba at this time coolness was required. Yet, the President said, he wished to stress that Soviet actions were extremely serious and he could find no satisfactory explanation for them. The Soviet Union was surely aware of US feelings with regard to Cuba, which was only 90 miles away from the United States. The President continued that the US planned no blockade of Cuba; it was only a question of ships taking arms to Cuba not being able to stop in the United States with their return cargo. Thus a very unfortunate situation had developed. The President said he did not know where it was taking us but it was the most dangerous situation since the end of the war. The US had taken the Soviet statement concerning the nature of armaments supplied to Cuba at its face value. He, the President, had attacked last Sunday in Indianapolis a Senator who was advocating invasion, and he had stated that the Cuban problem must be kept in perspective. The President reiterated that this was a dangerous situation, and said he did not know where the USSR planned to have it end.

Mr. Gromyko said that there had already been an invasion, and it was well known how it ended. It was well known now, both from facts and statements, including the President's own, under what circumstances and by whom that invasion had been organized. Everyone knew that if the United States had merely lifted its little finger, Cuban emigrees and smaller Caribbean countries which had helped them would not have dared undertake any invasion.

The President interjected that he had discussed with Mr. Khrushchev the April 1, 1961, invasion and had said that it was a mistake. He also pointed out he would have given assurances that there would be no further invasion, either by refugees or by US forces. But last July the Soviet Union took certain actions and the situation changed.

Mr. Gromyko continued that Cubans and the Cuban Government had before them the vital question of whether they should remain unprepared to resist attack or to take steps to defend their country. He said he wished to reiterate that the Soviet Union had responded to appeals for assistance only because that assistance pursued the sole objective of giving bread to Cuba and preventing hunger in that country; also, as far as armaments were concerned, Soviet specialists were training Cubans in handling certain types of armaments which were only defensive—and he wished to stress the word defensive—in character, and thus such training could not constitute a threat to the United States. He reiterated that if it were otherwise the Soviet Union would never have agreed to render such assistance.

The President said that in order to be clear on this Cuban problem he wanted to state the following: The US had no intention of invading Cuba. Introduction last July of intensive armanents had complicated the situation and created grave danger. His own actions had been to prevent, unless US security was endangered, anything from being done that might provoke the danger of war. The President then read a portion of his September 4 statement on Cuba and stated that this had been US position and policy on this question. He noted that the Attorney General had discussed the Cuban situation with Ambassador Dobrynin so that the latter must be aware of what it was. The President again recalled his Indianapolis speech of last Sunday and said that we were basing our present attitude on facts as they had been described by Mr. Gromyko; our presumption was that the armanents supplied by USSR were defensive.

Mr. Gromyko stated the Soviet Union proceeded from the assumption that on the basis of Soviet Government's statements and his own today the US Government and the President had a clear idea of the Soviet policy on this matter and of the Soviet evaluation of US action in relation to Cuba. He said he had nothing to add to what he had already said.

Memorandum

Washington, October 19, 1962.

Early in the morning of October 18th, Secretary McNamara called Mr. McCone at his residence expressing great concern over the reports from NPIC as a result of their examination of the two flights run on October 15th. Lundahl was at the house with the enlargements which indicated that, in addition to the three mobile MRBM sites detected on flight October 14th, there appeared to be now two IRBM sites with fixed launchers zeroed in on the Eastern United States. McNamara felt that this development demanded more prompt and decisive action.

The group which had been meeting on Tuesday met in the Cabinet Room at 11:00 a.m. on Wednesday with the President. State tabled revisions in their papers on covering a limited one-time strike and blockade, most of which are dated 10/18--11:00 a.m.

At the opening of the meeting, McCone gave a brief resume of current intelligence and Lundahl presented the most recent photography. President questioned Lundahl further if the uninitiated could be persuaded that the photographs presented offensive MRBM missiles. Lundahl stated probably not and that we must have low-level photography for public consumption.

Secretary Rusk then stated that developments in the last 24 hours had substantially changed his thinking. He first questioned whether, if it is necessary to move against Cuba, and then concluded that it was because Cuba can become a formidable military threat. He also referred to the President's recent public statements and indicated a feeling that if no action was taken, we would free the Soviets to act any place they wished and at their own will. Also, Rusk stated the failure on our part to act would make our situation unmanageable elsewhere in the world. He furthermore indicated that this would be an indication of weakness which would have serious effect on our Allies. Secretary pointed out to the President that action would involve risks. We could expect counter action and the cost may be heavy. The President must expect action in Berlin, Korea and possibly against the United States itself. Rusk felt a quick strike would minimize the risk of counter action. He raised the question of solidarity of the Alliance and seemed to dismiss this question, feeling that the Alliance would hold together. Rusk stated that if we enter upon positive action, we can not say for sure what the final Soviet response will be and therefore what the final outcome will be. However he felt that the American people will accept danger and suffering if they are convinced doing so is necessary and that they have a clear conscience. The Secretary reviewed the circumstances surrounding the outbreak of World War I, World War II, and the Korean war. These factors militated in favor of consulting with Khrushchev and depending on the Rio pact. This, he indicated, might have the possibility of prevention of action and settlement by political means. The other course open was the declaration of war. Rusk expressed himself in favor of leaning upon the Rio pact, but does not dismiss the alternative of a unilateral declaration of war as the ultimate action we must take. The alternate is a quick strike.

Ambassador Bohlen was not present but his views were expressed in a message which was read in which he strongly advocated diplomatic effort and stated that military action prior to this would be wrong. He urged against action first and then decisive value of discussion. He also stated that limited quick military action was an illusion and that any military action would rapidly escalate into an invasion. McNamara at this point presented the alternatives referred to the previous day, stating that alternatives one and two were not conclusive and that we would have to resort to alternative 3 and in fact this would lead us ultimately into an invasion.

General Taylor generally reviewed the situation stating that the Chiefs looked upon Cuba as a forward base of serious proportions, that it cannot be taken out totally by air; that the military operation would be sizeable, nevertheless necessary.

Ambassador Thompson urged that any action be preceded by a declaration of war; he strongly advocated that we institute a blockade and not resort to military action unless and until it is determined that Castro and Khrushchev refuse to reverse their activities and actually remove the missiles which are now in place.

Secretary Dillon questioned what would be accomplished by talking to Khrushchev. He pointed out that we would probably become engaged in discussions from which we could not extract ourselves and therefore our freedom of action would be frustrated. Dillon was very positive that whatever action we take should be done without consultation with Khrushchev. Rusk seemed to disagree indicating there was a possibility that Khrushchev might be persuaded to reduce his efforts but he admitted also that he might step them up as a result of discussions.

President Kennedy was non-committal, however he seemed to continually raise questions of reactions of our allies, NATO, South America, public opinion and others. Raised the question whether we should not move the missiles out of Turkey. All readily agreed they were not much use but a political question was involved. Bundy thought this a good idea either under conditions of a strike or during a preliminary talk.

McNamara discussed in some detail the effects of a strike indicating that we could expect several hundred Soviet citizens to be killed; he pointed out that all of the SAM sites were manned exclusively by Soviets and a great many Soviet technicians were working on the MRBMs and at the air fields. He agreed that we could move out of Turkey and Italy; pointed out the political complications. At this point McNamara seemed to be reconsidering his prior position of advocating military action and laid special emphasis on the fact that the price of Soviet retaliation, whether in Berlin or elsewhere, would be very high and we would not be able to control it.

Secretary Ball throughout the conversation maintained the position that strike without warning was not acceptable and that we should not proceed without discussion with Khrushchev. President Kennedy then said that he thought at some point Khrushchev would say that if we made a move against Cuba, he would take Berlin. McNamara surmised perhaps that was the price we must pay and perhaps we'd lose Berlin anyway. There followed an exchange of view on the possibility of the Soviets taking Berlin and our prospect of retaining it.

President Kennedy rather summed up the dilemma stating that action of a type contemplated would be opposed by the alliance — on the other hand, lack of action will create disunity, lack of confidence and disintegration of our several alliances and friendly relations with countries who have confidence in us.

As a result of discussions of the "price" of a strike, there followed a long discussion of the possibilities of a blockade, the advantages of it, and manner in which it would be carried out, etc. There seemed to be differences of opinion as to whether the blockade should be total, or should only involve military equipment which would mean blockading Soviet ships. Also there were continued references to blockading ships carrying offensive weapons and there seemed to be a differentiation in the minds of some in the policy of blockading offensive weapons as contrasted to blockading all weapons.

There followed discussion as to policies the President should follow with respect to calling Congress into session, asking for a declaration of war, advising the country and authorizing action. Thompson continued to insist that we must communicate with Khrushchev. There was a discussion concerning the President's meeting with Gromyko and the position he should take should the Cuban question come up. The President was advised to draw Gromyko out and it was indicated he probably would receive a flat denial that there were any offensive weapons in Cuba.

Meeting adjourned with the President requesting that we organize into two groups. One to study the advantages of what might be called a slow course of action which would involve a blockade to be followed by such further actions as appeared necessary as the situation evolved. Second would be referred to as a fast dynamic action which would involve the strike of substantial proportions with or without notice.

John A. McCone
Director

Record of Meeting

Washington, October 19, 1962, 11 a.m.
PARTICIPANTS
Secretary Rusk
Under Secretary Ball
Ambassador Thompson
Deputy Under Secretary Johnson
Assistant Secretary Martin
Leonard C. Meeker
Secretary Dillon
Secretary McNamara
Deputy Secretary Gilpatric
Assistant Secretary Nitze
General Taylor
Attorney General Kennedy
Deputy Attorney General Katzenbach
John A. McCone
Ray S. Cline
McGeorge Bundy
Theodore Sorensen
Dean Acheson

Secretary Rusk opened the meeting by asking Mr. Johnson if he was ready to lay a program before the group. Mr. Johnson said that he was not.

Then ensued a military photographic intelligence briefing on installations in Cuba, presented by a CIA representative (Arthur Lundahl). Following this, Mr. McCone called on Mr. Cline to give the most recent intelligence estimate conclusions of the United States Intelligence Board. Mr. Cline did so on the basis of three papers which were distributed to the group. (As he started, Mr. Cline spoke of China by inadvertence instead of Cuba; a few moments later this was called to his attention and corrected.)

Secretary Rusk then said he thought there should be an exposition of the legal framework surrounding possible military measures by the United States, turned to me, and seemed about to call on me, when the Attorney General signalled and said "Mr. Katzenbach." Secretary Rusk then called on the latter. Mr. Katzenbach said he believed the President had ample constitutional and statutory authority to take any needed military measures. He considered a declaration of war unnecessary. From the standpoint of international law, Mr. Katzenbach thought United States action could be justified on the principle of self-defense.

I said that my analysis ran along much the same lines. I did not think a declaration of war would improve our position, but indeed would impair it. I said that a defensive quarantine of Cuba would involve a use of force, and this had to be considered in relation to the United Nations Charter. The Charter contained a general prohibition against the use of force except in certain limited kinds of situation. One of these was "armed attack," but the situation in Cuba did not constitute armed attack on any country. Another exception was collective action voted by the competent United Nations organ to deal with a situation under Chapter VII of the Charter. Obviously, no resolution could be obtained from the Security Council. And it seemed quite problematical whether we could obtain a recommendation from the General Assembly.

The Charter also contained Chapter VIII on regional arrangements. Article 52 provided that regional arrangements could deal with "such matters relating to the maintenance of international peace and security as are appropriate for regional action". Thus a case could be made under the Charter for the use of force if it were sanctioned by the American Republics acting under the Rio Treaty. The Organ of Consultation, pursuant to Articles 6 and 8 of that Treaty, could recommend measures, including the use of armed force, to meet a situation endangering the peace of America. As to the prospects for securing the necessary two-thirds vote in the Organ of Consultation, Mr. Martin would have something to say about that.

If the contention were advanced that a defensive quarantine voted under the Rio Treaty constituted "enforcement action" under Article 53 of the United Nations Charter, and therefore required the authorization of the Security Council, we would be able to make a reasonably good argument to the contrary. While our ability to persuade seven members of the Security Council to vote with us on this issue might be uncertain, we would in any event be able to prevent a vote going against our position.

Mr. Martin then gave as his estimate that the United States could secure immediately a vote of 14 in the OAS. He thought the majority could be increased within 24 hours to 17 or perhaps even 18 or 19. He was hopeful in regard to Ecuador and Chile, and believed there was a good chance of getting Mexico. The Attorney General said the President would be placed in an impossible position if we went to the OAS and then failed to get the necessary votes, or if there were a delay. He asked if we could be perfectly sure of the outcome before seeking OAS concurrence. Mr. Martin said he hated to guarantee anything, but he had a lot of confidence about this. You couldn't go to the American Republics in advance without loss of security, but he felt that a last-minute approach to heads of state, laying the situation on the line, would produce the votes. The Attorney General again expressed his great concern at the possibility of a slip.

There followed a discussion covering the meeting held the night before with the President. One participant looked back on the meeting as having arrived at a tentative conclusion to institute a blockade, and thought the President had been satisfied at the consensus by then arrived at among his advisers. General Taylor quickly indicated that he had not concurred and that the Joint Chiefs had reserved their position.

Mr. Bundy then said that he had reflected a good deal upon the situation in the course of a sleepless night, and he doubted whether the strategy group was serving the President as well as it might, if it merely recommended a blockade. He had spoken with the President this morning, and he felt there was further work to be done. A blockade would not remove the missiles. Its effects were uncertain and in any event would be slow to be felt. Something more would be needed to get the missiles out of Cuba. This would be made more difficult by the prior publicity of a blockade and the consequent pressures from the United Nations for a negotiated settlement. An air strike would be quick and would take out the bases in a clean surgical operation. He favored decisive action with its advantages of surprises and confronting the world with a fait accompli.

Secretary Rusk asked Mr. Acheson for his views. Mr. Acheson said that Khrushchev had presented the United States with a direct challenge, we were involved in a test of wills, and the sooner we got to a showdown the better. He favored cleaning the missile bases out decisively with an air strike. There was something else to remember. This wasn't just another instance of Soviet missiles aimed at the United States. Here they were in the hands of a madman whose actions would be perfectly irresponsible; the usual restraints operating on the Soviets would not apply. We had better act, and act quickly. So far as questions of international law might be involved, Mr. Acheson agreed with Mr. Katzenbach's position that self-defense was an entirely sufficient justification. But if there were to be imported a qualification or requirement of approval by the OAS, as apparently suggested by Mr. Meeker, he could not go along with that.

Secretary Dillon said he agreed there should be a quick air strike. Mr. McCone was of the same opinion.

General Taylor said that a decision now to impose a blockade was a decision to abandon the possibility of an air strike. A strike would be feasible for only a few more days; after that the missiles would be operational. Thus it was now or never for an air strike. He favored a strike. If it were to take place Sunday morning, a decision would have to be made at once so that the necessary preparations could be ordered. For a Monday morning strike, a decision would have to be reached tomorrow. Forty-eight hours' notice was required.

Secretary McNamara said that he would give orders for the necessary military dispositions, so that if the decision were for a strike the Air Force would be ready. He did not, however, advocate an air strike, and favored the alternative of blockade.

Under Secretary Ball said that he was a waverer between the two courses of action.

The Attorney General said with a grin that he too had had a talk with the President, indeed very recently this morning. There seemed to be three main possibilities as the Attorney General analyzed the situation: one was to do nothing, and that would be unthinkable; another was an air strike; the third was a blockade. He thought it would be very, very difficult indeed for the President if the decision were to be for an air strike, with all the memory of Pearl Harbor and with all the implications this would have for us in whatever world there would be afterward. For 175 years we had not been that kind of country. A sneak attack was not in our traditions. Thousands of Cubans would be killed without warning, and a lot of Russians too. He favored action, to make known unmistakably the seriousness of United States determination to get the missiles out of Cuba, but he thought the action should allow the Soviets some room for maneuver to pull back from their over-extended position in Cuba.

Mr. Bundy, addressing himself to the Attorney General, said this was very well but a blockade would not eliminate the bases; an air strike would.

I asked at this point: who would be expected to be the government of Cuba after an air strike? Would it be anyone other than Castro? If not, would anything be solved, and would we not be in a worse situation than before? After a pause, Mr. Martin replied that, of course, a good deal might be different after a strike, and Castro might be toppled in the aftermath. Others expressed the view that we might have to proceed with invasion following a strike. Still another suggestion was that US armed forces seize the base areas alone in order to eliminate the missiles. Secretary McNamara thought this a very unattractive kind of undertaking from the military point of view.

Toward one o'clock Secretary Rusk said he thought this group could not make the decision as to what was to be done; that was for the President in consultation with his constitutional advisers. The Secretary thought the group's duty was to present to the President, for his consideration, fully staffed-out alternatives. Accordingly, two working groups should be formed, one to work up the blockade alternative and the other to work up air strike. Mr. Johnson was designated to head the former, and Mr. Bundy the latter. Mr. Johnson was to have with him Ambassador Thompson, Deputy Secretary Gilpatric, Mr. Martin, Mr. Nitze, and Mr. Meeker. Mr. Bundy was to have Secretary Dillon, Mr. Acheson, and General Taylor. Mr. McCone, when asked to serve with the air strike group, begged off on the ground that his position and duties on the US Intelligence Board made it undesirable for him to participate in the working group. Mr. Katzenbach was detailed to the Johnson group, later visiting the Bundy group to observe and possibly serve as a devil's advocate.

Mr. Sorensen commented that he thought he had absorbed enough to start on the draft of a speech for the President. There was some inconclusive discussion on the timing of such a speech, on the danger of leaks before then, and on the proper time for meeting with the President once more, in view of his current Western campaign trip.

Before the whole group dispersed, Ambassador Thompson said the Soviets attached importance to questions of legality and we should be able to present a strong legal case. The Attorney General, as he was about to leave the room, said he thought there was ample legal basis for a blockade. I said: yes, that is so provided the Organ of Consultation under the Rio Treaty adopted an appropriate resolution. The Attorney General said: "That's all political; it's not legal." On leaving the room, he said to Mr. Katzenbach, half humorously: "Remember now, you're working for me."

The two groups met separately until four o'clock. They then reconvened and were joined once more by the cabinet officers who had been away in the earlier afternoon.

The Johnson group scenario, which was more nearly complete and was ready earlier, was discussed first. Numerous criticisms were advanced. Some were answered; others led to changes. There was again a discussion of timing, now in relation to a Presidential radio address. Mr. Martin thought Sunday might be too early, as it would be virtually impossible to get to all the Latin American heads of state on Sunday. Ambassador Thompson made the point that 24 hours must be allowed to elapse between announcement of the blockade and enforcement, so as to give the Soviet Government time to get instructions to their ship captains.

Approximately two hours were spent on the Johnson scenario. About 6 o'clock the Bundy approach was taken up, its author saying, "It's been much more fun for us up to this point, since we've had a chance to poke holes in the blockade plan; now the roles will be reversed." Not much more than half an hour was spent on the Bundy scenario.

More than once during the afternoon Secretary McNamara voiced the opinion that the US would have to pay a price to get the Soviet missiles out of Cuba. He thought we would at least have to give up our missile bases in Italy and Turkey and would probably have to pay more besides. At different times the possibility of nuclear conflict breaking out was referred to. The point was made that, once the Cuban missile installations were complete and operational, a new strategic situation would exist, with the United States more directly and immediately under the gun than ever before. A striking Soviet military push into the Western Hemisphere would have succeeded and become effective. The clock could not be turned back, and things would never be the same again. During this discussion, the Attorney General said that in looking forward into the future it would be better for our children and grandchildren if we decided to face the Soviet threat, stand up to it, and eliminate it, now. The circumstances for doing so at some future time were bound to be more unfavorable, the risks would be greater, the chances of success less good.

Secretary Rusk, toward the end of the afternoon, stated his approach to the problem as follows: the US needed to move in a way such that a planned action would be followed by a pause in which the great powers could step back from the brink and have time to consider and work out a solution rather than be drawn inexorably from one action to another and escalate into general nuclear war. The implication of his statement was that he favored blockade rather than strike.

In the course of the afternoon discussion, the military representatives, especially Secretary McNamara, came to expressing the view that an air strike could be made some time after the blockade was instituted in the event the blockade did not produce results as to the missile bases in Cuba. The Attorney General took particular note of this shift, and toward the end of the day made clear that the firmly favored blockade as the first step; other steps subsequently were not precluded and could be considered; he thought it was now pretty clear what the decision should be.

At about six-thirty Governor Stevenson came into the room. After a few minutes, Secretary Rusk asked him if he had some views on the question of what to do. He replied: "Yes, most emphatic views." When queried as to them, he said that in view of the course the discussion was taking he didn't think it was necessary to express them then. When asked: "But you are in favor of blockade, aren't you?", he answered affirmatively. He went on to say he thought we must look beyond the particular immediate action of blockade; we need to develop a plan for solution of the problem—elements for negotiation designed to settle the current crisis in a stable and satisfactory way and enable us to move forward on wider problems; he was working on some ideas for a settlement. One possibility would be the demilitarization of Cuba under effective international supervision, perhaps accompanied by neutralization of the island under international guaranties and with UN observers to monitor compliance.

Once again there was discussion of when another meeting with the President should be held. It was generally agreed that the President should continue on his trip until Sunday morning. He would be reachable by telephone prior to that time.

The meeting broke up about seven o'clock.

Special National Intelligence Estimate

SNIE 11-18-62
Washington, October 19, 1962.
SUBJECT
SNIE 11-18-62: Soviet Reactions to Certain US Courses of Action on Cuba

The Problem
To estimate probable Soviet reactions to certain US courses of action with respect to Cuba.

The Estimate
1. A major Soviet objective in their military buildup in Cuba is to demonstrate that the world balance of forces has shifted so far in their favor that the US can no longer prevent the advance of Soviet offensive power even into its own hemisphere. In this connection they assume, of course, that these deployments sooner or later will become publicly known.

2. It is possible that the USSR is installing these missiles primarily in order to use them in bargaining for US concessions

elsewhere. We think this unlikely, however. The public withdrawal of Soviet missiles from Cuba would create serious problems in the USSR's relations with Castro; it would cast doubt on the firmness of the Soviet intention to protect the Castro regime and perhaps on their commitments elsewhere.

3. If the US accepts the strategic missile buildup in Cuba, the Soviets would continue the buildup of strategic weapons in Cuba. We have no basis for estimating the force level which they would wish to reach, but it seems clear already that they intend to go beyond a token capability. They would probably expect their missile forces in Cuba to make some contribution to their total strategic capability vis-a-vis the US. We consider in Annex B the possible effects of a missile buildup in Cuba upon the overall relationship of strategic military power.

4. US acceptance of the strategic missile buildup would provide strong encouragement to Communists, pro-Communists, and the more anti-American sectors of opinion in Latin America and elsewhere. Conversely, anti-Communists and those who relate their own interests to those of the US would be strongly discouraged. It seems clear that, especially over the long run, there would be a loss of confidence in US power and determination and a serious decline of US influence generally.

Effect of Warning

5. If the US confronts Khrushchev with its knowledge of the MRBM deployment and presses for a withdrawal, we do not believe the Soviets would halt the deployment. Instead, they would propose negotiations on the general question of foreign bases, claiming equal right to establish Soviet bases and assuring the US of tight control over the missiles. They would probably link Cuba with the Berlin situation and emphasize their patience and preference for negotiations, implying that Berlin was held hostage to US actions in Cuba.

6. There is some slight chance that a warning to Castro might make a difference, since the Soviets could regard this as a chance to stand aside, but it also would give time for offers to

negotiate, continued buildup, and counterpressures, and we think the result in the end would be the same.

7. Any warning would of course degrade the element of surprise in a subsequent US attack.

Effect of Blockade

8. While the effectiveness of Castro's military machine might be impaired by a total US blockade, Castro would be certain to tighten internal security and would take ruthless action against any attempts at revolt. There is no reason to believe that a blockade of itself would bring down the Castro regime. The Soviets would almost certainly exert strong direct pressures elsewhere to end the blockade. The attitudes of other states toward a blockade action are not considered in this paper. It is obvious that the Soviets would heavily exploit all adverse reactions.

Soviet Reaction to Use of Military Force

9. If the US takes direct military action against Cuba, the Soviets would be placed automatically under great pressure to respond in ways which, if they could not save Cuba, would inflict an offsetting injury to US interests. This would be true whether the action was limited to an effort to neutralize the strategic missiles, or these missiles plus airfields, surface-to-air missile sites, or cruise missile sites, or in fact an outright invasion designed to destroy the Castro regime.

10. In reaction to any of the various forms of US action, the Soviets would be alarmed and agitated, since they have to date estimated that the US would not take military action in the face of Soviet warnings of the danger of nuclear war. They would recognize that US military action posed a major challenge to the prestige of the USSR. We must of course recognize the possibility that the Soviets, under pressure to respond, would again miscalculate and respond in a way which, through a series of actions and reactions, could escalate to general war.

11. On the other hand, the Soviets have no public treaty with Cuba and have not acknowledged that Soviet bases are on the

island. This situation provides them with a pretext for treating US military action against Cuba as an affair which does not directly involve them, and thereby avoiding the risks of a strong response. We do not believe that the USSR would attack the US, either from Soviet bases or with its missiles in Cuba, even if the latter were operational and not put out of action before they could be readied for firing.

12. Since the USSR would not dare to resort to general war and could not hope to prevail locally, the Soviets would almost certainly consider retaliatory actions outside Cuba. The timing and selection of such moves would depend heavily upon the immediate context of events and the USSR's appreciation of US attitudes. The most likely location for broad retaliation outside Cuba appears to be Berlin. They might react here with major harassments, interruptions of access to the city or even a blockade, with or without the signing of a separate peace treaty.

13. We believe that whatever course of retaliation the USSR elected, the Soviet leaders would not deliberately initiate general war or take military measures, which in their calculation, would run the gravest risks of general war

Minutes

Washington, October 20, 1962, 2:30-5:10 p.m.
PARTICIPANTS
The President
Attorney General
Robert F. Kennedy

CIA
John A. McCone, Director
Mr. Ray Cline
Mr. Arthur Lundahl
Mr. Chamberlain

Defense
Robert S. McNamara, Secretary
Roswell Gilpatric, Deputy Secretary
Paul Nitze, Assistant Secretary (ISA)

JCS
General Maxwell D. Taylor, USA, Chairman
OEP
Edward A. McDermott, Director
State
Dean Rusk, Secretary
George Ball, Under Secretary
U. Alexis Johnson, Deputy Under Secretary for Political Affairs
Adlai Stevenson, U.S. Ambassador to the UN
Edwin Martin, Assistant Secretary, Inter-American Affairs
Llewellyn E. Thompson, Ambassador-at-Large
Treasury
Douglas Dillon, Secretary
White House
McGeorge Bundy, Special Assistant to the President for National Security Affairs
Theodore Sorensen, Special Counsel
Kenneth O'Donnell, Special Assistant to the President
Bromley Smith, Executive Secretary, National Security Council

Intelligence Briefing
The first twenty minutes were spent in the presentation and discussion of photographic intelligence establishing the presence in Cuba of Soviet intermediate-range and medium-range missiles, mobile missile launchers and missile sites.

Mr. Ray Cline of the Central Intelligence Agency summarized the report of the Guided Missile and Astronautics Intelligence Committee, the Joint Atomic Energy Intelligence Committee, and the National Photographic Interpretation Center, dated October 19, 1962 (SC 09538-62). Mr. Arthur

Lundahl of CIA described the various missile sites and launching pads, displaying enlarged pictures identical to those in the Committee report.

In response to the President's question, Mr. Cline stated that there were no U-2 photographic reconnaissance missions over Cuba from August 29th to October 14th. The gap in photographic coverage was in part due to bad weather and in part to a desire to avoid activating the SAM Air Defense installations which the Russians were hurriedly installing in Cuba during this period. Since October 14th, nine high altitude missions have been flown. Information from these missions is not fully processed, but will be available for presentation by Monday.

In summary, the Council was informed that sixteen SS-4 missiles, with a range of 1020 nautical miles were now operational in Cuba and could be fired approximately eighteen hours after a decision to fire was taken. The bearing of these launchers was 315 degrees, i.e. toward the central area of the United States.

The President summarized the discussion of the intelligence material as follows. There is something to destroy in Cuba now and, if it is destroyed, a strategic missile capability would be difficult to restore. (Specific details of the briefing are contained in the attached Committee report.)

Blockage Track

Secretary McNamara explained to the President that there were differences among his advisers which had resulted in the drafting of alternative courses of action. He added that the military planners are at work on measures to carry out all recommended courses of action in order that, following a Presidential decision, fast action could be taken.

Secretary McNamara described his view as the "blockade route." This route is aimed at preventing any addition to the strategic missiles already deployed to Cuba and eventually to eliminate these missiles. He said to do this we should institute a blockade of Cuba and be prepared to take armed action in specified instances.

(The President was handed a copy of Ted Sorensen's "blockade route" draft of a Presidential message, which he read.)

Secretary McNamara concluded by explaining that following the blockade, the United States would negotiate for the removal of the strategic missiles from Cuba. He said we would have to be prepared to accept the withdrawal of United States strategic missiles from Turkey and Italy and possibly agreement to limit our use of Guantanamo to a specified limited time. He added that we could obtain the removal of the missiles from Cuba only if we were prepared to offer something in return during negotiations. He opposed as too risky the suggestion that we should issue an ultimatum to the effect that we would order an air attack on Cuba if the missiles were not removed. He said he was prepared to tell Khrushchev we consider the missiles in Cuba as Soviet missiles and that if they were used against us, we would retaliate by launching missiles against the USSR.

Secretary McNamara pointed out that SNIE 11-19-62, dated October 20, 1962, estimates that the Russians will not use force to push their ships through our blockade. He cited Ambassador Bohlen's view that the USSR would not take military action, but would limit its reaction to political measures in the United Nations.

Secretary McNamara listed the disadvantages of the blockade route as follows:

1. It would take a long time to achieve the objective of eliminating strategic missiles from Cuba.

2. It would result in serious political trouble in the United States.

3. The world position of the United States might appear to be weakening.

The advantages which Secretary McNamara cited are:

1. It would cause us the least trouble with our allies.

2. It avoids any surprise air attack on Cuba, which is contrary to our tradition.

3. It is the only military course of action compatible with our position as a leader of the free world.

4. It avoids a sudden military move which might provoke a response from the USSR which could result in escalating actions leading to general war.

The President pointed out that during a blockade, more missiles would become operational, and upon the completion of sites and launching pads, the threat would increase. He asked General Taylor how many missiles we could destroy by air action on Monday.

General Taylor reported that the Joint Chiefs of Staff favor an air strike on Tuesday when United States forces could be in a state of readiness. He said he did not share Secretary McNamara's fear that if we used nuclear weapons in Cuba, nuclear weapons would be used against us.

Secretary Rusk asked General Taylor whether we dared to attack operational strategic missile sites in Cuba.

General Taylor responded that the risk of these missiles being used against us was less than if we permitted the missiles to remain there.

The President pointed out that on the basis of the intelligence estimate there would be some fifty strategic missiles operational in mid-December, if we went the blockade route and took no action to destroy the sites being developed.

General Taylor said that the principal argument he wished to make was that now was the time to act because this would be the last chance we would have to destroy these missiles. If we did not act now, the missiles would be camouflaged in such a way as to make it impossible for us to find them. Therefore, if they were not destroyed, we would have to live with them with all the consequent problems for the defense of the United States.

The President agreed that the missile threat became worse each day, adding that we might wish, looking back, that we had done earlier what we are now preparing to do.

Secretary Rusk said that a blockade would seriously affect the Cuban missile capability in that the Soviets would be unable to deploy to Cuba any missiles in addition to those now there.

Under Secretary Ball said that if an effective blockade was established, it was possible that our photographic intelligence would reveal that there were no nuclear warheads in Cuba; hence, none of the missiles now there could be made operational.

General Taylor indicated his doubt that it would be possible to prevent the Russians from deploying warheads to Cuba by means of a blockade because of the great difficulty of setting up an effective air blockade.

Secretary McNamara stated that if we knew that a plane was flying nuclear warheads to Cuba, we should immediately shoot it down. Parenthetically, he pointed out there are now 6000 to 8000 Soviet personnel in Cuba.

The President asked whether the institution of a blockade would appear to the free world as a strong response to the Soviet action. He is particularly concerned about whether the Latin American countries would think that the blockade was an appropriate response to the Soviet challenge.

The Attorney General returned to the point made by General Taylor, i.e. that now is the last chance we will have to destroy Castro and the Soviet missiles deployed in Cuba.

Mr. Sorensen said he did not agree with the Attorney General or with General Taylor that this was our last chance. He said a missile buildup would end if, as everyone seemed to agree, the Russians would not use force to penetrate the United States blockade.

Air Strike Route

Mr. Bundy handed to the President the "air strike alternative," which the President read. It was also referred to as the Bundy plan.

The Attorney General told the President that this plan was supported by Mr. Bundy, General Taylor, the Joint Chiefs of Staff, and with minor variations, by Secretary Dillon and Director McCone.

General Taylor emphasized the opportunity available now to take out not only all the missiles, but all the Soviet medium bombers (IL-28) which were neatly lined up in the open on airbases in Cuba.

Mr. McNamara cautioned that an air strike would not destroy all the missiles and launchers in Cuba, and, at best, we could knock out two-thirds of these missiles. Those missiles not destroyed could be fired from mobile launchers not destroyed. General Taylor said he was unable to explain why the IL-28 medium bombers had been left completely exposed on two airfields. The only way to explain this, he concluded, was on the ground that the Cubans and the Russians did not anticipate United States air strike.

Secretary Rusk said he hesitated to ask the question but he wondered whether these planes were decoys. He also wondered whether the Russians were trying to entice us into a trap. Secretary McNamara stated his strong doubt that these planes were decoys. Director McCone added that the Russians would not have sent one hundred shiploads of equipment to Cuba solely to play a "trick". General Taylor returned to the point he had made earlier, namely, that if we do not destroy the missiles and the bombers, we will have to change our entire military way of dealing with external threats.

The President raised the question of advance warning prior to military action—whether we should give a minimum of two hours notice of an air strike to permit Soviet personnel to leave the area to be attacked.

General Taylor said that the military would be prepared to live with a twenty-four hour advance notice or grace period if such advance notice was worthwhile politically. The President expressed his doubt that any notice beyond seven hours had any political value.

There was a brief discussion of the usefulness of sending a draft message to Castro, and a copy of such message was circulated.

The President stated flatly that the Soviet planes in Cuba did not concern him particularly. He said we must be prepared to live with the Soviet threat as represented by Soviet bombers. However, the existence of strategic missiles in Cuba had an entirely different impact throughout Latin America. In his view the existence of fifty planes in Cuba did not affect the balance of power, but the missiles already in Cuba were an entirely different matter.

The Attorney General said that in his opinion a combination of the blockade route and the air strike route was very attractive to him. He felt we should first institute the blockade. In the event that the Soviets continued to build up the missile capability in Cuba, then we should inform the Russians that we would destroy the missiles, the launchers, and the missile sites. He said he favored a short wait during which time the Russians could react to the blockade. If the Russians did not halt the development of the missile capability, then we would proceed to make an air strike. The advantage of proceeding in this way, he added, was that we would get away from the Pearl Harbor surprise attack aspect of the air strike route.

Mr. Bundy pointed out that there was a risk that we would act in such a way as to get Khrushchev to commit himself fully to the support of Castro.

Secretary Rusk doubted that a delay of twenty-four hours in initiating an air strike was of any value. He said he now favored proceeding on the blockade track.

Secretary Dillon mentioned seventy-two hours as the time between instituting the blockade and initiating an air strike in the event we receive no response to our initial action.

Director McCone stated his opposition to an air strike, but admitted that in his view a blockade was not enough. He argued that we should institute the blockade and tell the Russians that if the missiles were not dismantled within seventy-two hours, the United States would destroy the missiles by air attack. He called attention to the risk involved in a long drawn-out period during which the Cubans could, at will, launch the missiles against the United States. Secretary Dillon said that the existence of strategic missiles in Cuba was, in his opinion, not negotiable. He believed that any effort to negotiate the removal of the missiles would involve a price so high that the United States could not accept it. If the missiles are not removed or eliminated, he continued, the United States will lose all of its friends in Latin America, who will become convinced that our fear is such that we cannot act. He admitted that the limited use of force involved in a blockade would make the military task much harder and would involve the great danger of the launching of these missiles by the Cubans.

Deputy Secretary Gilpatric saw the choice as involving the use of limited force or of unlimited force. He was prepared to face the prospect of an air strike against Cuba later, but he opposed the initial use of all-out military force such as a surprise air attack. He defined a blockade as being the application of the limited use of force and doubted that such limited use could be combined with an air strike.

General Taylor argued that a blockade would not solve our problem or end the Cuban missile threat. He said that eventually we would have to use military force and, if we waited, the use of military force would be much more costly.

Secretary McNamara noted that the air strike planned by the Joint Chiefs involved 800 sorties. Such a strike would result in several thousand Russians being killed, chaos in Cuba, and efforts to overthrow the Castro government. In his view the probability was high that an air strike would lead inevitably to an invasion. He doubted that the Soviets would take an air strike on Cuba without resorting to a very major response. In such an event, the United States would lose control of the situation which could escalate to general war.

The President agreed that a United States air strike would lead to a major Soviet response, such as blockading Berlin. He agreed that at an appropriate time we would have to acknowledge that we were willing to take strategic missiles out of Turkey and Italy if this issue was raised by the Russians. He felt that implementation of a blockade would also result in Soviet reprisals, possibly the blockade of Berlin. If we instituted a blockade on Sunday, then by Monday or Tuesday we would know whether the missile development had ceased or whether it was continuing. Thus, we would be in a better position to know what move to make next.

Secretary Dillon called attention to the fact that even if the Russians agreed to dismantle the missiles now in Cuba, continuing inspection would be required to ensure that the missiles were not again made ready.

The President said that if it was decided to go the Bundy route, he would favor an air strike which would destroy only missiles. He repeated this view that we would have to live with the threat arising out of the stationing in Cuba of Soviet bombers.

Secretary Rusk referred to an air strike as chapter two. He did not think we should initiate such a strike because of the risk of escalating actions leading to general war. He doubted that we should act without consultation of our allies. He said a sudden air strike had no support in the law or morality, and, therefore, must be ruled out. Reading from notes, he urged that we start the blockade and only go on to an air attack when we knew the reaction of the Russians and of our allies.

At this point Director McCone acknowledged that we did not know positively that nuclear warheads for the missiles deployed had actually arrived in Cuba. Although we had evidence of the construction of storage places for nuclear weapons, such weapons may not yet have been sent to Cuba.

The President asked what we would say to those whose reaction to our instituting a blockade now would be to ask why we had not blockaded last July.

Both Mr. Sorensen and Mr. Ball made the point that we did not institute a blockade in July because we did not then know of the existence of the strategic missiles in Cuba.

Secretary Rusk suggested that our objective was an immediate freeze of the strategic missile capability in Cuba to be inspected by United Nations observation teams stationed at the missile sites. He referred to our bases in Turkey, Spain and Greece as being involved in any negotiation covering foreign bases. He said a United Nations group might be sent to Cuba to reassure those who might fear that the United States was planning an invasion.

Ambassador Stevenson stated his flat opposition to a surprise air strike, which he felt would ultimately lead to a United States invasion of Cuba. He supported the institution of the blockade and predicted that such action would reduce the chance of Soviet retaliation of a nature which would inevitably escalate. In his view our aim is to end the existing missile threat in Cuba without casualties and without escalation. He urged that we offer the Russians a settlement involving the withdrawal of our missiles from Turkey and our evacuation of Guantanamo base.

The President sharply rejected the thought of surrendering our base at Guantanamo in the present situation. He felt that such action would convey to the world that we had been frightened into abandoning our position. He was not opposed to discussing withdrawal of our missiles from Turkey and Greece, but he was firm in saying we should only make such a proposal in the future.

The Attorney General thought we should convey our firm intentions to the Russians clearly and suggested that we might tell the Russians that we were turning over nuclear weapons and missiles to the West Germans.

Ambassador Thompson stated his view that our first action should be the institution of a blockade. Following this, he thought we should launch an air strike to destroy the missiles and sites, after giving sufficient warning so that Russian nationals could leave the area to be attacked.

The President said he was ready to go ahead with the blockade and to take actions necessary to put us in a position to undertake an air strike on the missiles and missile sites by Monday or Tuesday.

General Taylor summarized the military actions already under way, including the quiet reinforcement of Guantanamo by infiltrating marines and the positioning of ships to take out United States dependents from Guantanamo on extremely short notice.

The Attorney General said we could implement a blockade very quickly and prepare for an air strike to be launched later if we so decided.

The President said he was prepared to authorize the military to take those preparatory actions which they would have to take in anticipation of the military invasion of Cuba. He suggested that we inform the Turks and the Italians that they should not fire the strategic missiles they have even if attacked. The warheads for missiles in Turkey and Italy could be dismantled. He agreed that we should move to institute a blockade as quickly as we possibly can.

In response to a question about further photographic surveillance of Cuba, Secretary McNamara recommended, and the President agreed, that no low level photographic reconnaissance should be undertaken now because we have decided to institute a blockade.

Secretary Rusk recommended that a blockade not be instituted before Monday in order to provide time required to consult our allies.

Mr. Bundy said the pressure from the press was becoming intense and suggested that one way of dealing with it was to announce shortly that we had obtained photographic evidence of the existence of strategic missiles in Cuba. This announcement would hold the press until the President made his television speech.

The President acknowledged that the domestic political heat following his television appearance would be terrific. He said he had opposed an invasion of Cuba but that now we were confronted with the possibility that by December there would be fifty strategic missiles deployed there. In explanation as to why we have not acted sooner to deal with the threat from Cuba, he pointed out that only now do we have the kind of evidence which we can make available to our allies in order to convince them of the necessity of acting. Only now do we have a way of avoiding a split with our allies.

It is possible that we may have to make an early strike with or without warning next week. He stressed again the difference between the conventional military buildup in Cuba and the psychological impact throughout the world of the Russian deployment of strategic missiles to Cuba. General Taylor repeated his recommendation that any air strike in Cuba included attacks on the MIGs and medium bombers.

The President repeated his view that our world position would be much better if we attack only the missiles. He directed that air strike plans include only missiles and missile sites, preparations to be ready three days from now.

Under Secretary Ball expressed his view that a blockade should include all shipments of POL to Cuba. Secretary Rusk thought that POL should not now be included because such a decision would break down the distinction which we want to make between elimination of strategic missiles and the downfall of the Castro government. Secretary Rusk repeated his view that our objective is to destroy the offensive capability of the missiles in Cuba, not, at this time, seeking to overthrow Castro!

The President acknowledged that the issue was whether POL should be included from the beginning or added at a later time. He preferred to delay possibly as long as a week.

Secretary Rusk called attention to the problem involved in referring to our action as a blockade. He preferred the use of the word "quarantine".

Parenthetically, the President asked Secretary Rusk to reconsider present policy of refusing to give nuclear weapons assistance to France. He expressed the view that in light of present circumstances a refusal to help the French was not worthwhile. He thought that in the days ahead we might be able to gain the needed support of France if we stopped refusing to help them with their nuclear weapons project.

There followed a discussion of several sentences in the "blockade route" draft of the President's speech. It was agreed that the President should define our objective in terms of halting "offensive missile preparations in Cuba". Reference to economic pressures on Cuba would not be made in this context.

The President made clear that in the United Nations we should emphasize the subterranean nature of the missile buildup in Cuba. Only if we were asked would we respond that we were prepared to talk about the withdrawal of missiles from Italy and Turkey. In such an eventuality, the President pointed out that we would have to make clear to the Italians and the Turks that withdrawing strategic missiles was not a retreat and that we would be prepared to replace these missiles by providing a more effective deterrent, such as the assignment of Polaris submarines. The President asked Mr. Nitze to study the problems arising out of the withdrawal of missiles from Italy and Turkey, with particular reference to complications which would arise in NATO. The President made clear that our emphasis should be on the missile threat from Cuba.

Ambassador Stevenson reiterated his belief that we must be more forthcoming about giving up our missile bases in Turkey and Italy. He stated again his belief that the present situation required that we offer to give up such bases in order to induce the Russians to remove the strategic missiles from Cuba.

Mr. Nitze flatly opposed making any such offer, but said he would not object to discussing this question in the event that negotiations developed from our institution of a blockade.

The President concluded the meeting by stating that we should be ready to meet criticism of our deployment of missiles abroad but we should not initiate negotiations with a base withdrawal proposal.

Notes

Washington, October 21, 1962.

1. The meeting was held in the Oval Room at the White House and lasted from 11:30 a.m. to approximately 12:30 p.m. In attendance were the Attorney General, General Taylor, General Sweeney and the Secretary of Defense.

2. The Secretary of Defense stated that following the start of an air attack, the initial units of the landing force could invade Cuba within 7 days. The movement of troops in preparation for

such an invasion will start at the time of the President's speech. No mobilization of Reserve forces is required for such an invasion until the start of the air strike. General LeMay had stated that the transport aircraft, from Reserve and Guard units, which would be required for participation in such an invasion can be fully operational within 24 to 48 hours after the call to active duty.

3. The Secretary of Defense reported that, based on information which became available during the night, it now appears that there is equipment in Cuba for approximately 40 MRBM or IRBM launchers. (Mr. McCone, who joined the group 15 or 20 minutes after the start of the discussion, confirmed this report.) The location of the sites for 36 of these launchers is known. 32 of the 36 known sites appear to have sufficient equipment on them to be included in any air strike directed against Cuba's missile capability.

4. We believe that 40 launchers would normally be equipped with 80 missiles. John McCone reported yesterday that a Soviet ship believed to be the vessel in which the Soviets have been sending missiles to Cuba has made a sufficient number of trips to that island within recent weeks to offload approximately 48 missiles. Therefore, we assume there are approximately that number on the Island today, although we have only located approximately 30 of these.

5. General Sweeney outlined the following plan of air attack, the object of which would be the destruction of the known Cuban missile capability.

a. The 5 surface-to-air missile installations in the vicinity of the known missile sites would each be attacked by approximately 8 aircraft; the 3 MIG airfields defending the missile sites would be covered by 12 U.S. aircraft per field. In total, the defense suppression operations, including the necessary replacement aircraft, would require approximately 100 sorties.

b. Each of the launchers at the 8 or 9 known sites (a total of approximately 32 to 36 launchers) would be attacked by 6 aircraft. For the purpose, a total of approximately 250 sorties would be flown.

c. The U.S. aircraft covering the 3 MIG airfields would attack the MIG's if they became airborne. General Sweeney strongly recommended attacks on each of the airfields to destroy the MIG aircraft.

6. General Sweeney stated that he was certain the air strike would be "successful"; however, even under optimum conditions, it was not likely that all of the known missiles would be destroyed. (As noted in 4 above, the known missiles are probably no more than 60% of the total missiles on the Island.) General Taylor stated, "The best we can offer you is to destroy 90% of the known missiles." General Taylor, General Sweeney and the Secretary of Defense all strongly emphasized that in their opinion the initial air strike must be followed by strikes on subsequent days and that these in turn would lead inevitably to an invasion.

7. CIA representatives, who joined the discussion at this point, stated that it is probable the missiles which are operational (it is estimated there are now between 8 and 12 operational missiles on the Island) can hold indefinitely a capability for firing with from 2-1/2 to 4 hours' notice. Included in the notice period is a countdown requiring 20 to 40 minutes. In relation to the countdown period, the first wave of our attacking aircraft would give 10 minutes of warning; the second wave, 40 minutes of warning; and the third wave a proportionately greater warning.

8. As noted above, General Sweeney strongly recommended that any air strike include attacks on the MIG aircraft and, in addition, the IL28s. To accomplish the destruction of these aircraft, the total number of sorties of such an air strike should be increased to 500. The President agreed that if an air strike is ordered, it should probably include in its objective the destruction of the MIG aircraft and the IL28s.

9. The President directed that we be prepared to carry out the air strike Monday morning or any time thereafter during the remainder of the week. The President recognized that the

Secretary of Defense was opposed to the air strike Monday morning, and that General Sweeney favored it. He asked the Attorney General and Mr. McCone for their opinions:

a. The Attorney General stated he was opposed to such a strike because:

(1) "It would be a Pearl Harbor type of attack."

(2) It would lead to unpredictable military responses by the Soviet Union which could be so serious as to lead to general nuclear war.

He stated we should start with the initiation of the blockade and thereafter "play for the breaks."

b. Mr. McCone agreed with the Attorney General, but emphasized he believed we should be prepared for an air strike and thereafter an invasion.

RSMc(2)

Minutes

Washington, October 21, 1962, 2:30-4:50 p.m.
PARTICIPANTS
The President
Attorney General Robert F. Kennedy

CIA
John A. McCone, Director
Mr. Ray Cline
Mr. Whelan
Mr. Arthur Lundahl

Defense
Robert S. McNamara, Secretary
Roswell Gilpatric, Deputy Secretary
Paul Nitze, Assistant Secretary (ISA)

JCS

General Maxwell D. Taylor

Admiral George W. Anderson, Jr., USN, Chief of Naval Operations

OEP

Edward A. McDermott, Director

State

Dean Rusk, Secretary

George Ball, Under Secretary

U. Alexis Johnson, Deputy Under Secretary for Political Affairs

Adlai Stevenson, U.S. Representative to the UN

Edwin Martin, Assistant Secretary, Inter-American Affairs

Llewellyn E. Thompson, Ambassador-at-Large

Treasury

Douglas Dillon, Secretary

USIA

Donald Wilson, Acting Director

White House

McGeorge Bundy, Special Assistant to the President for National Security Affairs

Theodore Sorensen, Special Counsel

Bromley Smith, Executive Secretary, National Security Council

Others:

Mr. Robert Lovett

(There is attached a tentative agenda for today's meeting, which was followed in large part.)

Introduction

Intelligence officers summarized new information which had become available since yesterday's meeting. Attached is a page highlighting the new facts presented to the Council.

Substantial Issues in a Draft Presidential Speech

The Council members read the third draft of the President's speech. (Copy attached.) There was some discussion of the date when positive information as to the existence of strategic missiles in Cuba became available. The draft was revised to state that such information became available Tuesday morning, October 16th.

The draft speech summarized the number of missiles and the number of sites known to exist in Cuba. Secretary McNamara recommended, and the President agreed, that specific numbers of missiles and sites be deleted.

The question was raised as to whether the speech should emphasize Soviet responsibility for the missile deployment or Castro's irresponsibility in accepting them. Secretary Rusk argued that we must hold the USSR responsible because it is important to emphasize the extra-hemispheric aspect of the missile deployment in order to increase support for our contemplated actions.

The President referred to the sentence mentioning the deployment of missiles by the Soviet Union and called attention to our deployment of missiles to Italy. Secretary Rusk pointed out that our missiles were deployed to NATO countries only after those countries were threatened by deployed Soviet missiles. Hence, our deployment was part of the confrontation of Soviet power, and, therefore, unrelated to the Cuban deployment by the USSR.

The President pointed out that Soviet missiles were in place, aimed at European countries, before we deployed United States missiles to Europe.

Secretary Dillon recalled that we sent United States missiles to Europe because we had so many of them we did not know where to put them.

The President referred to the sentence in the draft speech which states that the USSR secretly transferred weapons to Cuba. He said we should emphasize the clandestine manner in which the USSR had acted in Cuba.

The Attorney General wanted to be certain that the text as drafted did not preclude us from giving nuclear weapons to Western Germany, West Berlin, and France in the event we decided to do so.

It was agreed that no message would be sent to President Dorticos of Cuba at the present time and the draft speech was so revised.

The question of whether our actions should be described as a blockade or a quarantine was debated. Although the legal meaning of the two words is identical, Secretary Rusk said he preferred "quarantine" for political reasons in that it avoids comparison with the Berlin blockade. The President agreed to use "quarantine" and pointed out that if we so desired we could later institute a total blockade.

Both Secretary Dillon and Director McCone urged that the speech state that we were seeking to prevent all military equipment from reaching Cuba. They argued that later we might act to prevent all equipment from reaching Cuba even though at present our objective was to block offensive missile equipment.

The President preferred the phrase "offensive missile equipment" on the grounds that within forty-eight hours we will know the Soviet reaction. At such time we will know whether, as is expected, the Soviets turn back their ships rather than submit to inspection. Secretary McNamara agreed we should proceed in two stages. Initially our objective is to block offensive weapons and later we can extend our blockade to all weapons, if we so decide.

The President parenthetically pointed out that we were not taking action under the Monroe Doctrine.

General Taylor returned to a sentence in the earlier part of the draft (bottom of page 4) and asked whether we were firm on the phrase "whatever steps are necessary." The President agreed that these words should remain so that he would not be hindered from taking additional measures if we so decide at a later date.

(The President asked Under Secretary Ball to obtain assurances that Dakar would not be used by the Soviets for air shipments to Cuba.)

Secretary Rusk commented that our objective was to "put out the fire" in Cuba and get United Nations teams to inspect all missile activity in Cuba. The President felt that a better tactic was for us initially to frighten the United Nations representatives with the prospect of all kinds of actions and then, when a resolution calling for the withdrawal of missiles from Cuba, Turkey and Italy was proposed, we could consider supporting such a resolution.

Ambassador Stevenson said we should take the initiative by calling a U.N. Security Council meeting to demand an immediate missile standstill in Cuba. Secretary Rusk pointed out that following the President's speech we would either be in the posture of a complainant or of a defendant.

Mr. Sorensen said our posture should be to accuse the Soviets of being the aggressors and seek to persuade others to agree with us. He foresaw that some nations in the United Nations would immediately try to label us as the aggressors because of the actions which we had taken.

Secretary Rusk raised the question of whether we should move first in the United Nations or first in the OAS. He said our United Nations action should be aimed at removing the missile threat while our objective on the OAS would be to persuade other Latin American countries to act with us under the Rio Treaty.

In response to the President's question, Assistant Secretary Martin said that if there were a United Nations action before the OAS acted, the usefulness of the OAS would be seriously affected. Secretary Rusk felt we should act first in the OAS, then in the United Nations where our action program could be more flexible.

The President agreed that a reference in the draft speech to a Caribbean security force should be dropped.

The President said we should pin the responsibility for the developments in Cuba directly on Khrushchev. In response to the President's question, Ambassador Thompson agreed — naming Khrushchev would make it harder for him to reverse his actions in Cuba, but such reference to him would be more effective in producing favorable actions.

The President asked that the phrases describing the horrors of war should be deleted.

Ambassador Thompson urged, and the President agreed, that we should use the part of the TASS statement on Cuba which flatly states that the Russians have all the weapons they need and require no more for their defense. Therefore, the only reason for Soviet deployment of weapons to Cuba is the aim of dominating the Western hemisphere.

The President agreed that the invitation to a summit meeting should be deleted.

Ambassador Stevenson repeated that he favored an early conference with the Russians on terms acceptable to us, to be held in an atmos-phere free of threat. The President responded that he did not want to appear to be seeking a summit meeting as a result of Khrushchev's actions. Ambassador Thompson agreed. The President added that we should not look toward holding a meeting until it is clear to us what Khrushchev really thinks he will obtain worldwide as a result of his actions in Cuba.

Secretary Rusk said our first objective was to get a fully inspected missile standstill in Cuba before we sit down to talk with the Russians. Mr. McCone was concerned that if we let it be known that we are prepared to talk to the Russians now, it would appear to outsiders that our only response to Khrushchev's challenge was to negotiate.

The Attorney General said that in his view we should anticipate a Soviet reaction involving a movement in Berlin. Secretary Dillon felt that the Soviet reaction in Berlin would be governed by the actions we would take in response to the Russian missile deployment in Cuba.

Following a discussion of ways in which we could reach the Cuban people through television despite Cuban jamming efforts, the President told Mr. Wilson that we should go ahead with the television project involving the relay of signals via instruments aboard a ship at sea for use anywhere.

The Attorney General felt that the paragraphs in the President's draft speech addressed to the Cuban people were not personal enough. The President asked that these paragraphs be rewritten.

Following discussion of the pressure by the press for information, the President decided that no information on the missile deployment would be given out today.

In response to a Presidential question, General Taylor said an invasion of Cuba could be carried out seven days after the decision to invade had been taken. Secretary McNamara said the President had asked a question which was difficult to answer precisely. Present plans called for invasion to follow seven days after an initial air strike. The timing could be reduced, depending upon whether certain decisions were taken now. Some actions which were irreversible would have to be taken now in order to reduce the time when forces could be landed. He promised the President a breakdown of the decisions which he would have to take immediately in order to reduce the seven-day period.

The President said that in three or four days we might have to decide to act in order that we would not have to wait so long prior to the landing of our forces. As he understood the situation, a decision taken today would mean that an air strike could not be undertaken before seven days, and then seven days later the first forces could be ashore.

General Taylor explained that air action would be necessary to bring the situation under control prior to the dropping of paratroopers. He added that 90,000 men could be landed within an eleven-day period.

Secretary McNamara said that planning was being done under two assumptions. The first called for an air strike, and seven days later, landings would begin. Twenty-five thousand men would be put ashore the first day, and on the eighteenth day, 90,000 would be ashore. The second plan provided for the landing of 90,000 men in a twenty-three day period. The President told General Taylor that he wanted to do those things which would reduce the length of time between a decision to invade and the landing of the first troops.

The President said he believed that as soon as he had finished his speech, the Russians would: (a) hasten the construction and the development of their missile capability in Cuba, (b) announce that if we attack Cuba, Soviet rockets will fly, and (c) possibly make a move to squeeze us out of Berlin.

Secretary Dillon said that in his view a blockade would either inevitably lead to an invasion of Cuba or would result in negotiations, which he believes the Soviets would want very much. To agree to negotiations now would be a disaster for us. We would break up our alliances and convey to the world that we were impotent in the face of a Soviet challenge. Unless the Russians stop their missile buildup at once, we will have to invade Cuba in the next week, no matter what they say, if we are to save our world position. We cannot convey firm intentions to the Russians otherwise and we must not look to the world as if we were backing down.

Secretary McNamara expressed his doubt that an air strike would be necessary within the next week.

Admiral Anderson described, in response to the President's question, the way the blockade would be instituted. He added that the Navy did not need to call up reserves now to meet the immediate situation. He said that forty Navy ships were already in position. The Navy knew the positions of twenty-seven to thirty ships en route to Cuba. Eighteen ships were in Cuban ports, and fifteen were on their way home.

Admiral Anderson described the method to be used in the first interception of a Soviet ship. It was hoped that a cruiser rather than a destroyer would make this interception. It would follow accepted international rules. He favored a twenty-four hour grace period, beginning with the President's speech, during which the Russians could communicate with their ships, giving them instructions as to what to do in the event they were stopped by United States ships.

Secretary McNamara said he would recommend to the President later today which kinds of reserve forces should be called up. He felt that air reserves would be necessary if it were decided to make an air strike, but probably would not be needed if our action was limited to a blockade.

Admiral Anderson said we had a capability to protect United States ships in the Caribbean. If the Komar ships took any hostile action, they could be destroyed, thereby creating a new situation. If a MIG plane takes hostile action, he would like to be in a position to shoot it down, thereby creating again a new situation. He estimated that the Soviets could not get naval surface ships to the area in less than ten days and Soviet submarines could not get to the area in less than ten to fourteen days.

In response to a question, Admiral Anderson said that if the Navy received information that a Soviet submarine was en route to Havana, he would ask higher authority for permission to attack it.

Secretary McNamara said he favored rules of engagement which would permit responses to hostile actions, including attacks to destroy the source of the hostile action.

The President answered a question as to whether we were to stop all ships, including allied ships by saying that he favored stopping all ships in the expectation that allied ships would soon become discouraged and drop out of the Cuban trade.

Diplomatic Measures

Under Secretary Ball summarized a scenario (copy attached) providing for consultation with our allies. He said Dean Acheson would brief de Gaulle and the NATO Council, Ambassador Dowling would brief Adenauer, and Ambassador Bruce would brief Macmillan. Present at such briefings would be technical experts from CIA who could answer questions concerning the photographic intelligence which reveals the missile sites.

The President said we must assume that Khrushchev knows that we know of his missile deployments, and, therefore, he will be ready with a planned response. He asked that the draft speech emphasize his belief that the greatest danger to the United States in the present situation is doing nothing but acknowledging that in days to come we would be seriously threatened.

Ambassador Stevenson read from a list of problems which he foresaw in the United Nations. Secretary Rusk said we must decide on tactics for the Security Council meeting. He repeated his view that the aim of all our actions is to get a standstill of the missile development in Cuba to be inspected by United Nations observers and then be prepared to negotiate other issues.

The President asked Assistant Secretary of Defense Nitze to study the problem of withdrawing United States missiles from Turkey and Italy. Mr. Nitze said such a withdrawal was complicated because we must avoid giving the Europeans the impression that we are prepared to take nuclear weapons of all kinds out of Europe.

Secretary McNamara stated his firm view that the United States could not lift its blockade as long as the Soviet weapons remained in Cuba.

The President asked why we could not start with a demand for the removal or the withdrawal of the missiles and if at a later time we wanted to negotiate for a less favorable settlement, we could then decide to do so. The Attorney General said we should take the offensive in our presentation to the United Nations. Our attitude should not be defensive, especially in view of the fact that Soviet leaders had lied to us about the deployment of strategic missiles to Cuba.

The President interjected a directive that we reverse our policy on nuclear assistance to France in the light of the present situation.

Ambassador Stevenson repeated his view that the United States would be forced into a summit meeting and preferred to propose such a meeting.

The President disagreed, saying that we could not accept a neutral Cuba and the withdrawal from Guantanamo without indicating to Khrushchev that we were in a state of panic. An offer to accept Castro and give up Guantanamo must not be made because it would appear to be completely defensive. He said we should be clear that we would accept nothing less than the ending of the missile capability now in Cuba, no reinforcement of that capability, and no further construction of missile sites.

Secretary McNamara stated his view that in order to achieve such a result we would have to invade Cuba.

The President said what he was talking about was the dismantlement of missiles now in Cuba.

Ambassador Stevenson thought that we should institute a blockade, and when the Russians rejected our demand for a missile standstill in Cuba, we should defer any air strike until after we had talked to Khrushchev.

There followed a discussion as to whether we wanted to rely primarily on the United Nations or primarily on the OAS. Assistant Secretary of State Martin indicated that if we did not use the OAS in preference to the United Nations, we would jeopardize the entire hemispheric alliance. Under Secretary Ball agreed that we should put primary emphasis on the OAS and he preferred that any inspectors going to Cuba should be OAS inspectors rather than United Nations inspectors.

The President indicated a need for further discussion of this matter and suggested that Secretary Rusk speak to him later about it.

As the meeting concluded, the President asked that the word "miscalculate" be taken out of the draft letter prepared for him to send to Khrushchev. He recalled that in Vienna Khrushchev had revealed a misunderstanding of this word when translated into Russian. He also requested that reference to a meeting with Khrushchev be deleted from the draft letter.

Minutes

Washington, October 22, 1962, 3 p.m.

The President opened the meeting by asking Secretary Rusk to read the attached message from Prime Minister Macmillan which had just been received. Secretary Rusk observed that for a first reaction to information of our proposed blockade it was not bad. He added that it was comforting to learn that the British Prime Minister had not thought of anything we hadn't thought of.

The President commented that the Prime Minister's message contained the best argument for taking no action. What we now need are strong arguments to explain why we have to act as we are acting.

Secretary Rusk stated that the best legal basis for our blockade action was the Rio Treaty. The use of force would be justified on the ground of support for the principals of the United Nations Charter, not on the basis of Article 51, which might give the Russians a basis for attacking Turkey.

The Attorney General said that in his opinion our blockade action would be illegal if it were not supported by the OAS. In his view the greatest importance is attached to our obtaining the necessary fourteen favorable votes in the OAS. Secretary Rusk commented that if we do not win the support of the OAS, we are not necessarily acting illegally. He referred to the new situation created by modern weapons and he thought that rules of international law should not be taken as applying literally to a completely new situation. He said we need not abandon hope so early.

Mr. Salinger reported that Gromyko had departed from New York without making other than a usual departure statement containing nothing about Cuba.

Secretary Rusk said the Department had decided to hold off calling a Security Council meeting despite the possibility that the Russians might ask one first. The basis of this decision was that we would have to name Cuba in the documents requesting the Security Council meeting and this we did not wish to do.

Director McCone summarized the latest intelligence information and read from the attached document. He added that we have a report of a fleet of Soviet submarines which are in a position to reach Cuba in about a week. He also mentioned that the London Evening Standard had printed a great deal of information about the existence of Soviet strategic missiles in Cuba.

In response to a suggestion by Mr. Bundy, the President outlined the manner in which he expected Council Members to deal with the domestic aspects of the current situation. He said everyone should sing one song in order to make clear that there was now no difference among his advisers as to the proper course to follow. He pointed out the importance of fully supporting the course of action chosen which, in his view, represented a reasonable consensus. Any course is extremely troublesome and, as in the case of the Berlin wall, we are once again confronted with a difficult choice. If we undertake a tricky and unsatisfactory course, we do not even have the satisfaction of knowing what would have happened if we had acted differently. He mentioned that former Presidents, Eisenhower, Truman and Hoover had supported his decision during telephone conversations with each of them earlier in the day.

The President then summarized the arguments as to why we must act. We must reply to those whose reaction to the blockade would be to ask what had changed in view of the fact that we had been living in the past years under a threat of a missile nuclear attack by the USSR.

a. In September we had said we would react if certain actions were taken in Cuba. We have to carry out commitments which we had made publicly at that time.

b. The secret deployment by the Russians of strategic missiles to Cuba was such a complete change in their previous policy of not deploying such missiles outside the USSR that if we took no action in this case, we would convey to the Russians an impression that we would never act, no matter what they did anywhere.

c. Gromyko had left the impression that the Soviets were going to act in Berlin in the next few months. Therefore, if they acted now in response to our blockade action, we would only have brought on their Berlin squeeze earlier than expected.

d. The effect in Latin America would be very harmful to our interests if, by our failure to act, we gave the Latinos the impression that the Soviets were increasing their world position while ours was decreasing.

Two questions were raised which the President hoped would be discussed and settled the following day:

a. What is our response if one of our U-2 planes is shot down by a SAM missile?

b. If the missile development in Cuba continues, what is our next course of action?

The President concluded by acknowledging the difficulties which he was asking the military to accept because of the necessity of our taking action which warned Cuba of the possibility of an invasion.

Secretary Rusk commented that if anyone thought our response was weak, they were wrong because he believed that a "flaming crisis" was immediately ahead of us.

The President read from a list of questions and suggested answers which might be made public. The first question was why we had not acted earlier. The response is that we needed more evidence of the existence of Soviet strategic missiles in Cuba. This additional evidence was required in order to gain the necessary fourteen votes in the OAS. In addition, if we had acted earlier, we might have jeopardized our position in Berlin because our European Allies would have concluded that our preoccupation with Cuba was such as to reveal our lack of interest in Berlin, thus tempting the Russians to act in Berlin. Earlier action would undoubtedly have forced us to declare war on Cuba and this action, without the evidence we now have, would have thrown Latin American support to Castro.

There followed a discussion of why evidence of Soviet missiles was lacking. Information about the strategic missile sites was reported by the refugees but these reports could not be substantiated from aerial photography. Aerial photographs taken on August 29th revealed no missile sites. It was not until October 14th that photographic evidence of the sites and missiles was available. The cloud cover prevented photography for a period of time and the possibility of an attack on an overflying American plane led to a restriction on the number of U-2 flights. Mr. McCone felt that the information given to Senator Keating about the missile sites had come from refugee sources, which he had accepted without further substantiation. The Attorney General pointed out that even if there had been U-2 flights, construction at the missile sites was not far enough along to have been detected by photography much earlier than October 14. It was pointed out that all Soviet experts agreed that Khrushchev would not send strategic missiles to Cuba. Therefore, there was a tendency to downgrade the refugee reports.

Commenting on what should be said publicly about our actions in Cuba, Secretary Rusk cautioned that we should say nothing now which might tie our hands later in the event we wanted to take additional actions.

The President referred again to the question of distinguishing between Soviet missiles in Cuba and United States missiles in Turkey and Italy. Secretary Rusk read extracts from the NATO communique of 1959. The President thought that it was most important that everyone be fully briefed as to why these situations with respect to the deployment of missiles do not match. He again called attention to the secret deployment of the weapons and the TASS statement saying that the Russians had no need to position strategic missiles in foreign countries. Soviet missiles in Cuba have a quite different psychological effect than Soviet missiles positioned in the USSR in that the Soviet action in Cuba may in fact be a probing action to find out what we would be prepared to do in Berlin.

Secretary Rusk added that the threat to the United States from Soviet missiles in Cuba was of worldwide importance because this threat was to a country which in effect provided the sole defense of some forty Free World States.

The President suggested that we should make clear the difference between our Cuban blockade and the Berlin blockade by emphasizing that we were not preventing shipments of food and medicine to Cuba, but only preventing the delivery of offensive military equipment.

General Taylor asked how we should reply to the question: Are we preparing to invade? The President responded by saying that we should ask the press not to push this line of questioning and to accept our statement that we are taking all precautionary moves in anticipation of any contingency. Secretary McNamara agreed that we should say that the Defense Department had been ordered to be prepared for any contingency and that we were not now ready to say anything more than was in the President's speech.

In response to a Presidential question, Secretary McNamara said that an information group was working on the problem of voluntary press censorship based on experience during the Korean War.

[censored]

Secretary McNamara reported that the Defense Department was working on how we would prevent the introduction into Cuba of nuclear weapons by airplanes. He said some planes could fly non-stop from the Soviet Union if refueled en route. Present arrangements provided that we would be informed of any plane flying to Cuba and we would then decide what action to take against it.

It was agreed that no reserves would be called today, but that a review would be made tonight as to the necessity of such action.

Acting Secretary Fowler raised several questions involving domestic controls, including gold transfers, foreign exchange controls, and control of the stock market. He said, in response to the President's question, that another look would be taken the following day before any recommendation would be made as to closing the stock market.

Secretary Rusk said that if we were asked whether our blockade was an act of war, we should say that it was not. The President asked whether friendly ships would be halted and Admiral Anderson replied in the affirmative, saying that we would challenge all ships. The President agreed that we should stop all Soviet Bloc and non-Bloc ships when the order to institute the blockade was given.

The President discussed the reasons why he had decided against an air strike now. First, there was no certainty that an air strike would destroy all missiles now in Cuba. We would be able to get a large percentage of these missiles, but could not get them all.

In addition we would not know if any of these missiles were operationally ready with their nuclear warheads and we were not certain that our intelligence had discovered all the missiles in Cuba. Therefore, in attacking the ones we had located, we could not be certain that others unknown to us would not be launched against the United States. The President said an air strike would involve an action comparable to the Japanese attack on Pearl Harbor. Finally, an air strike would increase the danger of a worldwide nuclear war.

The President said he had given up the thought of making an air strike only yesterday morning. In summary, he said an air strike had all the disadvantages of Pearl Harbor. It would not insure the destruction of every strategic missile in Cuba, and would end up eventually in our having to invade.

Mr. Bundy added that we should not discuss the fact that we were not able to destroy all the missiles by means of an air strike because at some later time we might wish to make such an attack.

Soviet Archives

22 October 1962
TOP SECRET
TROSTNIK - to comrade PAVLOV
In connection with possible landing on Cuba of Americans participating in maneuvers in the Caribbean Sea, undertake urgent measures to increase combat readiness and to repel the enemy by joint efforts of the Cuban army and all Soviet troop units, excluding Statsenko's weapons and all of Beloborodov's cargo.
Director
4/389
October 22, 1962
23.30

Memorandum

Washington, October 24, 1962.
SUBJECT
Leadership meeting on October 22nd at 5:00 p.m.

ATTENDED BY
The Leadership, except for Senator Hayden,
The President, Rusk, McNamara, McCone and Ambassador Thompson

McCone read a summary of the situation, copy of which is attached. This statement had been discussed with the President, Attorney General and Bundy and had been modified to conform to their views.

There were a few questions of a substantive nature, Hickenlooper asked when missiles would be in operational status. McCone replied with the existing figures as reported in the morning report. Hickenlooper then asked if the Cuban situation is tied in to the China/India confrontation. McCone replied that we have no information one way or the other. Thompson then indicated it was more probable that Cuba may force a showdown on Berlin.

Secretary Rusk then reviewed his current appraisal of the Soviet Union indicating there had been some radical moves within the USSR which were indicating a tougher line. It appeared the hard-liners are coming in to ascendancy and the soft co-existent line seems to be disappearing. Peiping seems somewhat more satisfied with Moscow now. Rusk stated that he did not wish to underestimate the gravity of the situation; the Soviets were taking a very serious risk, but this in his opinion represents the philosophy of the "hard-liners". Russell questioned the Secretary as to whether things will get better in the future, whether we will have a more propitious time to act than now, the thrust of his questioning being, "Why wait." Rusk answered that he saw no opportunity for improvement.

The President then reviewed the chronology of the situation, starting on Tuesday, October 16th, when the first information was received from the photographic flight of October 14th. He stated that he immediately ordered extensive overflights; that McCone briefed President Eisenhower; that we must recognize that these missiles might be operational and therefore military action on our part might cause the firing of many of them with serious consequences to the United States; furthermore the actions taken, and further actions which might be required, might cause the Soviets to react in various areas, most particularly Berlin, which they could easily grab and if they do, our European Allies would lay the blame in our lap. The President concluded whatever we do involves a risk; however we must make careful calculations and take a chance. To do nothing would be a great mistake. The blockade of Cuba on the importation of offensive weapons was to be undertaken, all ships would be stopped and those containing offensive weapons would not be permitted to proceed. We have no idea how the Bloc will react but the indications are, from unconfirmed sources, they will attempt to run the blockade. Initially the blockade would not extend to petroleum. This might be a further step. We are taking all military preparations for either an air strike or an invasion. It was the President's considered judgment that if we have to resort to active military actions, then this would involve an invasion. Rusk then stated that our proposed action gave the other side a chance to pause. They may pull back or they may rapidly intensify the entire situation existing between the Soviet Union and the United States.

Senator Russell then demanded stronger steps, stated he did not think we needed time to pause. The President had warned them in September and no further warning was necessary. We must not take a gamble and must not temporize; Khrushchev has once again rattled his missiles; he can become firmer and firmer, and we must react. If we delay, if we give notification, if we telegraph our punches, the result will be more a difficult military action and more American lives will be sacrificed. The thrust of Senator Russell's remarks were to demand military action. He did not specifically say by surprise attack; however he did not advocate warning.

McNamara then described the blockade, indicating that this might lead to some form of military action; that there would be many alternative courses open to us. The President then reviewed in some detail time required to assemble an invasion force which would involve 90,000 men in the actual landings and a total of about 250,000 men. He stated this could not be done in 24 or 36 hours but would take a number of days and that many preliminary steps had been taken.

Halleck recalled a recent briefing by Secretary McNamara in which he stated it would take three months to prepare adequately to invade Cuba. McNamara then reaffirmed the 250,000-man figure, with 90,000 of them actually involved in the landing force. He stated that he could be ready in 7 days and that the landing would be preceded by substantial air strike. Russell again questioned the delay. He also seriously criticized any policy which involved extensive airborne alerts of SAC in the interests of our state of readiness, pointing out that the consequences would be the serious attrition of our SAC forces, most particularly the B-47s, which are now quite old. McNamara stated that we could carry on an airborne alert indefinitely because preliminary plans had been made, repair parts, etc., secured and were in position.

Vinson then asked if the Joint Chiefs of Staff actually approved the plans for the invasion. McNamara answered, "Yes." The plans had been developed over a 10-month period and had been submitted to the President by the JCS on a number of occasions.

Note: This question did not refer to whether the JCS did or did not approve the proposed actions of blockade against Cuba.

The President then reviewed matters again, read an intelligence note from a United Nations source which indicated Soviet intention to grab Berlin. Russell promptly replied that Berlin will always be a hostage. He then criticized the decision, stated we should go now and not wait.

Halleck questioned whether we were absolutely sure these weapons were offensive. The President answered affirmatively. McNamara then made a most unusual statement. He said, "One might question whether the missiles are or are not offensive. However there is no question about the IL 28s." Note: This was the first time anyone has raised doubt as to whether the MRBMs and the IRBMs are offensive missiles.

Questions were then raised concerning the attitude of our Allies. The President advised steps taken to inform our major Allies. He then read the message received from the Prime Minister which in effect agreed to support us in the United Nations and then raised many warnings including the dangers to Berlin, Turkey, Pakistan, Iran, etc., etc.

Senator Saltonstall brought up the question of the legality of the blockade. A great many Senators expressed concern over the proposed action with the OAS, indicating that they felt the OAS would delay rather than act. Saltonstall then asked whether a blockade would be legal if the OAS did not support it. The President answered that it probably would not; however we would proceed anyway.

Fulbright then stated that in his opinion the blockade was the worst of the alternatives open to us and it was a definite affront to Russia and that the moment that we had to damage or sink a Soviet ship because of their failure to recognize or respect the blockade we would be at war with Russia and the war would be caused because of our own initiative. The President disagreed with this thinking. Fulbright then repeated his position and stated in his opinion it would be far better to launch an attack and to take out the bases from Cuba. McNamara stated that this would involve the spilling of Russian blood since there were so many thousand Russians manning these bases. Fulbright responded that this made no difference because they were there in Cuba to help on Cuban bases. These were not Soviet bases. There was no mutual defense pact between the USSR and Cuba. Cuba was not a member of the Warsaw Pact. Therefore he felt the Soviets would not react if some Russians got killed in Cuba. The Russians in the final analysis placed little value on human life. The time has come for an invasion under the President's statement of February 13th. Fulbright repeated that an act on Russian ships is an act of war against Russia and on the other hand, an attack or an invasion of Cuba was an act against Cuba, not Russia. Fulbright also expressed reservations concerning the possible OAS action.

The President took issue with Fulbright, stating that he felt that an attack on these bases, which we knew were manned by Soviet personnel, would involve large numbers of Soviet casualties and this would be more provocative than a confrontation with a Soviet ship.

Vinson urged that if we strike, we strike with maximum force and wind the matter up quickly as this would involve the minimum of American losses and insure the maximum support by the Cuban people at large who, he reasoned, would very quickly go over to the side of the winner.

The meeting was concluded at 6:35 to permit the President to prepare for his 7:00 o'clock talk to the nation.

It was decided to hold a meeting on Wednesday, October 24th. During this meeting Senator Hickenlooper expressed himself as opposed to the action and in favor of direct military action. He stated that in his opinion ships which were accosted on the high sea and turned back would be a more humiliating blow to the Soviets and a more serious involvement to their pride than the losing of as many as 5,000 Soviet military personnel illegally and secretly stationed in Cuba.

John A. McCone
Director

Address by President Kennedy
October 22, 1962

Good evening, my fellow citizens. This Government, as promised, has maintained the closest surveillance of the Soviet military build-up on the island of Cuba. Within the past week unmistakable evidence had established the fact that a series of offensive missile sites is now in preparation on that imprisoned island. The purposes of these bases can be none other than to provide a nuclear strike capability against the Western Hemisphere.

Upon receiving the first preliminary hard information of this nature last Tuesday morning (October 16) at 9:00 A.M., I directed that our surveillance be stepped up. And having now confirmed and completed our evaluation of the evidence and our decision on a course of action, this Government feels obliged to report this new crisis to you in fullest detail.

The characteristics of these new missile sites indicate two distinct types of installations. Several of them include medium-range ballistic missiles capable of carrying a nuclear warhead for a distance of more than 1,000 nautical miles. Each of these missiles, in short, is capable of striking Washington, D.C., the Panama Canal, Cape Canaveral, Mexico City, or any other city on the southeastern part of the United States, in Central America, or in the Caribbean area.

Additional sites not yet completed appear to be designed for intermediate-range ballistic missiles capable of traveling more than twice as far — and thus capable of striking most of the major cities in the Western Hemisphere, ranging as far north as Hudson Bay, Canada, and as far south as Lima, Peru. In addition, jet bombers, capable of carrying nuclear weapons, are now being uncrated and assembled in Cuba, while the necessary air bases are being prepared.

This urgent transformation of Cuba into an important strategic base — by the presence of these large, long-range, and clearly offensive weapons of sudden mass destruction — constitutes an explicit threat to the peace and security of all the Americas, in flagrant and deliberate defiance of the Rio pact of 1947, the traditions of this nation and Hemisphere, the Joint Resolution of the 87th Congress, the Charter of the United Nations, and my own public warnings to the Soviet on September 4 and 13.

This action also contradicts the repeated assurances of Soviet spokesmen, both publicly and privately delivered, that the arms build-up in Cuba would retain its original defensive character and that the Soviet Union had no need or desire to station strategic missiles on the territory of any other nation.

The size of this undertaking makes clear that it has been planned for some months. Yet only last month, after I had made clear the distinction between any introduction of ground-to-ground missiles and the existence of defensive anti-aircraft missiles, the Soviet Government publicly stated on September 11 that, and I quote, "The armaments and military equipment sent to Cuba are designed exclusively for defensive purposes," and, and I quote the Soviet Government, "There is no need for the Soviet Government to shift its weapons for a retaliatory blow to any other country, for instance Cuba," and that, I quote the Government, "The Soviet Union has so powerful rockets to carry these nuclear warheads that there is no need to search for sites for them beyond the boundaries of the Soviet Union." That statement was false.

Only last Thursday, as evidence of this rapid offensive build-up was already in my hand, Soviet Foreign Minister Gromyko told me in my office that he was instructed to make it clear once again, as he said his Government had already done, that Soviet assistance to Cuba, and I quote, "pursued solely the purpose of contributing to the defense capabilities of Cuba," that, and I quote him, "training by Soviet specialists of Cuban nationals in handling defensive armaments was by no means offensive," and that "if it were otherwise," Mr. Gromyko went on, "the Soviet Government would never become involved in rendering such assistance." That statement also was false.

Neither the United States of America nor the world community of nations can tolerate deliberate deception and offensive threats on the part of any nation, large or small. We no longer live in world where only the actual firing of weapons represents a sufficient challenge to a nation's security tot constitute maximum peril. Nuclear weapons are so destructive and ballistic missiles are so swift that any substantially increased possibility of their use or any sudden change in their deployment may well be regarded as a definite threat to peace.

For many years both the Soviet Union and the United States, recognizing this fact, have deployed strategic nuclear weapons with great care, never upsetting the precarious status quo which insured that these weapons would not be used in the absence of some vital challenge. Our own strategic missiles have never been transferred to the territory of any other nation under a cloak of secrecy and deception; and our history, unlike that of the Soviets since the end of World War II, demonstrates that we have no desire to dominate or conquer any other nation or impose our system upon its people. Nevertheless, American citizens have become adjusted to living daily on the bull's eye of Soviet missiles located inside the U.S.S.R. or in submarines.

In that sense missiles in Cuba add to an already clear and present danger—although it should be noted the nations of Latin America have never previously been subjected to a potential nuclear threat.

But this secret, swift, and extraordinary build-up of Communist missiles—in an area well known to have a special and historical relationship to the United States and the nations of the Western Hemisphere, in violation of Soviet assurances, and in defiance of American and hemispheric policy—this sudden, clandestine decision to station strategic weapons for the first time outside of Soviet soil—is a deliberately provocative and unjustified change in the status quo which cannot be accepted by this country if our courage and our commitments are ever to be trusted again by either friend or foe.

The 1930's taught us a clear lesson: Aggressive conduct, if allowed to grow unchecked and unchallenged, ultimately leads to war. This nation is opposed to war. We are also true to our word. Our unswerving objective, therefore, must be to prevent the use of these missiles against this or any other country and to secure their withdrawal or elimination from the Western Hemisphere.

Our policy has been one of patience and restraint, as befits a peaceful and powerful nation, which leads a worldwide alliance. We have been determined not to be diverted from our central concerns by mere irritants and fanatics. But now further action is required—and it is underway; and those actions may only be the beginning. We will not prematurely or unnecessarily risk the costs of worldwide nuclear war in which even the fruits of victory would be ashes in our mouth—but neither will we shrink from that risk at any time it must be faced.

Acting, therefore, in the defense of our own security and of the entire Western Hemisphere, and under the authority entrusted to me by the Constitution as endorsed by the resolution of Congress, I have directed that the following initial steps be taken immediately:

First: To halt this offensive build-up, a strict quarantine on all offensive military equipment under shipment to Cuba is being initiated. All ships of any kind bound for Cuba from whatever nation or port will, if found to contain cargoes of offensive weapons, be turned back. This quarantine will be extended, if needed, to other types of cargo and carriers. We are not at this time, however, denying the necessities of life as the Soviets attempted to do in their Berlin blockade of 1948.

Second: I have directed the continued and increased close surveillance of Cuba and its military build-up. The Foreign Ministers of the Organization of American States in their communiqué of October 3 rejected secrecy on such matters in this Hemisphere. Should these offensive military preparations continue, thus increasing the threat to the Hemisphere, further action will be justified. I have directed the Armed Forces to prepare for any eventualities; and I trust that the interests of both the Cuban people and the Soviet technicians at the sites, the hazards to all concerned of continuing this threat will be recognized.

Third: It shall be the policy of this nation to regard any nuclear missile launched from Cuba against any nation in the Western Hemisphere as an attack by the Soviet Union on the United States, requiring a full retaliatory response upon the Soviet Union.

Fourth: As a necessary military precaution I have reinforced our base at Guantanamo, evacuated today the dependents of our personnel there, and ordered additional military units to be on a stand-by alert basis.

Fifth: We are calling tonight for an immediate meeting of the Organ of Consultation, under the Organization of American States, to consider this threat to hemispheric security and to invoke articles six and eight of the Rio Treaty in support of all necessary action. The United Nations Charter allows for regional security arrangements—and the nations of this Hemisphere decided long ago against the military presence of outside powers. Our other allies around the world have also been alerted.

Sixth: Under the Charter of the United Nations, we are asking tonight that an emergency meeting of the Security Council be convoked without delay to take action against this latest Soviet threat to world peace. Our resolution will call for the prompt dismantling and withdrawal of all offensive weapons in Cuba, under the supervision of United Nations observers, before the quarantine can be lifted.

Seventh and finally: I call upon Chairman Khrushchev to halt and eliminate this clandestine, reckless, and provocative threat to world peace and to stable relations between our two nations. I call upon him further to abandon this course of world domination and to join in an historic effort to end the perilous arms race and transform the history of man. He has an opportunity now to move the world back from the abyss of destruction—by returning to his Government's own words that it had no need to station missiles outside its own territory, and withdrawing these weapons from Cuba—by refraining from any action which will widen or deepen the present crisis—and then by participating in a search for peaceful and permanent solutions. This nation is prepared to present its case against the Soviet threat to peace, and our own proposals for a peaceful world, at any time and in any forum in the Organization of American States, in the United Nations, or in any other meeting that could be useful—without limiting our freedom of action.

We have in the past made strenuous efforts to limit the spread of nuclear weapons. We have proposed the elimination of all arms and military bases in a fair and effective disarmament treaty. We are prepared to discuss new proposals for the removal of tensions on both sides—including the possibilities of a genuinely independent Cuba, free to determine its own destiny. We have no wish to war with the Soviet Union, for we are a peaceful people who desire to live in peace with all other peoples.

But it is difficult to settle or even discuss these problems in an atmosphere of intimidation. That is why this latest Soviet threat—or any other threat which is made either independently or in response to our actions this weekmust and will be met with determination. Any hostile move anywhere in the world against the safety and freedom of peoples to whom we are committed—including in particular the brave people of West Berlin—will be met by whatever action is needed.

Finally, I want to say a few words to the captive people of Cuba, to whom this speech is being directly carried by special radio facilities. I speak to you as a friend, as one who knows of your deep attachment to your fatherland, as one who shares your aspirations for liberty and justice for all. And I have watched and the American people have watched with deep sorrow how your nationalist revolution was betrayed and how your fatherland fell under foreign domination. Now your leaders are no longer Cuban leaders inspired by Cuban ideals. They are puppets and agents of an international conspiracy which has turned Cuba against your friends and neighbors in the Americas—and turned it into the first Latin American country to become a target for nuclear war, the first Latin American country to have these weapons on its soil.

These new weapons are not in your interest. They contribute nothing to your peace and well being. They can only undermine it. But this country has no wish to cause you to suffer or to impose any system upon you. We know that your lives and land are being used as pawns by those who deny you freedom.

Many times in the past Cuban people have risen to throw out tyrants who destroyed their liberty. And I have no doubt that most Cubans today look forward to the time when they will be truly free—free from foreign domination, free to choose their own leaders, free to select their own system, free to own their own land, free to speak and write and worship without fear or degradation. And then shall Cuba be welcomed back to the society of free nations and to the associations of this Hemisphere.

My fellow citizens, let no one doubt that this is a difficult and dangerous effort on which we have set out. No one can foresee precisely what course it will take or what costs or casualties will be incurred. Many months of sacrifice and self-discipline lie ahead—months in which many threats and denunciations will keep us aware of our dangers. But the greatest danger of all would be to do nothing.

The path we have chosen for the present is full of hazards, as all paths are; but it is the one most consistent with our character and courage as a nation and our commitments around the world. The cost of freedom is always high—but Americans have always paid it. And one path we shall never choose, and that is the path of surrender or submission.

Our goal is not the victory of might but the vindication of right—not peace at the expense of freedom, but both peace and freedom, here in this Hemisphere and, we hope, around the world. God willing, that goal will be achieved.

Letter From President Kennedy to Chairman Khrushchev

October 22, 1962.

Dear Mr. Chairman: A copy of the statement I am making tonight concerning developments in Cuba and the reaction of my Government thereto has been handed to your Ambassador in Washington. In view of the gravity of the developments to which I refer, I want you to know immediately and accurately the position of my Government in this matter.

In our discussions and exchanges on Berlin and other international questions, the one thing that has most concerned me has been the possibility that your Government would not correctly understand the will and determination of the United States in any given situation, since I have not assumed that you or any other sane man would, in this nuclear age, deliberately plunge the world into war which it is crystal clear no country could win and which could only result in catastrophic consequences to the whole world, including the aggressor.

At our meeting in Vienna and subsequently, I expressed our readiness and desire to find, through peaceful negotiation, a solution to any and all problems that divide us. At the same time, I made clear that in view of the objectives of the ideology to which you adhere, the United States could not tolerate any action on your part which in a major way disturbed the existing over-all balance of power in the world. I stated that an attempt to force abandonment of our responsibilities and commitments in Berlin would constitute such an action and that the United States would resist with all the power at its command.

It was in order to avoid any incorrect assessment on the part of your Government with respect to Cuba that I publicly stated that if certain developments in Cuba took place, the United States would do whatever must be done to protect its own security and that of its allies.

Moreover, the Congress adopted a resolution expressing its support of this declared policy. Despite this, the rapid development of long-range missile bases and other offensive weapons systems in Cuba has proceeded. I must tell you that the United States is determined that this threat to the security of this hemisphere be removed. At the same time, I wish to point out that the action we are taking is the minimum necessary to remove the threat to the security of the nations of this hemisphere. The fact of this minimum response should not be taken as a basis, however, for any misjudgment on your part.

I hope that your Government will refrain from any action which would widen or deepen this already grave crisis and that we can agree to resume the path of peaceful negotiation.

Sincerely,

JFK

Memorandum, Telephone Conversation Between President Kennedy and British Prime Minister Macmillan

October 22, 1962.

The clandestine way that the Soviets have made their build-up in Cuba would have unhinged us in all of Latin America. To allow it to continue would have thrown into question all our statements about Berlin.

PM spoke.

We have the potential to occupy Cuba but we didn't start that way.

There would be a gap of some days before invasion could be mounted. Preparations for invasion would have public notice. This way provides action without immediate escalation to war.

Action is limited now. Greater force would give him the same excuse in Berlin.

It may be necessary to expand blockade to include fuel, lubricants and so forth.

PM spoke. (about possible Russian actions)

He may require us to seize their ships by force.

There is no telling what he will do—probably it will be something in Berlin.

PM spoke.

We have had no plan to invade Cuba. We must get their missiles out. What exchange possible is not known. But getting the missiles out is the object of our policy.

We are aware that this action is not complete application of force—does not immediately solve the problem.

The alternatives were air strike or invasion. These may be necessary but going completely into Cuba now invites him into Berlin.

PM spoke.

If we had the force on hand to take Cuba tonight that would be okay, but it would take a week to build up.

Prime Minister spoke.

We are attempting to begin the escalation in a way to prevent WW III. Maybe this will result anyway, but we cannot accept his actions.

PM spoke. (about talking to K on phone)

No, but I sent a letter to him one hour ago.

Khrushchev is playing a double game. He said he wasn't going to do anything until after the election. He said weapons in Cuba were not offensive.

It is obvious that he was attempting to face us in November with a bad situation.

PM answered.

Mr. Bundy suggested the following point which the President made.

The build-up in Cuba, if completed, would double the number of missiles the Soviets could bring to bear on the U.S. They would also overcome our warning system which does not face south. Furthermore, the short distance involving short times of flight would tempt them to make a first strike.

PM spoke.

Some action was necessary. It could result in WW III; we could lose Berlin.

PM spoke.

Invasion may yet be required. It requires seven days for mobilization of the necessary forces. In any event we won't invade until I speak again with you.

PM spoke.

It faces Khrushchev with action taken which has unpleasant options for him also.

From Soviet Statement To U.N. Security Council

October 23, 1962

I should now like to speak in my capacity as the representative of the Soviet Union.

Before proceeding with the statement of the position of the Soviet Government on the question which has been introduced by the Soviet Union for discussion in the Security Council, I should like to say a few words on the speech made by the representative of the United States who was defending the position of the United States on the question which that Government deemed it essential to place before the Security Council.

I must say that even a cursory examination of what was said by Mr. Stevenson betokens the total paucity of argument in the position of the United States Government in a question which it deems essential to place before the Security Council, the total helplessness of the Government of the United States to defend its position in the face of the Council and of world public opinion.

Mr. Stevenson has touched upon numerous subjects. He gave a falsified—let us be frank about this—account of the history of postwar relations and has represented the whole position of the United States as being beneficent. He has tried to denigrate in every means possible the position of the Soviet Union. He has spoken of the history of the Cuban Revolution, although one might well wonder what relationship there was between the United States and the internal affairs of the sovereign Cuban State. He drew an idyllic picture of the history of the Western Hemisphere during the past 150 years, but he seemed to have overlooked the policy of the "big stick" of a President of the United States, President McKinley, the Monroe Doctrine, the action of Theodore Roosevelt in connection with the Panama Canal and the actions taken there; the boastful statements of the American General Butler to the effect that with his soldiers and marines he could hold elections in any Latin

American country. This is something he was silent about. The policy of the "big stick" is now being sought to be carried out by the United States on this occasion too. But Mr. Stevenson has apparently forgotten that times have changed since then.

Mr. Stevenson touched upon the question of bases in various parts of the world. However, he failed to mention that the United States has these bases in thirty-five countries of the world, appropriating to itself the role of world policeman. What is surprising is that Mr. Stevenson has said practically nothing about the political, legal and moral grounds, based on the United Nations Charter for those aggressive acts that were undertaken by the United States Government during the past twenty-four hours against the small Cuban State.

This is not by accident, since in fact the Government of the United States has nothing to say in defense of its aggressive position. The Government of the United States has no positive ideas. If I may be excused the expression, it seemed to me that during the statement of the representative of the United States, Mr. Stevenson, we were look-ing at a completely naked man, bereft of any of the adornments of a civilized man, for in the eyes of the entire world and in the eyes of this Council, Mr. Stevenson stood here as the representative of an aggressive American brand of imperialism which rattles the sabre and demands that its own order be set up in the Western Hemisphere and throughout the whole world.

I do not wish to go off into polemics with Mr. Stevenson and with the Government of the United States generally on those subjects that have been touched upon in the long statement of the representative of the United States; I understand full well that all of these matters raised by Mr. Stevenson are but a smoke screen, an attempt to distract the attention of the Council from the substance of the matter under discussion, a matter involving the provisions of the Charter of the United Nations and the flagrant violations of those provisions that have been committed by the United States before the eyes of the whole world. Accordingly I shall not follow Mr. Stevenson in that course and I shall not answer all of his bold and false statements concerning the position of the Soviet Union. The position of the Soviet Union is clear and definite; it is known to the whole world. I shall not minimize or downgrade my statement by answering these minor and insignificant issues that Mr. Stevenson has attempted to raise before the Council.

The Security Council has convened today in circumstances which can but give rise to the gravest concern for the fate of peace in the Caribbean region and in the whole world. It is not a trivial matter that is involved; it is a matter of a unilateral and arbitrary action by a great Power which constitutes a direct infringement of the freedom and independence of a small country. This involves a new and extremely dangerous act of aggression in a chain of acts of aggression committed earlier by the United States against Cuba. It involves the violation of the most elementary rules and principles of international law. It involves the violation of the fundamental provisions of the Charter of the United Nations and of the spirit and letter of that Charter at the end of which stand the signature and seal of the United States.

Yesterday the United States in fact instituted a naval blockade of the Republic of Cuba, thus trampling underfoot the norms of inter-national behaviour and the principles enshrined in the Charter of the United Nations. The United States has appropriated to itself the right—and has stated so—to attack ships of other countries on the open seas, and this constitutes nothing other than undisguised piracy. At the same time, at the Guantanamo Base, a base located on the territory of Cuba, landings of additional troops have been effected and the armed forces of the United States brought to combat readiness. Such venturesome enterprises, together with the statements of the President of the United States to explain them, statements made yesterday on the radio and on television, give evidence of the fact that American imperialist circles will balk at nothing in their attempts to throttle a sovereign state, a Member of the United Nations, as that little country is. They are prepared, for the sake of this, to push the world to the brink of a military catastrophe.

As is known, a request for an urgent convening of the Security Council in view of the act of war committed unilaterally by the actions of the United States, which has declared a naval blockade of Cuba, was submitted to the Security Council by the representative of Cuba, Mr. Garcia-Inchaustegui.

These are the clear-cut requests addressed to the Security Council by two States whose actions are permeated with a conviction of the extreme gravity of the highly dangerous situation created by the United States, and permeated with the desire to strengthen inter-national peace and security, now so gravely threatened by the aggressive actions of the United States. These two letters differ as night differs from day, from the hypocritical letter addressed by the United States to the Security Council while, behind the backs of the Security Council, it tramples upon the principles of the Charter of the United Nations and of international law, having already begun military ac-tions against a small nation, a Member of the United Nations, while at the same time cynically attempting to wrap itself in the raiments of the peacemaker.

The present actions of the United States against Cuba are the logical link in that aggressive policy — fraught with the direst consequences — carried out by the United States with respect to Cuba as early as the Eisenhower Administration, and which was continued and intensified by the present Government of the United States, a Government which proclaimed at the very outset of its entry into office, the era of the "New Frontier." These actions constitute the most eloquent and tragic evidence for the world of the justification of the accusations that have been advanced on numerous occasions by the Revolutionary Government of Cuba in the organs of the United Nations, accusations that the Government of the United States has made preparations for the unleashing of aggression against Cuba and has made that the principal objective of all of its hostile actions against that small country.

The complaint of Cuba against the policy of constant threats and aggressive actions by the United States was first discussed by the Security Council, as is known, as early as July 1960. Cuba also applied to the Security Council, unmasking further aggressive actions of the United States and the preparation by them of direct military aggres-sion in January 1961, and the Security Council once again was obliged to revert to the consideration of the important actions that were brought to it at that time. The representative of the United States in the Security Council then had baldly denied all of these accusations. The genuine value of the false statements of the United States at that time, that they never had any plan whatsoever for any kind of aggression or for intervention in Cuba—these are the actual statements of the representatives of the United States—became quite clear, as to how bald they were, when three months after these statements the United States, in April of 1961, organized, prepared and carried out an intervention by mercenaries in Cuba.

The United Nations again, this time at the fifteenth session of the General Assembly, was obliged to consider the question of the ag-gressive actions of the United States against Cuba, the responsibility for which was officially assumed by the President of the United States. The April fiasco nevertheless had taught no lesson to the United States. Not only did they make preparations for a new and greater intervention in Cuba, but they first tried to isolate Cuba and attract to their aggressive actions against Cuba the Organization of American States. Cuba at that time already was indicating the danger of the continuation and intensification of that course for the work of peace in the world.

The complaints of Cuba against the aggressive actions by the United States, through the illegitimate use of the Organization of American States, was discussed at the sixteenth session of the General Assembly and at meetings of the Security Council in February and March of the present year. If there was any need for further proof of the justification or the justness of those accusations, they are more than amply provided, as we have indicated, in those aggressive actions of the Government of the United States against Cuba which were proclaimed yesterday and the component part of which is the campaign for creating a smoke screen for the justification of those aggressive actions, which is here being unfolded, quite cynically, by the delegation of the United States.

As a matter of fact, the covering role that is being carried out in the halls of the United Nations by the representatives of the United States is not new to them, as is known. One can but refer to the fact that Mr. Stevenson personally has already spoken, in this rather ungainly role, in the halls of this building in April of 1961 when United States ships were landing trained, armed and prepared mercenaries on the shores of Cuba, all of them trained and equipped from America. And Mr. Stevenson at that very moment was hypocritically denying the existence of such an aggression.

Everybody will remember the statement of Mr. Stevenson of 15 April to the effect that the United States was planning no aggression against Cuba; and on the 17th the mercenaries of the United States were landing at Playa Girón. What worth is there then in the statements of a representative of a great Power who dared to deceive world public opinion and the official organs of the United Nations; trying to salvage the errors of the Intelligence Agency of the United States which had ordered Stevenson not to say anything about it?

The delegation of the United States today, of course, has somewhat changed its tune. Today it is not denying any more the fact that the United States has undertaken unilateral arbitrary action of a military character against Cuba, and the argument used by the United States against Cuba is found to be a new one. Having searched in the pile of junk, the so-called detectives of the State Department proposed to their Government a variant involving the setting up of so-called rocket bases in Cuba. In other words, there might have been an order to find some cause for the justification of aggression. That is all that would have mattered and the rest is a question of the resourcefulness of the officials concerned. Let them find a good enough excuse. There we have emerging as clear as the light of day, in the statement of President Kennedy and in the letter of the representative of the United States, Mr. Stevenson, the thesis of some incontrovertible evi-dence of the presence in Cuba of Soviet rockets, the falsity of which is all too obvious.

If the Government of the United States has after all decided in these circumstances to embark upon open falsehood, if it has not shirked before the advancing of the completely false and slanderous thesis of the presence of offensive Soviet rockets in Cuba, this simply illustrates and proves the extent to which it has absolutely no value with respect to what sort of excuse should serve as the justification for the new aggressive acts against Cuba which they are already com-mitting. This simply illustrates the depth to which the United States has fallen and the depth of cynicism of the present new policy of the United States labeled the "New Frontier."

The falsity of the accusations advanced now by the United States against the Soviet Union—which consist of the fact that the Soviet Union has allegedly set up offensive armaments in Cuba—is clear from the outset. The Soviet delegation first of all officially confirms the statement already made by the Soviet Union in this connection that the Soviet Government has not directed and is not directing to Cuba any offensive armaments. The Soviet delegation recalls in particular the statement of TASS of 11 September of this year in which, on the instructions of the Soviet Government the following was stated:

"The armaments and military materiel sent to Cuba is designed exclusively for defensive purposes. The Soviet Union does not need to relocate in any other country, for instance, in Cuba, the means available to it for repelling aggression and for a retaliatory blow. The Soviet Union has so powerful a series of rockets and missile carriers that there is no need to seek a location for their launching anywhere outside the territory of the Soviet Union."

The observers of the United States in the Pacific recently were able to be convinced of the accuracy of the firing of Soviet rockets.

The Soviet delegation recalls also the statement of the Minister for Foreign Affairs, Mr. Gromyko, made by him on 21 September 1962 in the General Assembly, when he said:

"Any sober-minded man knows that Cuba is not. . . building up her forces to such a degree that she can pose a threat to the United States or to the passage of the United States to the Panama Canal, or else a threat to any State of the Western Hemisphere."

Mr. Gromyko went on to say:

"They know full well that the aid rendered by the Soviet Union to Cuba to strengthen her independence does not pursue any of these goals either, since they are alien to our foreign policy."

We should also recall the statement made on 8 October 1962 at the plenary meeting of the General Assembly by the President of the Republic of Cuba, Mr. Osvaldo Dorticós — to which the representa-tive of Cuba here has partly referred:

"We were forced to arm — not to attack anyone, not to assault any nation, but only to defend ourselves... Cuba constitutes a danger to the security of no nation whatsoever of our continent, nor has Cuba harboured, in the past or at the present time, any aggressive intentions against any of them."

And finally, the Soviet Government only today in its official statement which was circulated to the members of the Council once again declared the following:

"With regard to the Soviet Union's assistance to Cuba, this assistance is exclusively designed to improve Cuba's defensive capacity. As was stated on 3 September 1962 in the joint Soviet-Cuban communiqué on the visit to the Soviet Union of a Cuban delegation composed of Mr. E. Guevara and Mr. E. Aragones, the Soviet Government has responded to the Cuban Government's request to help Cuba with arms. The communiqué states that such arms and military equipment are intended solely for defensive purposes. The Governments of the two countries still firmly adhere to that position."

Soviet assistance in strengthening Cuba's defences is necessitated by the fact that, from the outset of its existence, the

Republic of Cuba has been subjected to continuous threats and acts of provocation by the United States.

In the light of these clear-cut statements it is obvious that the assertion — let us call things by their proper names — these completely false statements, which are being disseminated by the United States of some alleged intentions on the part of Cuba or on the part of the Soviet Union, are but a fabrication and a tissue of imaginary dreams. They are utilized and have been raised in the United States to the level of Government statements for the sole purpose of shielding, justifying and finding at least some sort of excuse for the committing of further and much more far-reaching acts of aggression by the United States, which is violating the Charter of the United Nations and which is creating a direct threat to peace.

Mr. Stevenson quoted Article 2, paragraph 4 of the Charter of the United Nations. This Article states:

"All Members shall refrain in their international relations from the threat or use of force against the territorial integrity or political independence of any state, or in any other manner inconsistent with the Purposes of the United Nations."

But the declaring of a naval blockade of Cuba and all those military measures that have been put into effect on the instructions of the President of the United States since yesterday, all these measures, are they not threats or use of force against the territorial integrity or political independence of a State—of Cuba in this instance? Every sensible person will understand that this is the most flagrant violation of this principle of the Charter of the United Nations, a principle to which the representative of the United States dared refer.

The delegation of the United States is now trying to utilize fabrications in the Security Council for horrendous purposes and in order to try to compel the Security Council to approve retroactively those un-lawful, aggressive actions of the United States which have already been adopted by the United States against Cuba, and which the United States is carrying out unilaterally, in clear violation of the Charter of the United Nations and of the elementary norms and principles of international law. The peoples of the world, however, must have a clear idea of the fact that in embarking upon an open adventure of this kind, the United States of America is taking a step toward the unleashing of a world thermonuclear war. This is the great terrible price which the world may have to pay for the present reckless and irresponsible actions of the United States.

Why did the United States begin its new aggressive action against Cuba in such haste, and why is it trying to pretend that it is appeal-ing to the Security Council? The answer to that question is dictated by logic. The very priority of the actions of the United States Govern-ment demonstrates this. Such a course can be taken only by someone who is sure in advance that the Security Council will never support—indeed, it will never be able to support—the aggressive actions in question. The purpose of the United States is in fact to place before the Security Council the fait accompli of United States aggression. The appeal to the Council is only a gesture to satisfy the public. To speak bluntly, this gesture is intended to disorient public opinion.

Of course, when one indulges in such a cynical gesture one does not really need any proof whatsoever. A mere declaration about some alleged incontrovertible evidence will do.

Thus, in the present position of the United States delegation in the Security Council there is a sorry logic of sorts. There is no proof, no evidence. But the United States does not need any evidence, because the United States—and this is openly mentioned in the Press of the United States—is not counting on the Security Council's being able to justify or approve its aggressive actions against Cuba. As is known, the United States is already carrying out these actions in practice—and the Security Council has been apprised of all this simply for the sake of appearances.

What is the fait accompli before which the United States is placing the Security Council? First, the United States unilaterally has declared the implementation of an actual blockade of Cuba by the United States. Secondly, the United

States has directed large-scale military forces not only to the Cuban area but to the very territory of Cuba, to the United States base at Guantanamo, and has ordered them to be in a state of combat readiness. Thirdly, the United States has officially stated that it intends not to limit itself to this, but to take further action against Cuba — and this was stated in Mr. Stevenson's letter — if and when it finds that necessary. In other words, the United States is trying to reserve its right to continue open military aggression against Cuba. However great the danger is today that is hovering over Cuba as a result of these aggressive actions on the part of the United States, it does not fully cover the seriousness of the critical situation that has been produced.

The principal aspect of the present reckless actions of the United States against Cuba lies in the fact that on the basis of official United States statements the Government of the United States is prepared to move to the direct unleashing of a world thermonuclear war for the purpose of achieving its aggressive designs against Cuba.

In the letter addressed by Mr. Stevenson to the President of the Security Council we find this direct statement: "What is at stake is the peace and security both of a single region and of the whole world." Thus the whole world is confronted with the readiness of the United States to go to the brink, where the stake is the fate of the world, where the stake is millions and millions of human lives.

The peace-loving countries and peoples have for a long time now had fears that the reckless and aggressive policies of the United States with respect to Cuba might bring the world to the brink of catastrophe. The apprehensions of the peace-loving forces and their attempts to call upon the United States Government to heed the voice of reason and to settle the dispute with Cuba peacefully are clearly shown in the records of the general debate which the seventeenth session of the General Assembly has only recently completed. I shall mention only a few of the statements made in the course of that debate by the heads of delegations, statements made at the highest level on behalf of the Governments of the various countries.

The Foreign Minister of the United Arab Republic, Mr. Fawzi, said: "The situation around Cuba is a source of worry to many lovers of peace and of the rule of law in international relations."

The Minister for Foreign Affairs of Algeria, Mr. Khemisti, said the following:

"...each State, great or small, rich or poor, must recognize this right to its own political system and have that right recognized by others."

It is because of this necessity that we feel that the efforts made to attack and undermine a political regime chosen by the friendly people of Cuba are dangerous for international peace. The people of Cuba have no aggressive intentions, and they have the right to wish for their economic and social liberation.

But the United States is preventing the Cubans from thinking of that.

The Foreign Minister of Iraq, Mr. Jawad, said:

"We are all neighbours of countries with differing social and political systems and none has the right to impose its system upon others"—except the United States, which wishes to arrogate to itself such a right.

Mr. Jawad continued:

"This is the essence of the accepted policy of peaceful coexistence, and any other policy would inevitably lead to aggression. "

The people of Cuba are free to choose their own system of government and no State, however big and powerful, has the right to interfere in the internal affairs of other States.

In order to achieve the observance, by the United States, of the sovereign rights of the Cuban people to choose a regime that it likes, the need to settle peacefully the dispute between the United States and Cuba, the need to cause the United States to waive the use of force in solving this dispute, was something that found the adherence of these countries and many others. Now, after the effecting, by the United States, of the recent and far-reaching aggressive actions against Cuba, it is clearly obvious how cynical was the attitude of the United States towards these and many other invocations and appeals to adhere, in its policy in the international arena and in relations with Cuba, to the lofty principles of the Charter of the United Nations.

In declaring the introduction of a blockade against Cuba, the United States has committed an unprecedented step in relations between States—between which there is no formal state of war.

By this arbitrary, piratical act, the United States has placed under threat the shipping of many countries of the world, including shipping of its allies who do not agree with this reckless and dangerous policy with respect to Cuba.

By this aggressive action of theirs, which creates a threat to peace in the whole world, they have launched a direct challenge at the United Nations, and to the Security Council as the principal organ of the United Nations responsible for the maintenance of international peace and security.

In stating its intention to draw into the implementation of its aggressive actions against Cuba the Organization of American States—to which it is already dictating the effecting of collective sanctions against Cuba—the United States is openly violating the prerogatives of the Security Council which alone can offer powers for the carrying out of any enforcement measures. In throwing their armed forces around Cuba and upon the territory of Cuba itself, and in having declared their intention to use force when they deem that appropriate, the United States is committing an act of uncovered aggression. They have openly violated the Charter of the United Nations, which prohibits to States—Members of the United Nations—the threat or use of force in international relations.

In showing total indifference to the serious international consequences that may stem from their unilateral action against Cuba, the United States has directly placed international peace and security under threat, and automatically, by their actions, has raised the ques-tion of urgent convening of die Security

Council for the consideration of the critical stipulation that has been produced.

The fact that the United States itself has applied to the Security Council is but trying to maintain composure while losing the game. The United States realizes full well that, after having committed such clearly aggressive actions against Cuba, it will in any event have to appear before the Security Council, to be accountable for these defiant, adventuresome actions. Indeed, could the Security Council ignore the fact that the United States is arbitrarily setting up a block-ade around Cuba and is committing a definitely provocative step in its unprecedented and unheard-of violation of international law; are trampling underfoot the whole of the Charter of the United Nations; and are throwing a challenge to all of the peace-loving peoples? Could the Security Council overlook the fact that the United States of America is openly installing the law of the jungle in international relations by its actions—that it has reached such a state of cynicism that, not only does it commit aggressive actions against a small country such as Cuba, but it is even demanding that Cuba explain itself to the United States as to the fashion in which it has organized its defense and, at the same time, that it remove from its territory the technology that is needed by it for its defence against United States aggression?

Mr. Stevenson has, in his statement today, permitted himself to use a series of sentences to the effect that Castro, as you will see, has done with impunity this, that and the other thing, that he has estab-lished relations with the Soviet Union—and all this with impunity—as if the United States were called upon to punish someone, whoever he may be, who is establishing new relations with any country of the world, including the Soviet Union.

Mr. Stevenson, perhaps you yourself will punish yourself for having set up relations with the Soviet Union and holding negotiations with it.

The Security Council would fail in its direct duty as the principal organ responsible for the maintenance of international peace and security if it were to ignore or overlook the aggressive actions of the United States, which are nothing else than the fact that the United States has openly embarked upon the course of liquidation of the United Nations, a course of unleashing of world war.

Thus, what are the realistic facts facing the Security Council? These facts can be summarized in the following fashion:

First, the Government of the United States has declared that it will use such measures in regard to the shipping of other countries in the high seas — which action can be qualified in no fashion other than piracy. The decision of the United States to stop and inspect the ships of other countries which are headed for the shores of Cuba leads to a great intensification of the tension in the international situation, and constitutes a step towards the unleashing of world thermonuclear war, because no self-respecting State will permit its shipping to be tampered with.

Secondly, for the concealment of its actions, the United States is advancing a completely fabricated set of excuses. The United States is trying to represent as distorted the measures undertaken by the Cuban Government—measures designed to achieve or enhance the defense of its State. As any country and government concerned over its sovereignty and independence, Cuba in the face of aggression can-not but show serious apprehension and concern over its own safety.

Thirdly, from the very first days of its existence, the Revolutionary Government of Cuba is subjected to continual threats and provocations on the part of the United States, which is not balking at any actions—including the armed intervention in Cuba in April of 1961.

Fourth, the American imperialists have openly declared that they do not force their proposals upon other countries. Yet they are blatantly demanding that military facilities be removed from the territory of Cuba, when these facilities have been designed for the defense of that country.

Fifth, the Soviet Union Government has consistently spoken in favour, and now speaks in favour, of the withdrawal of all foreign forces and armaments from foreign territories back to their own coun-try. This Soviet proposal is designed to normalize the international climate and to create an atmosphere of confidence in relations between States. Yet the Government of the United States, which has deployed its armaments and forces throughout the whole world, stubbornly refuses to adopt this Soviet proposal. The United States utilizes the presence of its armed forces on foreign territories for interference in the domestic affairs of other States and for carrying out its aggressive plans. The Soviet Union Government has stood and still stands by the position that it is necessary to liquidate all bases on foreign territories and to withdraw from them all foreign military forces and facilities. The Soviet Union Government will not object to this being done under the observance of observers appointed by the United Nations.

Sixth, the United States has no right whatsoever to make the demands that were contained in President Kennedy's speech, either from the point of view of the normal practices of international law in regard to the freedom of shipping or from the point of view of the principles and provisions of the Charter. No State, however powerful it may be, has any right at all to define or determine what form of armaments may be required by another State for its defense. Each State, according to the Charter of the United Nations, has the right of self-defense and the right to the necessary weapons to secure that defense. The Soviet Union, at the request of the Cuban Government, is supplying military material to Cuba designed for defensive purposes and defensive purposes only. In this connection the Soviet Union Government does not seek to obtain any advantage for itself in Cuba. The Soviet Union Government is not threatening anyone. It is not pursuing any military objectives in this region, or in any other region of the world. The Soviet Union does not possess military bases in thirty-five of the world's countries. The Soviet Union is merely striving very sincerely towards giving assistance to the young Cuban Republic for the maintenance and strengthening of its sovereignty and independence.

Seventh, the position of the United States, as set out in President Kennedy's statement, is flagrantly at variance with the Charter of the United Nations and other universally recognized norms of international law. The Charter of the United Nations requires that all States, independently of their social structure, base their relations on a footing of equality and that they do not interfere in the domestic affairs of other States. The course which the United States has embarked upon with respect to Cuba and the Soviet Union is a course which would involve the liquidation of the United Nations. It is the course involving an unleashing of war.

Eighth, the Soviet Union Government appeals to all the peoples of the world to raise their voices in defense of the United Nations and not to permit the disintegration of this Organization. It appeals to them to vote against the United States policy of piracy, banditry, and the unleashing of a new war. Realizing the great responsibility resting upon the Security Council at this moment, the Soviet Union delegation considers that it is necessary first of all urgently to halt and repeal all the aggressive measures put into effect by the United States against Cuba and other countries. Understanding the urgent need for the adoption of such measures, the Soviet Union delegation, on the instructions of the Soviet Government, is introducing for the consideration of the Security Council the following draft resolution on the violation of the Charter of the United Nations and the threat to peace by the United States of America.

Telegram From US Embassy

Moscow, October 23, 1962, 5 p.m.
1042. Policy. Embtel 1041.
Embassy translation follows of Khrushchev's letter of October 23 to President. Kuznetsov informed me letter would not be published "for time being."

Begin Text.

Mr. President.

I have just received your letter, and have also acquainted myself with text of your speech of October 22 regarding Cuba.

I should say frankly that measures outlined in your statement represent serious threat to peace and security of peoples. United States has openly taken path of gross violation of Charter of United Nations, path of violation of international norms of freedom of navigation on high seas, path of aggressive actions both against Cuba and against Soviet Union.

Statement of Government of United States America cannot be evaluated in any other way than as naked interference in domestic affairs of Cuban Republic, Soviet Union, and other states. Charter of United Nations and international norms do not give right to any state whatsoever to establish in international waters control of vessels bound for shores of Cuban Republic.

It is self-understood that we also cannot recognize right of United States to establish control over armaments essential to Republic of Cuba for strengthening of its defensive capacity.

We confirm that armaments now on Cuba, regardless of classification to which they belong, are destined exclusively for defensive purposes, in order to secure Cuban Republic from attack of aggressor.

I hope that Government of United States will show prudence and renounce actions pursued by you, which would lead to catastrophic consequences for peace throughout world.

Viewpoint of Soviet Government with regard to your statement of October 22 is set forth in statement of Soviet Government, which is being conveyed to you through your Ambassador in Moscow.

/s/ N. Khrushchev. End text.

Original of letter being airpouched today.
Kohler

Minutes

Washington, October 23, 1962, 10 a.m.

1. Intelligence
The meeting began with a briefing by Mr. McCone in which, in addition to written material, he emphasized the strength of evidence substantiating the non-participation of Cubans in Soviet missile installations in Cuba.

2. Unity on the Home Front
There was general discussion of the problem of adequate briefing of Members of the Congress and of the press on the way in which the crisis had developed and on the reasons for the decisions which had been taken. A number of assignments were given to individual members of the Committee for further work on this problem.

3. Blockade Effects Estimates
The President asked the Director of Central Intelligence for an analysis of effects of the blockade on Cuba, not to include food and medicine, and for a comparable analysis of the effects of a comparable blockade on Berlin.

4. Items Presented by the Department of Defense
a. The President approved plans for the issue of the Proclamation of Interdiction of ship delivery of offensive weapons to Cuba. The Proclamation was to be issued at 6:00 pm and the Interdiction to become effective at dawn October 24.
b. The President approved and later signed an Executive Order authorizing the extension of tours of duty of certain members of the Armed Forces.
c. The President approved the following contingency plan for action in the event of an incident affecting U-2 overflights. The President will be informed through SAC/DOD channels, and it is expected that if there is clear indication that the incident is the result of hostile action, the recommendation will

be for immediate retaliation upon the most likely surface-to-air site involved in this action. The President delegated authority for decision on this point to the Secretary of Defense under the following conditions:

(1) that the President himself should be unavailable

(2) that evidence of hostile Cuban action should be very clear.

d. It was expected, but not definitely decided, that if hostile actions should continue after such a single incident and single retaliation, it would become necessary to take action to eliminate the effectiveness of surface-to-air missiles in Cuba.

e. The Secretary reported that he was not ready to make a recommendation on air intercept of Soviet flights to Cuba, that he was maintaining aircraft on alert for prompt reaction against known missile sites, that preparations for invasion were proceeding at full speed, that the quarantine would initially exclude POL, though this decision should be reexamined continuously.

f. The Attorney General was delegated to check the problem of the legal possibility of permitting foreign flag ships to participate in U.S. coastwise trade, in order to prevent shipping requirements for an invasion from disrupting U.S. commerce.

g. The Secretary of Defense recommended, and the President approved, about six low-level reconnaissance flights for the purpose of obtaining still more persuasive photography of Soviet missile sites.

h. The President, on hearing these reports, asked whether U.S. air forces in Southeastern United States were properly deployed against possible hostile reaction, and after discussion he directed that photographs be taken of U.S. airfields to show their current condition.

5. State Department Business

a. Secretary Ball reported the urgent need for persuasive evidence in New York as described by Ambassador Stevenson and Mr. McCloy, and the President directed Secretary Ball and

Mr. McCone to work together to meet this requirement as well as possible.

b. There was a brief discussion of possible reactions in Berlin, and the President indicated that he would wish to consider whether additional Soviet inspection of convoys would be acceptable. After the meeting, the President designated Assistant Secretary Nitze to be Chairman of a Subcommittee of the Executive Committee, for Berlin Contingencies.

c. The President decided that it would be advisable not to make his forthcoming trip to Brazil, and the assignment of diplomatic disengagement was given to the Department of State.

6. There was discussion of the problem of effective communications and it was agreed that for the present, Dr. Wiesner will be asked informally to lead an inter-departmental review of this matter and to report on the problem on Wednesday, October 24.

McGeorge Bundy

Telegram to US Embassy in Moscow

Washington, October 23, 1962, 6:51 p.m.

You should deliver following letter addressed by the President to Chairman Khrushchev immediately. This replaces message contained Deptel 982.

"Dear Mr. Chairman:

I have received your letter of October twenty-third. I think you will recognize that the steps which started the current chain of events was the action of your Government in secretly furnishing offensive weapons to Cuba. We will be discussing this matter in the Security Council. In the meantime, I am concerned that we both show prudence and do nothing to allow events to make the situation more difficult to control than it already is.

I hope that you will issue immediately the necessary instructions to your ships to observe the terms of the quarantine, the basis of which was established by the vote of the Organization of American States this afternoon, and which will go into effect at 1400 hours Greenwich time October twenty-four.

Sincerely, JFK"
Rusk

Soviet Archives

Date: 10/24/1962

Secret
Copy No. 1

CC CPSU

We report on work undertaken in connection with the announcement of the Soviet government about the aggressive actions of American imperialism against the Cuban republic.

The Ministry of Defense, fulfilling the Council of Ministers decision of 23 October 1962, has taken supplementary measures to support the Armed Forces at the highest state of military readiness. Commanders and military councils of military regions, groups of troops, Air Defense districts and fleets are ordered to delay the discharge of soldiers, sailors and sergeants in the last year of service, troops of the strategic rocket forces, Air Defense forces, and the submarine fleet; to cancel all leaves, and to increase military readiness and vigilance in all units and on every ship.

At the present time commanders of the Armed Forces together with local party organs work on explaining to military men the Declaration of the Soviet government. In detachments, on ships, in military schools and in military institutions the Declaration of the USSR government was listened to collectively on the radio, talks, meetings and gatherings are taking place, where members of military councils, commanders and heads of political organs speak. In the country's Air Defense units, Secretaries of the Sakhalin regional CPSU committee (comrade Evstratov), the Khabarovsk provincial committee (comrade Klepikov), Berezovsk City Party Committee (comrade Uglov) spoke. In the military regions special leaflets with the text of the Declaration of the Soviet government were published and transferred by air to far-away detachments and garrisons.

All servicemen passionately approve of the policies of the USSR government, support additional measures which it has undertaken and which are aimed at maintaining the troops in the state of maximum military readiness. At the same time Soviet soldiers express readiness to fulfill without delay every order of the Motherland aimed at the crushing defeat of the American aggressors.

Captain Padalko and Captain Sorkov, pilots of the Second Independent Air Defense Army, and senior technical lieutenants Aziamov and Ovcharov declared: "At this alarming hour we are at the highest state of military readiness. If the American adventurists unleash a war, they will be dealt the most powerful crippling blow. In response to the ugly provcation of the warmonger, we will strengthen even more our vigilance and military preparedness, we will fulfill without delay any order of the Soviet government."

The announcement of the Soviet Government received broad support among soldiers, sergeants and sailors due to be discharged from the Armed Forces. They all declare that they will serve as much as required in the interests of the strengthening of the preparedness of the troops.

Private Kovalenko (415th Air Force Combat Air Wing), prematurely released into the reserves, returned to his base, gave back his documents and announced, "At such a troubling time, my responsibility is to be at my military post, and to defend the interests of the Motherland with a weapon in my hands."

Many senior soldiers, striving with all their strength and knowledge to the increase in military readiness, declare their willingness to remain for additional service. After a meeting of the 15th Division of the Moscow District Air Defense Forces 20 soldiers reported with a request to enlist for additional service. Following the example of Communists Sergeant Kaplin and Junior Sergeant Afanas'ev, 18 soldiers who had been discharged from the 345th anti-aircraft detachment of the Bakinsk District Air Defense Forces requested permission to remain in the army.

After the declaration of the Soviet government, at the bases and on the ships there was a strengthened desire of individual soldiers to defend Cuba as volunteers. On just one day in the 78th motorized infantry training division of the Ural Military District, 1240 requests to be sent to the Cuban Republic were received. At a meeting of the 300 and 302nd detachment (sic) of the Second Independent Air Defense Army of the Air Defense Forces the decision was made about the readiness of the entire unit to leave for Cuba.

In response to the directions of the Soviet government relating to the aggressive actions of the American government, military personnel heighten their vigilance and increase their personal responsibility for the maintenance of military readiness. In the 3rd Corps of the Air Defense Forces of the Moscow Military District, soldiers work at night in fulfillment of daytime norms. In the 201st anti-aircraft detachment of the Ural Military District there has been a significant reduction in the time required for maintenance work on military equipment.

As an expression of the unprecedented trust of the individuals of the Armed Forces in the CPSU there is a strengthened desire among front-line soldiers to join the ranks of the Party and the Komsomol. Following the declaration of the Government of the USSR, the number of applications to join the Party and the Komsomol grew.

During the explanation of the declaration of the Soviet Government, no sorts of negative manifestations were noted.

We are reporting for your information.
(signed) R. Malinovskii
(signed) A. Epishev
24 October 1962

Memorandum

October 24, 1962

I met with Ambassador Dobrynin last evening on the third floor of the Russian Embassy and as you suggested made the following points:

I told him first that I was there on my own and not on the instructions of the President. I said that I wanted to give him some background on the decision of the United States Government and wanted him to know that the duplicity of the Russians had been a major contributing factor. When I had met with him some six weeks before, I said, he had told me that the Russians had not placed any long-range missiles in Cuba and had no intention to do so in the future. He interrupted at that point and confirmed this statement and said he specifically told me they would not put missiles in Cuba which would be able to reach the continental United States.

I said based on that statement which I had related to the President plus independent intelligence information at that time, the President had gone to the American people and assured them that the weapons being furnished by the Communists to Cuba were defensive and that it was not necessary for the United States to blockade or take any military action. I pointed out that this assurance of Dobrynin to me had been confirmed by the TASS statement and then finally, in substance, by Gromyko when he visited the President on Thursday. I said that based on these assurances the President had taken a different and far less belligerent position than people like Senators Keating and Capehart, and he had assured the American people that there was nothing to be concerned about.

I pointed out, in addition, that the President felt he had a very helpful personal relationship with Mr. Khrushchev. Obviously, they did not agree on many issues, but he did feel that there was a mutual trust and confidence between them on which he could rely. As an example of this statement I related the time that Mr. Khrushchev requested the President to withdraw the troops from Thailand and that step was taken within 24 hours.

I said that with the background of this relationship, plus the specific assurances that had been given to us, and then the statement of Dobrynin from Khrushchev to Ted Sorensen and to me that no incident would occur before the American elections were completed, we felt the action by Khrushchev and the Russians at this time was hypocritical, misleading and false. I said this should be clearly understood by them as it was by us.

Dobrynin's only answer was that he had told me no missiles were in Cuba but that Khrushchev had also given similar assurances through TASS and as far as he (Dobrynin) knew, there were still no missiles in Cuba.

Dobrynin in the course of the conversation made several other points. The one he stressed was why the President did not tell Gromyko the facts on Thursday. He said this was something they could not understand and that if we had the information at the time why didn't we tell Gromyko.

I answered this by making two points:

Number one, there wasn't anything the President could tell Gromyko that Gromyko didn't know already and after all, why didn't Gromyko tell the President this instead of, in fact, denying it. I said in addition the President was so shocked at Gromyko's presentation and his failure to recite these facts that he felt that any effort to have an intelligent and honest conversation would not be profitable.

Dobrynin went on to say that from his conversations with Gromyko he doesn't believe Gromyko thought there were any missiles in Cuba. He said he was going to contact his government to find out about this matter.

I expressed surprise that after all that had appeared in the papers, and the President's speech, that he had not had a communication on that question already.

Dobrynin seemed extremely concerned. When I left I asked him if ships were going to go through to Cuba. He replied that was their instructions last month and he assumed they had the same instructions at the present time. He also made the point that although we might have pictures, all we really knew about were the sites and not missiles and that there was a lot of difference between sites and the actual missile itself. I said I did not have to argue the point—there were missiles in Cuba—we knew that they were there and that I hoped he would inform himself also.

I left around 10:15 p.m. and went to the White House and gave a verbal report to the President.

RFK

Telegram to US Embassy in Turkey

October 24, 1962

445. For Ambassadors Hare and Finletter from Secretary.

Soviet reaction Cuban quarantine likely involve efforts compare missiles in Cuba with Jupiters in Turkey. While such comparison refutable, possible that negotiated solution for removal Cuban offensive threat may involve dismantling and removal Jupiters. Recognize this would create serious politico-military problems for US-Turkish relations and with regard to Turkey's place in NATO Alliance. Therefore need prepare carefully for such contingency order not harm our relations with this important ally.

Urgently request Ambassador Hare's assessment political consequences such removal under various assumptions, including outright removal, removal accompanied by stationing of Polaris submarine in area, or removal with some other significant military offset, such as seaborn multilateral nuclear force within NATO.

Ambassador Finletter also requested comment standpoint NATO aspect problem. Do not discuss with any foreigners.

Rusk

Letter From Chairman Khrushchev to President Kennedy

October 24, 1962

Moscow, October 24, 1962.

Dear Mr. President: I have received your letter of October 23, have studied it, and am answering you.

Just imagine, Mr. President, that we had presented you with the conditions of an ultimatum which you have presented us by your action. How would you have reacted to this? I think that you would have been indignant at such a step on our part. And this would have been understandable to us.

In presenting us with these conditions, you, Mr. President, have flung a challenge at us. Who asked you to do this? By what right did you do this? Our ties with the Republic of Cuba, like our relations with other states, regardless of what kind of states they may be, concern only the two countries between which these relations exist. And if we now speak of the quarantine to which your letter refers, a quarantine may be established, according to accepted international practice, only by agreement of states between themselves, and not by some third party. Quarantines exist, for example, on agricultural goods and products. But in this case the question is in no way one of quarantine, but rather of far more serious things, and you yourself understand this.

You, Mr. President, are not declaring a quarantine, but rather are setting forth an ultimatum and threatening that if we do not give in to your demands you will use force. Consider what you are saying! And you want to persuade me to agree to this! What would it mean to agree to these demands? It would mean guiding oneself in one's relations with other countries not by reason, but by submitting to arbitrariness. You are no longer appealing to reason, but wish to intimidate us.

No, Mr. President, I cannot agree to this, and I think that in your own heart you recognize that I am correct. I am convinced that in my place you would act the same way.

Reference to the decision of the Organization of American States cannot in any way substantiate the demands now advanced by the United States. This Organization has absolutely no authority or basis for adopting decisions such as the one you speak of in your letter. Therefore, we do not recognize these decisions. International law exists and universally recognized norms of conduct exist. We firmly adhere to the principles of international law and observe strictly the norms which regulate navigation on the high seas, in international waters. We observe these norms and enjoy the rights recognized by all states.

You wish to compel us to renounce the rights that every sovereign state enjoys, you are trying to legislate in questions of international law, and you are violating the universally accepted norms of that law. And you are doing all this not only out of hatred for the Cuban people and its government, but also because of considerations of the election campaign in the United States. What morality, what law can justify such an approach by the American Government to international affairs? No such morality or law can be found, because the actions of the United States with regard to Cuba constitute outright banditry or, if you like, the folly of degenerate imperialism. Unfortunately, such folly can bring grave suffering to the peoples of all countries, and to no lesser degree to the American people themselves, since the United States has completely lost its former isolation with the advent of modern types of armament.

Therefore, Mr. President, if you coolly weigh the situation which has developed, not giving way to passions, you will understand that the Soviet Union cannot fail to reject the arbitrary demands of the United States. When you confront us with such conditions, try to put yourself in our place and consider how the United States would react to these conditions. I do not doubt that if someone attempted to dictate similar conditions to you—the United States—you would reject such an attempt. And we also say—no.

The Soviet Government considers that the violation of the freedom to use international waters and international air space is an act of aggression which pushes mankind toward the abyss of a world nuclear-missile war. Therefore, the Soviet Government cannot instruct the captains of Soviet vessels bound for Cuba to observe the orders of American naval forces blockading that Island. Our instructions to Soviet mariners are to observe strictly the universally accepted norms of navigation in international waters and not to retreat one step from them. And if the American side violates these rules, it must realize what responsibility will rest upon it in that case. Naturally we will not simply be bystanders with regard to piratical acts by American ships on the high seas. We will then be forced on our part to take the measures we consider necessary and adequate in order to protect our rights. We have everything necessary to do so.

Respectfully,

N. Khrushchev

Memorandum

October 24, 1962, 11:45 p.m.

Ball—We've got another idea that I would like to try out on you. Do you think there is any chance that U Thant would be willing to send Mr. K a letter?. Let me bring you up to date. We've had a message from K in which he says in effect that he can't give instructions to his ships to abide by the blockade and that if we violate these rules, that will be our fault and they will be forced to take measures that they deem necessary and adequate to protect their rights, and they have what's necessary to do that. Implications being knowing that there may be a submarine or two in the waters, that could be an attempt to torpedo one of our ships. Would U Thant under all the circumstances knowing the possibility of a confrontation tomorrow be prepared to send a message to K along the lines that he is very concerned about possibility of a confrontation in connection with this quarantine, and that he asked K to hold his ships away from Cuban waters on the condition that we will not molest them while there is a discussion of the modalities of a possible negotiation.

Stevenson — Yes, I think he might do something like this.

Ball — If we could get something out like that tonight, I think we would hold off, because all we've got is a tanker coming through. We've just given instructions not to touch the thing tonight. We can buy a day or two here and see how it goes.

Stevenson — I think it would be a lot more helpful for me in trying to get U Thant to do this if I could have a copy of the message that we have from K.

Ball — I can give you. It's a garbled message, and it hasn't been cleaned up yet.

Stevenson — Well, if you could put on the wire to me, so that I would have it first thing in the morning a substantial text of it.

Ball — I think it would have to be done tonight if we're going to do it because we've got a time dislocation and things are moving so swiftly. Is there a chance of getting hold of Thant tonight.

Stevenson — He's awful hard to get when he goes home. I am afraid it will be almost impossible to do anything with him tonight.

Ball — If you could even talk to him tonight.

Stevenson — I could talk to him on the phone and tell him what the burden of this thing is and that I'm going to be around in the morning with a suggestion that he send a message to K saying that he. I don't know whether he should say that he has this word.

Ball—I don't think he needs to say that he has any word.

Stevenson—See, what he's already said is please hold off on everything.

Ball—What he can say is that he is disturbed about the possibility of a confrontation at sea under the quarantine before further action could be taken toward trying to get this into political channels and he would therefore like an agreement from K that he will hold his ships off on the condition, away from Cuban waters, we won't molest them while the discussion of modalities goes forward.

Stevenson—He says that all concerned should refrain from any actions which may aggravate the situation and bring with it the risk of war. He will say, well I've already said that.

Ball—Yes, but this is giving specific content to it in terms of what the real danger, an immediate confrontation, may be.

Stevenson—I think if he had some feeling that we were likely to present this thing in general subject or conditions, which he knows about, I think maybe he would send such a message.

Ball—This position, I don't want to misrepresent the President on it, but this position that I have from him is that we could hold off for a while while there is some discussions on the modalities of the thing if they will hold their ships away while we do that.

Stevenson—As I understand it, are there any ships nearby?

Ball—There is a ship which was going to be challenged at 2 o'clock tomorrow morning, which is just about 2-1/2 hours from now. We have got that held off.

Stevenson—That was a tanker?

Ball—Yes, and we can continue to hold that one off until we can see if something like this would work.

Stevenson—Would we stop it anyway?

Ball—Yes, we were going to stop it.

Stevenson—Although it was not carrying—

Ball—That is on the theory that we stop everything and challenge it and find out what's on board.

Stevenson—Let me call him. I think he may have trouble getting this message off tonight.

Ball—You know, there is a little flexibility in this because we are challenging these ships 5 hundred miles out; we could outrun most of them and we could challenge them 200 miles out if necessary.

Stevenson—What's next . . . .

Ball—I'm not very clear just what comes how soon. But we could adjust that. We don't want to let ships go through because this discredits our firmness of attention. What I think, if we could get an agreement from the Russians to hold their ships off while we talk about this, the modalities.

Stevenson—For a couple of days?

Ball—Yes, I think it would be that long probably before we get something settled. We won't take any action as long as their ships are held off, that way we avoid a confrontation until we can see if we can get the modalities with negotiation.

Stevenson—He has diverted the armed ships?

Ball—Yes.

Stevenson—Let me call him and see what I get.

Telegram to US Embassy in Moscow

Washington, October 25, 1962, 1:59 a.m.

997. Ref: Embtel 1070. Signed original following message from President to Khrushchev delivered to Soviet Embassy 1:45 a.m. Washington time October 25. Please deliver to highest ranking Soviet official immediately available.

October 25, 1962

"Dear Mr. Chairman:

I have received your letter of October 24, and I regret very much that you still do not appear to understand what it is that has moved us in this matter.

The sequence of events is clear. In August there were reports of important shipments of military equipment and technicians from the Soviet Union to Cuba. In early September I indicated very plainly that the United States would regard any shipment of offensive weapons as presenting the gravest issues. After that time, this Government received the most explicit assurance from your Government and its representatives, both publicly and privately, that no offensive weapons were being sent to Cuba. If you will review the statement issued by TASS in September, you will see how clearly this assurance was given.

In reliance on these solemn assurances I urged restraint upon those in this country who were urging action in this matter at that time. And then I learned beyond doubt what you have not denied — namely, that all these public assurances were false and that your military people had set out recently to establish a set of missile bases in Cuba. I ask you to recognize clearly, Mr. Chairman, that it was not I who issued the first challenge in this case, and that in the light of this record these activities in Cuba required the responses I have announced.

I repeat my regret that these events should cause a deterioration in our relations. I hope that your Government will take the necessary action to permit a restoration of the earlier situation.

Sincerely yours, John F. Kennedy"
Please report time delivery.
Rusk

Memorandum

Washington, October 25, 1962.

SUBJECT

Executive Committee Meeting 10/25/62--10:00 a.m. All Members present

McCone reported on intelligence, reviewing summary of 25 October, including penciled memorandums as indicated, plus Cline memorandum of 25 October on talks with Sir Kenneth Strong, and the Watch Report of same date.

I called special attention to the Belovodsk and reported on page II-5 and the searching of the Cubana airplane by Canadians as reported on page IV-2. Also the shipping schedule.

McNamara reported that at 7:00 o'clock a destroyer intercepted the tanker Bucharest which responded destination was Havana, cargo was petroleum and the Bucharest was permitted to proceed under surveillance. He stated that no United States Navy ships had orders to board. He recommended orders be issued to immediately board Bloc ships and then the Bucharest be boarded. Decision was reached that Navy be instructed to board the next Soviet ship contacted which would be the Graznyy, a tanker, but which was carrying a deck load which might be missile field tanks. Later in the meeting decision was reached not to board the Bucharest. Contact was to be made with the Graznyy as early as possible and that was estimated to be about 8:00 o'clock in the evening, Friday, October 26th.

McNamara recommended several recurring low-level surveillance strikes of multiple aircraft in an operation that would resemble an air strike. [censored] It was the Secretary's opinion that since all of these were indicators of some indecision on the part of the Soviets, that we should pursue low-level surveillance in the interests of gathering intelligence, simulating air attack, demonstrating our intention to watch construction, familiarizing ourselves with camouflage and to determine whether the Soviets are building additional sites. This recommendation was approved and 8 sorties were ordered immediately to cover the nine missile sites, the IL 28 site, the MIG 21 airfield, and the nuclear storage sites and the KOMAR missile ship sites. It was decided this reconnaissance should not be announced but, if questioned, we should refer to the President's statement.

McCone then noted the number of ships in the Eastern Atlantic and in the Baltic and Mediterranean which had turned back. Dillon asked about ships in the Pacific. The President asked whether Soviet ships bound elsewhere than Cuba had changed course. McCone said he would report on this in the afternoon.

There was a further discussion of the policy of stopping or hailing non-Bloc ships. It was decided that all ships must be hailed.

Rusk raised the question of discussions with the United Nations. Draft of U.S. reply to the U Thant letter was approved with modifications. It was agreed at the meeting that we must insist upon the removal of missiles from Cuba in addition to demands that construction be stopped and that UN inspectors be permitted at once.

Bundy reviewed Khrushchev letter to the President of the 24th of October and the Kennedy reply. McNamara raised the question of accelerating or raising the escalation of the actions we have so far taken, expressing concern over the plateau, indicating determination to meet our ultimate objective of taking out the missile sites.

Rusk then asked certain actions on the part of CIA as follows: (1) An answer to questions of the effect on Cuba because ships were turned about as indicated in recent reports; (2) What had happened to Soviet ships which were bound elsewhere than Cuba; (3) The general Cuban reaction to our actions to date:

(a) Do they know about Soviet missiles?
(b) Have they heard the President's speech?
(c) What is the morale in Cuba?
McCone promised answers.

John A. McCone
Director

Record of Action

Washington, October 25, 1962.

1. Mr. McCone presented the intelligence briefing.

2. The President requested Mr. McCone to prepare a careful analysis of the present situation inside Cuba, and he asked for further consideration by USIA of the possibility of dropping propaganda leaflets.

3. The Secretary of Defense reported the current military situation, and on the President's direction instructions were issued for selective investigation and boarding of non-bloc ships, excluding tankers.

4. The Secretary reported that all armed forces in Cuba have been instructed to fire only in response to attack. Many installations are so camouflaged as to be in a low state of readiness. The Secretary recommended a program of low-level reconnaissance for the purpose of improving intelligence, camouflaging the possibility of a later low-level attack, and emphasizing our concern with offensive installations already in Cuba. The President approved an immediate daylight mission of 8 low-level reconnaissance aircraft to cover missile sites, airfields holding IL28's and MIG's, KOMAR naval vessels, coastal installations, nuclear storage sites, and selected SAM sites.

5. The President directed that the tanker Bucharest not be intercepted for the present. Her status as a tanker with no contraband cargo made it desirable to allow her to proceed. He directed further that the Defense Department be prepared to make an intercept of an appropriate bloc ship on Friday in daylight.

6. The President approved a version of an answer to U Thant, but in later discussion a revised version was worked out between New York and Washington and approved by the President at 1:15 p.m.

7. There was preliminary discussion of alternative courses of action in the immediate future, and the President asked the

other members of the Committee to make appropriate arrangements for preparing alternative courses of action for discussion with him at a later meeting.

8. The President approved the recommendation of the Secretary of Defense that missile fuel be added to the list of contraband goods under the Proclamation of Interdiction.

McGeorge Bundy

Soviet Statement to UN Secuity Council

United Nations Security Council Meeting
October 25, 1962

When Mr. Stevenson today attempted to accuse the Soviet Union as the prime cause for these aggressive actions on the part of the United States, I should like to draw attention of the Council to a completely surprising fact.

In the statement of President Kennedy of the 22nd of October, Mr. Kennedy said that during the last week unmistakable evidence has established the fact that a series of offensive missile sites is now in preparation on that island.

On the 16th of October the President of the United States had in his hands incontrovertible information. What happened after that? On the 18th of October the President of the United States was receiving the representative of the Soviet Union, the Minister of Foreign Affairs, Mr. Gromyko, two days after he had already in his hands incontrovertible evidence.

One may well ask why did the President of the United States in receiving the minister of another power which the Government of the United States is now accusing of dispatching offensive arms to Cuba against the United States, why then did he not say a word to the Minister of Foreign Affairs of the Soviet Union with respect to these incontrovertible facts?

Why? Because no such facts exist. The Government of the United States has no such fact in its hands except these falsified information of the United States Intelligence Agency, which are being displayed for review in halls and which are sent to the press.

Falsity is what the United States has in its hands, false evidence.

The Government of the United States has deliberately intensified the crisis, has deliberately prepared this provocation and had tried to cover up this provocation by means of a discussion in the Security Council.

You cannot conduct world policies and politics on such an opportunistic matter. Such steps can lead you to catastrophic consequences for the whole world, and the Soviet Government has issued a warning to the United States and to the world on that score.

The Soviet Union considers that the Government of the United States of America must display reserve and stay the execution of its piratical threats, which are fraught with the most serious consequence.

The question of war and peace is so vital that we should consider useful a top level meeting in order to discuss all the problems which have arisen to do everything to remove the danger of unleashing a thermonuclear war.

US Statement To U.N. Security Council

October 25, 1962

I want to say to you, Mr. Zorin, that I do not have your talent for obfuscation, for distortion, for confusing language, and for doubletalk. And I must confess to you that I am glad that I do not!

But if I understood what you said, you said that my position had changed, that today I was defensive because we did not have the evidence to prove our assertions, that your Government had installed long-range missiles in Cuba.

Well, let me say something to you, Mr. Ambassador—we do have the evidence. We have it, and it is clear and it is incontrovertible. And let me say something else—those weapons must be taken out of Cuba.

Next, let me say to you that, if I understood you, with a trespass on credibility that excels your best, you said that our position had changed since I spoke here the other day because of the pressures of world opinion and the majority of the United Nations. Well, let me say to you, sir, you are wrong again. We have had no pressure from anyone whatsoever. We came in here today to indicate our willingness to discuss Mr. U Thant's proposals, and that is the only change that has taken place.

But let me also say to you, sir, that there has been a change. You—the Soviet Union has sent these weapons to Cuba. You—the Soviet Union has upset the balance of power in the world. You—the Soviet Union has created this new danger, not the United States.

And you ask with a fine show of indignation why the President did not tell Mr. Gromyko on last Thursday about our evidence, at the very time that Mr. Gromyko was blandly denying to the President that the U.S.S.R. was placing such weapons on sites in the new world.

Well, I will tell you why—because we were assembling the evidence, and perhaps it would be instructive to the world to see how a Soviet official—how far he would go in perfidy. Perhaps we wanted to know if this country faced another example of nuclear deceit like that one a year ago, when in stealth, the Soviet Union broke the nuclear test moratorium.

And while we are asking questions, let me ask you why your Government—your Foreign Minister—deliberately, cynically deceived us about the nuclear build-up in Cuba.

And, finally, the other day, Mr. Zorin, I remind you that you did not deny the existence of these weapons. Instead, we heard that they had suddenly become defensive weapons. But today again if I heard you correctly, you now say that they do not exist, or that we haven't proved they exist, with another fine flood of rhetorical scorn.

All right, sir, let me ask you one simple question: Do you, Ambassador Zorin, deny that the U.S.S.R. has placed and is placing medium- and intermediate-range missiles and sites in Cuba? Yes or no—don't wait for the translation—yes or no?

(The Soviet representative refused to answer.)

You can answer yes or no. You have denied they exist. I want to know if I understood you correctly. I am prepared to wait for my answer until hell freezes over, if that's your decision. And I am also prepared to present the evidence in this room.

(The President called on the representative of Chile to speak, but Ambassador Stevenson continued as follows.)

I have not finished my statement. I asked you a question. I have had no reply to the question, and I will now proceed, if I may, to finish my statement.

I doubt if anyone in this room, except possibly the representative of the Soviet Union, has any doubt about the facts. But in view of his statements and the statements of the Soviet Government up until last Thursday, when Mr. Gromyko denied the existence or any intention of installing such weapons in Cuba, I am going to make a portion of the evidence available right now. If you will indulge me for a moment, we will set up an easel here in the back of the room where I hope it will be visible to everyone.

The first of these exhibits shows an area north of the village of Candelaria, near San Cristóbal, southwest of Habana. A map, together with a small photograph, shows precisely where the area is in Cuba.

The first photograph shows the area in late August 1962; it was then, if you can see from where you are sitting, only a peaceful countryside.

The second photograph shows the same area one day last week. A few tents and vehicles had come into the area, new spur roads had appeared, and the main road had been improved.

The third photograph, taken only twenty-four hours later, shows facilities for a medium-range missile battalion installed. There are tents for 400 or 500 men. At the end of the new spur road there are seven 1,000-mile missile trailers. There are four launcher-erector mechanisms for placing these missiles in erect firing position. This missile is a mobile weapon, which can be moved rapidly from one place to another. It is identical with the 1,000-mile missiles which have been displayed in Moscow parades. All of this, I remind you, took place in twenty-four hours.

The second exhibit, which you can all examine at your leisure, shows three successive photographic enlargements of another missile base of the same type in the area of San Cristóbal. These enlarged photographs clearly show six of these missiles on trailers and three erectors.

And that is only one example of the first type of ballistic missile installation in Cuba.

A second type of installation is designed for a missile of intermediate range—a range of about 2,200 miles. Each site of this type has four launching pads.

The exhibit on this type of missile shows a launching area being constructed near Guanajay, southwest of the city of Habana. As in the first exhibit, a map and small photograph show this area as it appeared in late August 1962, when no military activities were apparent.

A second large photograph shows the same area about six weeks later. Here you will see a very heavy construction effort to push the launching area to rapid completion. The pictures show two large concrete bunkers or control centers in process of construction, one between each pair of launching pads. They show heavy concrete retaining walls being erected to shelter vehicles and equipment from rocket blast-off. They show cable scars leading from the launch pads to the bunkers. They show a large reinforced concrete building under construction. A building with a heavy arch may well be intended as the storage area for the nuclear warheads. The installation is not yet complete, and no warheads are yet visible.

The next photograph shows a closer view of the same intermediate-range launch site. You can clearly see one of the pairs of large concrete launch pads, with a concrete building from which launching operations for three pads are controlled. Other details are visible, such as fuel tanks.

And that is only one example, one illustration, of the work being furnished in Cuba on intermediate-range missile bases.

Now, in addition to missiles, the Soviet Union is installing other offensive weapons in Cuba. The next photograph is of an airfield at San Julián in western Cuba. On this field you will see twenty-two crates designed to transport the fuselages of Soviet llyushin-28 bombers. Four of the aircraft are uncrated, and one is partially assembled. These bombers, sometimes known as Beagles, have an operating radius of about 750 miles and are capable of carrying nuclear weapons. At the same field you can see one of the surface-to-air anti-aircraft guided missile bases, with six missiles per base, which now ring the entire coastline of Cuba.

Another set of two photographs covers still another area of deployment of medium-range missiles in Cuba. These photographs are on a larger scale than the others and reveal many details of an improved field-type launch site. One photograph provides an overall view of most of the site; you can see clearly three of the four launching pads. The second photograph displays details of two of these pads. Even an eye untrained in photographic interpretation can clearly see the buildings in which the missiles are checked out and maintained ready to fire, a missile trailer, trucks to move missiles out to the launching pad, erectors to raise the missiles to launching position, tank trucks to provide fuel, vans from which the missile firing is controlled, in short, all of the requirements to maintain, load, and fire these terrible weapons.

These weapons, gentlemen, these launching pads, these planes—of which we have illustrated only a fragment—are a part of a much larger weapons complex, what is called a weapons system.

To support this build-up, to operate these advanced weapons systems, the Soviet Union has sent a large number of military personnel to Cuba—a force now amounting to several thousand men.

These photographs, as I say, are available to members for detailed examination in the Trusteeship Council room following this meeting. There I will have one of my aides who will gladly explain them to you in such detail as you may require.

I have nothing further to say at this time.

(After another statement by the Soviet representative, Ambassador Stevenson replied as follows:)

Mr. President and gentlemen, I won't detain you but one minute.

I have not had a direct answer to my question. The representative of the Soviet Union says that the official answer of the U.S.S.R. was the Tass statement that they don't need to locate missiles in Cuba. Well, I agree—they don't need to. But the question is, have they missiles in Cuba—and that question remains unanswered. I knew it would be.

As to the authenticity of the photographs, which Mr. Zorin has spoken about with such scorn, I wonder if the Soviet Union would ask its Cuban colleague to permit a U.N. team to go to these sites. If so, I can assure you that we can direct them to the proper places very quickly.

And now I hope that we can get down to business, that we can atop this sparring. We know the facts, and so do you, sir, and we are ready to talk about them. Our job here is not to score debating points. Our job, Mr. Zorin, is to save the peace. And if you are ready to try, we are.

Memorandum

Washington, undated.

Alexander S. Fomin, Sov Emby Counselor, at lunch which he sought urgently, asks if State would be interested in settlement of Cuban crisis along these lines:

Bases would be dismantled under United Nations supervision and Castro would pledge not to accept offensive weapons of any kind, ever, in return for US pledge not to invade Cuba.

I said I didn't know but that perhaps this is something that could be talked about. He said if Stevenson pursued this line, Zorin would be interested. Asked that I check with State and let him know. He gave me his home telephone number so I could call him tonight, if necessary.

Fomin claimed that Cuban delegate to UN during Security Council debate asked for such no-invasion assurances in return for dismantling but that he got no reply. I told him I'd followed the UN debate very carefully but could not recall any such remarks on Cuban's part.

Fomin also said Russia had been forced "to make some concessions" to Communist China in order to convince them to stop the fighting against India. He declined to say what under my questioning. But he recalled they hadn't helped the ChiComs with nuclear weapons or conventional weapons in the past, even tanks, and hinted it might be aid in the conventional field.

Scali

Telegram From US Embassy in Moscow ("The First Message")

October 26, 1962

1101. Policy. Embassy translation follows of letter from Khrushchev to President delivered to Embassy by messenger 4:43 p.m. Moscow time October 26, under cover of letter from Gromyko to me.

Begin text.

Dear Mr. President:

I have received your letter of October 25. From your letter, I got the feeling that you have some understanding of the situation which has developed and a sense of responsibility. I value this.

Now we have already publicly exchanged our evaluations of the events around Cuba and each of us has set forth his explanation and his understanding of these events. Consequently, I would think that, apparently, a continuation of an exchange of opinions at such a distance, even in the form of secret letters, will hardly add anything to that which one side has already said to the other.

I think you will understand me correctly if you are really concerned about the welfare of the world. Everyone needs peace: both capitalists, if they have not lost their reason, and, still more, Communists, people who know how to value not only their own lives but, more than anything, the lives of the peoples. We, Communists, are against all wars between states in general and have been defending the cause of peace since we came into the world. We have always regarded war as a calamity, and not as a game nor as a means for the attainment of definite goals, nor, all the more, as a goal in itself. Our goals are clear, and the means to attain them is labor. War is our enemy and a calamity for all the peoples.

It is thus that we, Soviet people, and, together with US, other peoples as well, understand the questions of war and peace. I can, in any case, firmly say this for the peoples of the socialist countries, as well as for all progressive people who want peace, happiness, and friendship among peoples.

I see, Mr. President, that you too are not devoid of a sense of anxiety for the fate of the world, understanding, and of what war entails. What would a war give you? You are threatening us with war. But you well know that the very least which you would receive in reply would be that you would experience the same consequences as those which you sent us. And that must be clear to us, people invested with authority, trust, and responsibility. We must not succumb to intoxication and petty passions, regardless of whether elections are impending in this or that country, or not impending. These are all transient things, but if indeed war should break out, then it would not be in our power to contain or stop it, for such is the logic of war. I have participated in two wars and know that war ends when it has rolled through cities and villages, everywhere sowing death and destruction.

In the name of the Soviet Government and the Soviet people, I assure you that your arguments regarding offensive weapons on Cuba are groundless. It is apparent from what you have written me that our conceptions are different on this score, or rather, we have different definitions for these or those military means, indeed, in reality, the same forms of weapons can have different interpretations.

You are a military man and, I hope, will understand me. Let us take for example a simple cannon. What sort of means is this: offensive or defensive? A cannon is a defensive means if it is set up to defend boundaries or a fortified area. But if one concentrates artillery, and adds to it the necessary number of troops, then the same cannons do become an offensive means, because they prepare and clear the way for infantry to advance. The same happens with missile-nuclear weapons as well, with any type of this weapon.

You are mistaken if you think that any of our means on Cuba are offensive. However, let us not argue now, it is apparent that I will not be able to convince you of this, but I say to you: You, Mr. President, are a military man and should understand: can one advance, if one has on one's territory even an enormous quantity of missiles of various effective radiuses and various power, but using only these means. These missiles are a means of extermination and destruction, but one cannot advance with these missiles, even nuclear missiles of a power of 100 megatons because only people, troops, can advance, without people, any means however powerful cannot be offensive.

How can one, consequently, give such a completely incorrect interpretation as you are now giving, to the effect that some sort of means on Cuba are offensive. All the means located there, and I assure you of this, have a defensive character, are on Cuba solely for the purposes of defense, and we have sent them to Cuba at the request of the Cuban Government. You, however, say that these are offensive means.

But, Mr. President, do you really seriously think that Cuba can attack the United States and that even we together with Cuba can advance upon you from the territory of Cuba? Can you really think that way? How is it possible? We do not understand this. Has something so new appeared in military strategy that one can think that it is possible to advance thus. I say precisely advance, and not destroy, since barbarians, people who have lost their sense, destroy.

I believe that you have no basis to think this way. You can regard us with distrust, but, in any case, you can be calm in this regard, that we are of sound mind and understand perfectly well that if we attack you, you will respond the same way. But you too will receive the same that you hurl against us. And I think that you also understand this. My conversation with you in Vienna gives me the right to talk to you this way.

This indicates that we are normal people, that we correctly understand and correctly evaluate the situation. Consequently, how can we permit the incorrect actions which you ascribe to us? Only lunatics or suicides, who themselves want to perish and to destroy the whole world before they die, could do this. We, however, want to live and do not at all want to destroy your country. We want something quite different: to compete with your country on a peaceful endeavor. We quarrel with you, we have differences in ideological questions. But our view of the world consists in this, that ideological questions, as well as economic problems, should be solved not by military means, they must be solved on the basis of peaceful competition, i.e., as this is understood in capitalist society, on the basis of competition. We have proceeded and are proceeding from the fact that the peaceful co-existence of the two different social-political systems, now existing in the world, is necessary, that it is necessary to assure a stable peace. That is the sort of principle we hold.

You have now proclaimed piratical measures, which were employed in the Middle Ages, when ships proceeding in international waters were attacked, and you have called this "a quarantine" around Cuba. Our vessels, apparently, will soon enter the zone which your Navy is patrolling. I assure you that these vessels, now bound for Cuba, are carrying the most innocent peaceful cargoes. Do you really think that we only occupy ourselves with the carriage of so-called offensive weapons, atomic and hydrogen bombs? Although perhaps your military people imagine that these (cargoes) are some sort of special type of weapon, I assure you that they are the most ordinary peaceful products.

Consequently, Mr. President, let us show good sense. I assure you that on those ships, which are bound for Cuba, there are no weapons at all. The weapons which were necessary for the defense of Cuba are already there. I do not want to say that there were not any shipments of weapons at all. No, there were such shipments. But now Cuba has already received the necessary means of defense.

I don't know whether you can understand me and believe me. But I should like to have you believe in yourself and to agree that one cannot give way to passions; it is necessary to control them. And in what direction are events now developing? If you stop the vessels, then, as you yourself know, that would be piracy. If we started to do that with regard to your ships, then you would also be as indignant as we and the whole world now are. One cannot give another interpretation to such actions, because one cannot legalize lawlessness. If this were permitted, then there would be no peace, there would also be no peaceful coexistence. We should then be forced to put into effect the necessary measures of a defensive character to protect our interest in accordance with international law. Why should this be done? To what would all this lead?

Let us normalize relations. We have received an appeal from the Acting Secretary General of the UN, U Thant, with his proposals. I have already answered him. His proposals come to this, that our side should not transport armaments of any kind to Cuba during a certain period of time, while negotiations are being conducted—and we are ready to enter such negotiations—and the other side should not undertake any sort of piratical actions against vessels engaged in navigation on the high seas. I consider these proposals reasonable. This would be a way out of the situation which has been created, which would give the peoples the possibility of breathing calmly. You have asked what happened, what evoked the delivery of weapons to Cuba? You have spoken about this to our Minister of Foreign Affairs. I will tell you frankly, Mr. President, what evoked it.

We were very grieved by the fact—I spoke about it in Vienna—that a landing took place, that an attack on Cuba was committed, as a result of which many Cubans perished. You yourself told me then that this had been a mistake. I respected that explanation. You repeated it to me several times, hinting that not everybody occupying a high position would acknowledge his mistakes as you had done. I value such frankness. For my part, I told you that we too possess no less courage; we also acknowledged those mistakes which had been committed during the history of our state, and not only acknowledged, but sharply condemned them.

If you are really concerned about the peace and welfare of your people, and this is your responsibility as President, then I, as the Chairman of the Council of Ministers, am concerned for my people. Moreover, the preservation of world peace should be our joint concern, since if, under contemporary conditions, war should break out, it would be a war not only between the Soviet Union and the United States which have no contentions between them, but a worldwide cruel and destructive war.

Why have we proceeded to assist Cuba with military and economic aid? The answer is: we have proceeded to do so only for reasons of humanitarianism. At one time, our people itself had a revolution, when Russia was still a backward country, we were attacked then. We were the target of attack by many countries. The USA participated in that adventure. This has been recorded by participants in the aggression against our country. A whole book has been written about this by General Graves, who, at that time, commanded the US Expeditionary Corps. Graves called it "The American Adventure in Siberia."

We know how difficult it is to accomplish a revolution and how difficult it is to reconstruct a country on new foundations. We sincerely sympathize with Cuba and the Cuban people, but we are not interfering in questions of domestic structure, we are not interfering in their affairs. The Soviet Union desires to help the Cubans build their life as they themselves wish and that others should not hinder them.

You once said that the United States was not preparing an invasion. But you also declared that you sympathized with the Cuban counter-revolutionary emigrants, that you support them and would help them to realize their plans against the present Government of Cuba. It is also not a secret to anyone that the threat of armed attack, aggression, has constantly hung, and continues to hand over Cuba. It was only this which impelled us to respond to the request of the Cuban Government to furnish it aid for the strengthening of the defensive capacity of this country.

If assurances were given by the President and the Government of the United States that the USA itself would not participate in an attack on Cuba and would restrain others from actions of this sort, if you would recall your fleet, this would immediately change everything. I am not speaking for Fidel Castro, but I think that he and the Government of Cuba, evidently, would declare demobilization and would appeal to the people to get down to peaceful labor. Then, too, the question of armaments would disappear, since, if there is no threat, then armaments are a burden for every people. Then, too, the question of the destruction, not only of the armaments which you call offensive, but of all other armaments as well, would look different.

I spoke in the name of the Soviet Government in the United Nations and introduced a proposal for the disbandment of all armies and for the destruction of all armaments. How then can I now count on those armaments?

Armaments bring only disasters. When one accumulates them, this damages the economy, and if one puts them to use, then they destroy people on both sides. Consequently, only a madman can believe that armaments are the principal means in the life of society. No, they are an enforced loss of human energy, and what is more are for the destruction of man himself. If people do not show wisdom, then in the final analysis they will come to a clash, like blind moles, and then reciprocal extermination will begin.

Let us therefore show statesmanlike wisdom. I propose: we, for our part, will declare that our ships, bound for Cuba, are not carrying any armaments. You would declare that the United States will not invade Cuba with its forces and will not support any sort of forces which might intend to carry out an invasion of Cuba. Then the necessity for the presence of our military specialists in Cuba would disappear.

Mr. President, I appeal to you to weigh well what the aggressive, piratical actions, which you have declared the USA intends to carry out in international waters, would lead to. You yourself know that any sensible man simply cannot agree with this, cannot recognize your right to such actions.

If you did this as the first step towards the unleashing of war, well then, it is evident that nothing else is left to us but to accept this challenge of yours. If, however, you have not lost your self-control and sensibly conceive what this might lead to, then, Mr. President, we and you ought not now to pull on the ends of the rope in which you have tied the knot of war, because the more the two of us pull, the tighter that knot will be tied. And a moment may come when that knot will be tied so tight that even he who tied it will not have the strength to untie it, and then it will be necessary to cut that knot. And what that would mean is not for me to explain to you, because you yourself understand perfectly of what terrible forces our countries dispose.

Consequently, if there is no intention to tighten that knot and thereby to doom the world to the catastrophe of thermonuclear war, then let us not only relax the forces pulling on the ends of the rope, let us take measures to untie that knot. We are ready for this.

We welcome all forces which stand on positions of peace. Consequently, I both expressed gratitude to Mr. Bertrand Russell, who manifests alarm and concern for the fate of the world, and readily responded to the appeal of the Acting Secretary General of the UN, U Thant.

There, Mr. President, are my thoughts, which, if you agreed with them, could put an end to that tense situation which is disturbing all peoples.

These thoughts are dictated by a sincere desire to relieve the situation, to remove the threat of war.

Respectfully yours,

N. Khrushchev

October 26, 1962. End text.
Original of letter being air pouched today under transmittal slip to Executive Secretariat.

Kohler

White House Statement

October 26, 1962

The development of ballistic missile sites in Cuba continues at a rapid pace. Through the process of continued surveillance directed by the President, additional evidence has been acquired which clearly reflects that as of Thursday, October 25, definite build-ups in these offensive missile sites continued to be made. The activity at these sites apparently is directed at achieving a full operational capability as soon as possible.

There is evidence that as of yesterday, October 25, considerable construction activity was being engaged in at the intermediate-range ballistic missile sites. Bulldozers and cranes were observed as late as Thursday actively clearing new areas within the sites and improving the approach roads to the launch pads.

Since Tuesday, October 23, missile-related activities have continued at the medium-range ballistic missile sites resulting in progressive refinements at these facilities. For example, missiles were observed parked in the open on October 23. Surveillance on October 25 revealed that some of these same missiles have now been moved from their original parked positions. Cabling can be seen running from the missile-ready tents to power generators nearby.

In summary, there is no evidence to date indicating that there is any intention to dismantle or discontinue work on these missile sites. On the contrary the Soviets are rapidly continuing their construction of missile support and launch facilities, and serious attempts are under way to camouflage their efforts.

Letter From Khrushchev to Kennedy ("The Second Message")

October 26, 1962

Dear Mr. President:

It is with great satisfaction that I studied your reply to Mr. U Thant on the adoption of measures in order to avoid contact by our ships and thus avoid irreparable fatal consequences. This reasonable step on your part persuades me that you are showing solicitude for the preservation of peace, and I note this with satisfaction.

I have already said that the only concern of our people and government and myself personally as chairman of the Council of Ministers is to develop our country and have it hold a worthy place among all people of the world in economic competition, advance of culture and arts, and the rise in people's living standards. This is the loftiest and most necessary field for competition which will only benefit both the winner and loser, because this benefit is peace and an increase in the facilities by means of which man lives and obtains pleasure.

In your statement, you said that the main aim lies not only in reaching agreement and adopting measures to avert contact of our ships, and, consequently, a deepening of the crisis, which because of this contact, can spark off the fire of military conflict after which any talks would be superfluous because other forces and other laws would begin to operate – the laws of war. I agree with you that this is only a first step. The main thing is to normalize and stabilize the situation in the world between states and between people.

I understand your concern for the security of the United States, Mr. President, because this is the first duty of the president. However, these questions are also uppermost in our minds. The same duties rest with me as chairman of the U.S.S.R. Council of Ministers. You have been worried over our assisting Cuba with arms designed to strengthen its defensive potential - precisely defensive potential – because Cuba, no matter what weapons it had, could not compare with you since these are different dimensions, the more so given up-to-date means of extermination.

Our purpose has been and is to help Cuba, and no one can challenge the humanity of our motives aimed at allowing Cuba to live peacefully and develop as its people desire. You want to relieve your country from danger and this is understandable. however, Cuba also wants this. All countries want to relieve themselves from danger, but how can we, the Soviet Union and our government, assess your actions which, in effect, mean that you have surrounded the Soviet Union with military bases, surrounded our allies with military bases, set up military bases literally around our country, and stationed your rocket weapons at them? This is no secret. High-placed American officials demonstratively declare this. Your rockets are stationed in Britain and in Italy and pointed at us. Your rockets are stationed in Turkey.

You are worried over Cuba. You say that it worries you because it lies at a distance of ninety miles across the sea from the shores of the United States. However, Turkey lies next to us. Our sentinels are pacing up and down and watching each other. Do you believe that you have the right to demand security for your country and the removal of such weapons that you qualify as offensive, while not recognizing this right for us?

You have stationed devastating rocket weapons, which you call offensive, in Turkey literally right next to us. How then does recognition of our equal military possibilities tally with such unequal relations between our great states? This does not tally at all.

It is good, Mr. President, that you agreed for our representatives to meet and begin talks, apparently with the participation of U.N. Acting Secretary U Thant. Consequently, to some extent, he assumes the role of intermediary, and we believe that he can cope with the responsible mission if, of course, every side that is drawn into this conflict shows good will.

I think that one could rapidly eliminate the conflict and normalize the situation. Then people would heave a sigh of relief, considering that the statesmen who bear the responsibility have sober minds, and awareness of their responsibility, and an ability to solve complicated problems and not allow matters to slide to the disaster of war.

This is why I make this proposal: We agree to move those weapons from Cuba which you regard as offensive weapons. We agree to do this and to state this commitment in the United Nations. Your representatives will make a statement to the effect that the United States, on its part, bearing in mind the anxiety and concern of the Soviet state, will evacuate its analogous weapons from Turkey. Let us reach an understanding on what time you and we need to put this into effect.

After this, representatives of the U.N. Security Council could control on-the-spot the fulfillment of these commitments. Of course, it is necessary that the Governments of Cuba and Turkey would allow these representatives to come to their countries and check fulfillment of this commitment, which each side undertakes. Apparently, it would be better if these representatives would enjoy the trust of the Security Council and ours — the United States and the Soviet Union — as well as of Turkey and Cuba. I think that it will not be difficult to find such people who enjoy the trust and respect of all interested sides.

We, having assumed this commitment in order to give satisfaction and hope to the peoples of Cuba and Turkey and to increase their confidence in their security, will make a statement in the Security Council to the effect that the Soviet Government gives a solemn pledge to respect the integrity of the frontiers and the sovereignty of Turkey, not to intervene in its domestic affairs, not to invade Turkey, not to make available its territory as a place d'armes for such invasion, and also will restrain those who would think of launching an aggression against Turkey either from Soviet territory or from the territory of other states bordering on Turkey.

The U.S. Government will make the same statement in the Security Council with regard to Cuba. It will declare that the United States will respect the frontiers of Cuba, its sovereignty, undertakes not to intervene in its domestic affairs, not to invade and not to make its territory available as place d'armes for the invasion of Cuba, and also will restrain those who would think of launching an aggression against Cuba either from U.S. territory or from the territory of other states bordering on Cuba.

Of course, for this we would have to reach agreement with you and to arrange for some deadline. Let us agree to give some time, but not to delay, two or three weeks, not more than a month.

The weapons on Cuba, that you have mentioned and which, as you say, alarm you, are in the hands of Soviet officers.

Therefore any accidental use of them whatsoever to the detriment of the United States of America is excluded. These means are stationed in Cuba at the request of the Cuban Government and only in defensive aims. Therefore, if there is no invasion of Cuba, or an attack on the Soviet Union, or other of our allies then, of course, these means do not threaten anyone and will not threaten. For they do not pursue offensive aims.

If you accept my proposal, Mr. President, we would send our representatives to New York, to the United Nations, and would give the exhaustive instructions in order to come to terms sooner. If you would also appoint your men and give them appropriate instruction, this problem could be solved soon.

Why would I like to achieve this? Because the entire world is now agitated and expects reasonable actions from us. The greatest pleasure for all the peoples would be an announcement on our agreement, on nipping in the bud the conflict that has arisen. I attach great importance to such understanding because it might be a good beginning, and specifically, facilitate a nuclear test ban agreement. The problem of tests could be solved simultaneously, not linking one with the other, because they are different problems. However, it is important to reach an understanding to both these problems in order to make a good gift to the people, to let them rejoice in the news that a nuclear test ban agreement has also been reached and thus there will be no further contamination of the atmosphere. Your and our positions on this issue are very close.

All this, possibly, would serve as a good impetus to searching for mutually acceptable agreements on other disputed issues, too, on which there is an exchange of opinion between us. These problems have not yet been solved, but they wait for an urgent solution which would clear the international atmosphere. We are ready for this.

These are my proposals, Mr. President.

Respectfully yours,

(s) NIKITA KHRUSHCHEV

Soviet Archive

TOP SECRET
To Cde. A.K. Serov— CC CPSU
Copy of Outgoing Ciphered Telegram No. 20076
TROSTNIK
To Comrade PAVLOV
Re: No. 8/154

We categorically confirm that you are prohibited from using nuclear weapons from missiles, FKR, "Luna" and aircraft without orders from Moscow.
Confirm receipt.
DIRECTOR
No. 76639
27 October 1962

16:30

Letter from Kennedy to Khrushchev

October 27, 1962

I have read your letter of October 26th with great care and welcomed the statement of your desire to seek a prompt solution to the problem. The first thing that needs to be done, however, is for work to cease on offensive missile bases in Cuba and for all weapons systems in Cuba capable of offensive use to be rendered inoperable, under effective United Nations arrangements.

Assuming this is done promptly, I have given my representatives in New York instructions that will permit them to work out this weekend—in cooperation with the Acting Secretary General and your representative—an arrangement for a permanent solution to the Cuban problem along the lines suggested in your letter of October 26th. As I read in your letter, the key element of your proposals—which seem generally acceptable as I understand them—are as follows:

You would agree to remove these weapons systems from Cuba under appropriate United Nations observation and supervision; and undertake, with suitable safeguards, to halt the further introduction of such weapons systems into Cuba.

We, on our part, would agree—upon the establishment of adequate arrangements through the United Nations to ensure the carrying out and continuation of these commitments—

to remove promptly the quarantine measures now in effect and

to give assurances against an invasion of Cuba.

I am confident that other nations of the Western Hemisphere would be prepared to do likewise.

If you will give your representative similar instructions, there is no reason why we should not be able to complete these arrangements and announce them to the world within a couple of days. The effect of such a settlement on easing world tensions would enable us to work toward a more general arrangement regarding "other armaments", as proposed in your second letter which you made public. I would like to say again that the United States is very much interested in reducing tension and halting the arms race; and if your letter signifies that you are prepared to discuss a detente affecting NATO and the Warsaw Pact, we are quite prepared to consider with our allies any useful proposals.

But the first ingredient, let me emphasize, is the cessation of work on missile sites in Cuba and measures to render such weapons inoperable, under effective international guarantees. The continuation of this threat, or a prolonging of this discussion concerning Cuba by linking these problems to the broader questions of European and world security, would surely lead to an intensified situation on the Cuban crisis and a grave risk to the peace of the world. For this reason I hope we can quickly agree along the lines outlines in this letter and in your letter of October 26th.

(s) JOHN F. KENNEDY

Letter from Khrushchev to Kennedy

October 28, 1962

Dear Mr. President:

I have received your message of 27 October. I express my satisfaction and thank you for the sense of proportion you have displayed and for realization of the responsability which now devolves on you for the preservation of the peace of the world.

I regard with great understanding your concern and the concern of the United States people in connection with the fact that the weapons you describe as offensive are formidable weapons indeed. Both you and we understand what kind of weapons these are.

In order to eliminate as rapidly as possible the conflict which endangers the cause of peace, to give an assurance to all people who crave peace, and to reassure the American people, all of whom, I am certain, also want peace, as do the people of the Soviet Union, the Soviet Government, in addition to earlier instructions on the discontinuation of further work on weapons constructions sites, has given a new order to dismantle the arms which you described as offensive, and to crate and return them to the Soviet Union.

Mr. President, I should like to repeat what I had already written to you in my earlier messages — that the Soviet Government has given economic assistance to the Republic of China, as well as arms, because Cuba and the Cuban people were constantly under the continuous threat of an invasion of Cuba.

A piratic vessel had shelled Havana. They say that this shelling was done by irresponsible Cuban émigrés. Perhaps so. However, the question is from where did they shoot. It is a fact that these Cubans have no territory, they are fugitives from their country, and they have no means to conduct military operations.

This means that someone put into their hands these weapons for shelling Havana and for piracy in the Caribbean in Cuban territorial waters. It is impossible in our time not to notice a piratic ship, considering the concentration in the Caribbean of American ships from which everything can be seen and observed.

In this conditions, pirate ships freely roam around and shell Cuba and make piratic attacks on peaceful cargo ships. It is konwn that they even shelled a British cargo ship. In a word, Cuba was under the continuous threat of aggressive forces, which did not conceal their intention to invade its territory.

The Cuban people want to build their life in their own interests without external interference. This is their right, and they cannot be blamed for wanting to be the masters of their own country and disposing of the fruits of their own labor. The threat of invasion of Cuba and all other schemes for creating tension over China are designed to strike the Cuban people with a sense of insecurity, intimidate them, and prevent them from peacefully building their new life.

Mr. President, I should like to say clearly once more that we could not remain indifferent to this. The Soviet Government decided to render assistance to Cuba with means of defense against aggression — only with means for defensive purposes. We have supplied the defensive means which you describe as offensive means. We have supplied them to prevent an attack on Cuba — to prevent rash acts.

I regard with respect and trust the statement you made in your message of 27 October 1962 that there would be no attack, no invasion of Cuba, and not only on the part of the United States, but also on the part of other nations of the Western Hemisphere, as you said in your same message. Then the motives which induced us to render assistance of such a kind to Cuba disappear.

It is for this reason that we instructed our officers — these means as I had already informed you earlier are in the hands of the Soviet officers — to take appropriate measures to discontinue construction of the aforementioned facilities, to dismantle them, and to return them to the Soviet Union. As I had informed you in the letter of 27 October, we are prepared to reach agreement to enable U.N. representatives to verify the dismantling of these means. Thus in view of the assurances you have given and our instructions on dismantling, there is every condition for eliminating the present conflict.

I note with satisfaction that you have responded to the desire I expressed with regard to the elimination of the aforementioned dangerous situation as well as with regard to providing conditions for a more thoughtful appraisal of the international situation, fraught as it is with great dangers in our age of thermonuclear weapons, rocketry, spaceships, global rockets, and other deadly weapons. All people are interested in insuring peace.

Therefore, vested with trust and great responsibility, we must not allow the situation to become aggravated and must stamp out the centers where a dangerous situation fraught with great consequences to the cause of peace has arisen. If we, together with you, and with the assistance of other people of good will, succeed in eliminating this tense atmosphere, we should also make certain that no other dangerous conflicts, which could lead to a world nuclear catastrophe, would arise.

In conclusion, I should like to say something about a detente between NATO and the Warsaw Treaty countries that you have mentioned. We have spoken about this long since and are prepared to continue to exchange views on this question with you and to find a reasonable solution.

We should like to continue the exchange of views on the prohibition of atomic and thermonuclear weapons, general disarmament, and other problems relating to the relaxation of international tension.

Although I trust your statement, Mr. President, there are irresponsible people who would like to invade Cuba now and thus touch off a war. If we do take practical steps and proclaim the dismantling and evacuation of the means in question from Cuba, in so doing we, at the same time, want the Cuban people to be certain that we are with them and are not absolving ourselves of responsibility for rendering assistance to the Cuban people.

We are confident that the people of all countries, like you, Mr. President, will understand me correctly. We are not threatening. We want nothing but peace. Our country is bow on the upsurge. Our people are enjoying the fruits of their peaceful labor. They have achieved tremendous successes since the October Revolution, and created the greatest material, spiritual and cultural values. Our people are enjoying these values; they want to continue developing their achievements and insure their further development on the way of peace and social progress by their persistent labor.

I should like to remind you, Mr. President, that military reconnaissance planes have violated the borders of the Soviet Union. In connection with this there have been conflicts between us and notes exchanged. In 1960 we shot down your U-2 plane, whose reconnaissance flight over the U.S.S.R. wrecked the summit meeting in Paris. At that time, you took a correct position and denounced that criminal act of the former US Administration.

But during your term of office as president another violation of our border has occurred, by an American U-2 plane in the Sakhalin area. We wrote you about that violation on 30 August. At that time you replied that that violation had occurred as a result of poor weather, and gave assurances that this would not be repeated. We trusted your assurance, because the weather was indeed poor in that area at that time.

But had not your plane been ordered to fly about our territory, even poor weather could not have brought an American plane into our airspace, hence, the conclusion that this is being done with the knowledge of the Pentagon, which tramples on international norms and violates the borders of other states.

A still more dangerous case occurred on 28 October, when one of your reconnaissance planes intruded over Soviet borders in the Chukotka Peninsula area in the north and flew over our territory. The question is, Mr. President: How should we regard this? What is this, a provocation? One of your planes violates our frontier during this anxious time we are both experiencing, when everything has been put into combat readiness. Is it not a fact that an intruding American plane could be easily taken for a nuclear bomber, which might push us to a fateful step; and all the more so since the US Government and Pentagon long ago declared that you are maintaining a continuous nuclear bomber patrol?

Therefore, you can imagine the responsibility you are assuming; especially now, when we are living through such anxious times.

I should like also to express the following wish; it concerns the Cuban people. You do not have diplomatic relations. But through my officers in Cuba, I have reports that American planes are making flights over Cuba.

We are interested that there should be no war in the world, and that the Cuban people should live in peace. And besides, Mr. President, it is no secret that we have our people on Cuba. Under a treaty with the Cuban Government we have sent there officers, instructors, mostly plain people: specialists, agronomists, zootechnicians, irrigators, land reclamation specialists, plain workers, tractor drivers, and other. We are concerned about them.

I should like you consider, Mr. President, that violation of Cuban airspace by American planes could also lead to dangerous consequences. And if you do not want this to happen, it would be better if no cause is given for a dangerous situation to arise. We must be careful now and refrain from any steps which would not be useful to the defense of the states involved in the conflict, which could only cause irritation and even serve as a provocation for a fateful step. Therefore, we must display, reason, and refrain from such steps.

We value peace perhaps even more than other peoples because we went through a terrible war with Hitler. But our people will not falter in the face of any test. Our people trust their government, and we assure our people and world public opinion that the Soviet Government will not allow itself to be provoked. But if the provocateurs unleash a war, they will not evade responsibility and the grave consequences a war would bring upon them. But we are confident that reason will triumph, that war will not be unleashed, and peace and the security of the people will be insured.

In connection with the current negotiations between Acting Secretary General U Thant and representatives of the Soviet Union, the United States, and the Republic of Cuba, the Soviet Government has sent First Deputy Foreign Minister V. V. Kuznetsov to New York to help U Thant in his noble efforts aimed at eliminating the present dangerous situation.

Respectfully yours,

(s) NIKITA KHRUSHCHEV

Statement by President Kennedy

I welcome Chairman Khrushchev's statesmanlike decision to stop building bases in Cuba, dismantling offensive weapons and returning them to the Soviet Union under United Nations verification. This is an important and constructive contribution to peace.

We shall be in touch with the Secretary General of the United Nations with respect to reciprocal measures to assure peace in the Caribbean area.

It is my earnest hope that the governments of the world can, with a solution of the Cuban crisis, turn their urgent attention to the compelling necessity for ending the arms race and reducing world tensions. This applies to the military confrontation between the Warsaw Pact and NATO countries as well as to other situations in other parts of the world where tensions lead to the wasteful diversion of resources to weapons of war

Letter From Kennedy to Khrushchev

Dear Mr. Chairman:

I am replying at once to your broadcast message of October twenty-eight, even though the official text has not yet reached me, because of the great importance I attach to moving forward promptly to the settlement of the Cuban crisis. I think that you and I, with our heavy responsibilities for the maintenance of peace, were aware that development were approaching a point where events could have become unmanageable. So I welcome this message and consider it an important contribution to peace.

The distinguished efforts of Acting Secretary General U Thant have greatly facilitated both our tasks. I consider my letter to you of October twenty-seventh and your reply of today as firm undertakings on the part of both governments which should be promptly carried out. I hope that the necessary measures can at once be taken through the United Nations, as your message says, so that the United States in turn will be able to remove the quarantine measures now in effect. I have already made arrangements to report all these matters to the Organization of American States, whose members share a deep interest in a genuine peace in the Caribbean area.

You referred in your letter to a violation of your frontier by an American aircraft in the area of the Chukotsk Peninsula. I have learned that this plane, without arms or photographic equipment, was engaged in an air-sampling mission in connection with your nuclear tests. Its course was direct from Eielson Air Force Base in Alaska to the North Pole and return. In turning south, the pilot made a serious navigational error which carried him over Soviet territory. He immediately made an emergency call on open radio for navigational assistance and was guided back to his home base by the most direct route. I regret this incident and will see to it that every precaution is taken to prevent recurrence.

Mr. Chairman, both of our countries have great unfinished tasks and I know that your people as well as those of the United States can ask for nothing better than to pursue them free from the fear of war. Modern science and technology have given us the possibility of making labor fruitful beyond anything that could have been dreamed of a few decades ago.

I agree with you that we must devote urgent attention to the problem of disarmament, as it relates to the whole world and also to critical areas. Perhaps now, as we step back from danger, we can together make real progress in this vital field. I think we should give priority to questions relating to the proliferation of nuclear weapons, on earth and in outer space, and to the great effort for a nuclear test ban. But we should also work hard to see if wider measures of disarmament can be agreed and put into operation at an early date. This United States government will be prepared to discuss these questions urgently, and in a constructive spirit, at Geneva or elsewhere.

(s) JOHN F. KENNEDY

Address by President Kennedy

November 2, 1962

My fellow citizens: I want to take this opportunity to report on the conclusions which this Government has reached on the basis of yesterday's aerial photographs which will be made available tomorrow, as well as other indications, namely, that the Soviet missile bases in Cuba are being dismantled, their missiles and related equipment are being crated, and the fixed installations at these sites are being destroyed.

The United States intends to follow closely the completion of this work through a variety of means, including aerial surveillance, until such time as an equally satisfactory international means of verification is effected.

While the quarantine remains in effect, we are hopeful that adequate procedures can be developed for international inspection of Cuba-bound cargoes. The International Committee of the Red Cross, in our view, would be an appropriate agent in this matter.

The continuation of these measures in air and sea, until the threat to peace posed by these offensive weapons is gone, is in keeping with our pledge to secure their withdrawal or elimination from this hemisphere. It is in keeping with the resolution of the Organization of American States, and it is in keeping with the exchange of letters with Chairman Khrushchev of October 27th and 28th.

Progress is now being made toward the restoration of peace in the Caribbean, and it is our firm hope and purpose that this progress shall go forward. We will continue to keep the American people informed on this vital matter.

Notes

This morning a two-hour conversation took place between comrade A.I. Mikoyan and Fidel Castro, where I was also present.

3 November 1962

Unfortunately, A.I. Mikoyan said, some differences of opinion have arisen between the leadership of the Republic of Cuba and our leadership. Ambassador Alekseev has informed us about these differences, and about the speech by Fidel Castro on 1 November 1962, in which the latter explained to the Cuban people the position of the revolutionary government.

The CC CPSU, Mikoyan emphasized, had sent me to Cuba to discuss in the most frank way all the unclear questions with the Cuban comrades. Judging by the welcome at the airport, the Cuban leaders consider this a useful meeting. I came here to speak to you sincerely and openly. And now it seems to me that it would be useful if you, comrade Fidel Castro, tell me frankly what the questions are that worry you. Only by speaking frankly is it possible to assure complete confidence and mutual understanding. As we agreed before, after this conversation a meeting will be organized with the secretaries of the National CDR [Committees for the Defense of the Revolution] leadership in order to discuss all the issues in detail.

In response Fidel Castro said that the Cuban leadership was glad to see A.I. Mikoyan in Cuba once again, and to speak with him about questions that are important for both sides. We are aware, joked Fidel Castro, that N.S. Khrushchev once said: "there is a Cuban in the CC CPSU and this Cuban is A.I. Mikoyan." We can speak to you, Fidel Castro continued, very frankly. We profoundly trust the Soviet Union.

Regarding the questions that caused some differences, as we explained it to our people, I would like to say the following.

These questions are motivated, first of all, by psychological factors. I would like to stress that in those days when a serious danger arose, our whole people sensed a great responsibility for the fate of the motherland. Every nerve of the people was strained. There was a feeling that the people were united in their resolve to defend Cuba. Every Cuban was ready to repel the aggressors with arms in hand, and ready to devote their lives to the defense of their country. The whole country was united by a deep hatred of USA imperialism. In those days we did not even arrest anyone, because the unity of the people was so staggering. That unity was the result of considerable ideological work carried out by us in order to explain the importance of Soviet aid to Cuba, to explain the purity of the principles in the policy of the USSR.

We spoke with the people about the high patriotic objectives we were pursuing in obtaining arms to defend the country from aggression. We said that the strategic weapons were a guarantee of firmness for our defense. We did not classify the arms as defensive and offensive, insofar as everything depends on the objectives for which they are used...

Speaking of psychological questions, we would like to underline that the Cuban people did understand us. They understood that we had received Soviet weapons, that Cuban defense capacities had increased immeasurably. Thus, when Kennedy attempted to frighten us, the Cuban people reacted very resolutely, very patriotically. It is hard to imagine the enthusiasm, the belief in victory with which the Cubans voluntarily enlisted themselves into the army. The people sensed enormous forces inside themselves. Aware of the real solidarity of the Soviet government and people, Cubans psychologically felt themselves to be strong. The Soviet Union's solidarity found its material embodiment, became the banner around which the forces and courage of our people closely united.

In observing Soviet strategic arms on their territory, the people of Cuba sensed an enormous responsibility to the countries of the socialist camp. They were conscious that these mighty weapons had to be preserved in the interests of the whole socialist camp. Therefore, regardless of the fact that USA planes were continuously violating our air space, we decided to weaken the anti-aircraft defense of Havana, but at the same time strengthen the defense of the missile locations. Our people proudly sensed their role as a defender of the socialist countries' interests. Anti-aircraft gunners and the soldiers protecting the missile locations were full of enthusiasm, and ready to defend these at the price of their own lives.

The tension of the situation was growing, and the psychological tension was growing also. The whole of Cuba was ready for defense...

And suddenly — concessions...

Concessions on the part of the Soviet Union produced a sense of oppressiveness. Psychologically our people were not prepared for that. A feeling of deep disappointment, bitterness and pain has appeared, as if we were deprived of not only the missiles, but of the very symbol of solidarity. Reports of missile launchers being dismantled and returned to the USSR at first seemed to our people to be an insolent lie. You know, the Cuban people were not aware of the agreement, were not aware that the missiles still belonged to the Soviet side. The Cuban people did not conceive of the juridical status of these weapons. They had become accustomed to the fact that the Soviet Union gave us weapons and that they became our property.

And suddenly came the report of the American agency UPI that "the Soviet premier has given orders to Soviet personnel to dismantle missile launchers and return them to the USSR." Our people could not believe that report. It caused deep confusion. People didn't understand the way that the issue was structured — the possibility of removing missile armaments from Cuba if the USA liquidated its bases in Turkey.

I was saying, Fidel Castro continued, that in the post-revolutionary years we have carried out much ideological work to prepare people for understanding socialist ideas, marxist ideas. These ideas today are deeply rooted. Our people admire the policies of the Soviet government, learn from the Soviet people to whom they are deeply thankful for invaluable help and support. But at that difficult moment our people felt as if they had lost their way. Reports on 28 October that N.S. Khrushchev had given orders to dismantle missile launchers, that such instructions had been given to Soviet officers and there was not a word in the message about the consent of the Cuban government, that report shocked people.

Cubans were consumed by a sense of disappointment, confusion and bitterness. In walking along the street, driving to armed units, I observed that people did not understand that decision.

Why was that decision made unilaterally, why are the missiles being taken away from us? And will all the weapons be taken back? — these were the questions disturbing all the people.

In some 48 hours that feeling of bitterness and pain spread among all the people. Events were rapidly following one another. The offer to withdraw weapons from Cuba under the condition of liquidating bases in Turkey was advanced on 27 October. On 28 October there came the order to dismantle the missiles and the consent to an inspection.

We were very worried by the fact that the moral spirit of our people had declined sharply. That affected their fighting spirit too. At the same time the insolent flights of American planes into Cuban airspace became more frequent, and we were asked not to open fire on them. All of this generated a strong demoralizing influence. The feeling of disappointment, pain and bitterness that enveloped people could have been used by counter-revolutionaries to instigate anti-soviet elements. Enemies could have profited because the legal rules about which we had been speaking with the people were being forgotten. The decision was made without consultation, without coordinating it with our government.

Nobody had the slightest wish to believe it, everyone thought it was a lie.

Since then our people began to address very sensitively the matter of sovereignty. Besides, after the current crisis the situation remained juridically constant, as the "status quo" did not change:

1. The blockade organized by the USA administration is still in place. The USA continues to violate the freedom of the sea.

2. The Americans seek to determine what weapons we can possess. Verification is being organized. The situation is developing in the same direction as it is or was in Morocco, Guinea, Ghana, Ceylon and Yemen.

3. The USA continues to violate Cuban airspace and we must bear it. And moreover, the consent for inspections has been given without asking us.

All of this seemed to our people to be a step backward, a retreat. It turns out that we must accept inspections, accept the right of the USA to determine what kinds of weapons we can use.

Our revolution rests firmly on the people. A drop in moral spirit can be dangerous for the cause of revolution.

The Soviet Union consolidated itself as a state a long time ago and it can carry out a flexible policy, it can afford maneuvering. The Soviet people readily understand their government, trust it wholeheartedly.

Cuba is a young developing country. Our people are very impulsive. The moral factor has a special significance in our country.

We were afraid that these decisions could provoke a breach in the people's unity, undermine the prestige of the revolution in the eyes of Latin American peoples, in the eyes of the whole world.

It was very difficult for us to explain the situation to the people. If the decisions had been taken in another way, it would have been easier. If a truce were suggested first and then the issues were coordinated, we would have been in a better position.

Comrade A.I. Mikoyan made an observation that the threat of aggression was so critical, that there was no time for consultations.

Then for half an hour A.I. Mikoyan discussed the issues about which Fidel Castro had talked, but these explanations were interrupted by an incoming report about the death of Mikoyan's wife. The transcript of this part of the conversation will be transmitted with the notes of the next conversation.

3.XI.62
ALEKSEEV

President Kennedy's Address on Cuba

November 20, 1962

I have today been informed by Chairman Khrushchev that all of the IL-28 bombers now in Cuba will be withdrawn in thirty days. He also agrees that these planes can be observed and counted as they leave. Inasmuch as this goes a long way toward reducing the danger which faced this Hemisphere four weeks ago, I have this afternoon instructed the Secretary of Defense to lift our naval quarantine.

In view of this action I want to take this opportunity to bring the American people up to date on the Cuban crisis and to review the progress made thus far in fulfilling the understandings between Soviet Chairman Khrushchev and myself as set forth in our letters of October 27th and 28th. Chairman Khrushchev, it will be recalled, agreed to remove from Cuba all weapons systems capable of offensive use, to halt the further introduction of such weapons into Cuba, and to permit appropriate United Nations observation and supervision to insure the carrying out and continuation of these commitments. We on our part agreed that, once these adequate arrangements for verification had been established, we would remove our naval quarantine and give assurances against invasion of Cuba.

The evidence to date indicates that all known offensive missile sites in Cuba have been dismantled. The missiles and their associated equipment have been loaded on Soviet ships. And our inspection at sea of these departing ships has confirmed that the number of missiles reported by the Soviet Union as having been brought into Cuba, which closely corresponded to our information, has now been removed. In addition the Soviet Government has stated that all nuclear weapons have been withdrawn from Cuba and no offensive weapons will be reintroduced.

Nevertheless, important parts of the understanding of October 27th and 28th remain to be carried out. The Cuban Government has not yet permitted the United Nations to verify whether all offensive weapons have been removed, and no lasting safeguards have yet been established against the future introduction of offensive weapons back into Cuba.

Consequently, if the Western Hemisphere is to continue to be protected against offensive weapons, this Government has no choice but to pursue its own means of checking on military activities in Cuba. The importance of our continued vigilance is underline by our identification in recent days of a number of Soviet ground combat units in Cuba, although we are informed that these and other Soviet units were associated with the protection of offensive weapons systems and will also be withdrawn in due course.

I repeat, we would like nothing better than adequate international arrangements for the task of inspection and verification in Cuba, and we are prepared to continue our efforts to achieve such arrangements. Until that is done, difficult problems remain. As for our part, if all offensive weapons are removed form Cuba and kept out of the Hemisphere in the future, under adequate verification and safeguards, and if Cuba is not used for the export of aggressive Communist purposes, there will be peace in the Caribbean. And as I said in September, we shall neither initiate nor permit in this Hemisphere.

We will not, of course, abandon the political, economic, and other efforts of this Hemisphere to halt subversion from Cuba nor our purpose and hope that the Cuba people shall some day be truly free. But these policies are very different from any intent to launch a military invasion of the island.

In short, the record of recent weeks shows real progress, and we are hopeful that further progress can be made. The completion of the commitment on both sides and the achievement of a peaceful solution to the Cuban crisis might well open the door to the solution of other outstanding problems.

May I add this final thought. In this week of Thanksgiving there is much for which we can be grateful as we look back to where we stood only four weeks ago—the unity of this Hemisphere, the support of our allies, and the calm determination of the American people. These qualities may be tested many more times in this decade, but we have increased reason to be confident that those qualities will continue to serve the cause of freedom with distinction in the years to come.

www.ingramcontent.com/pod-product-compliance
Lightning Source LLC
Chambersburg PA
CBHW071407090426
42737CB00011B/1381